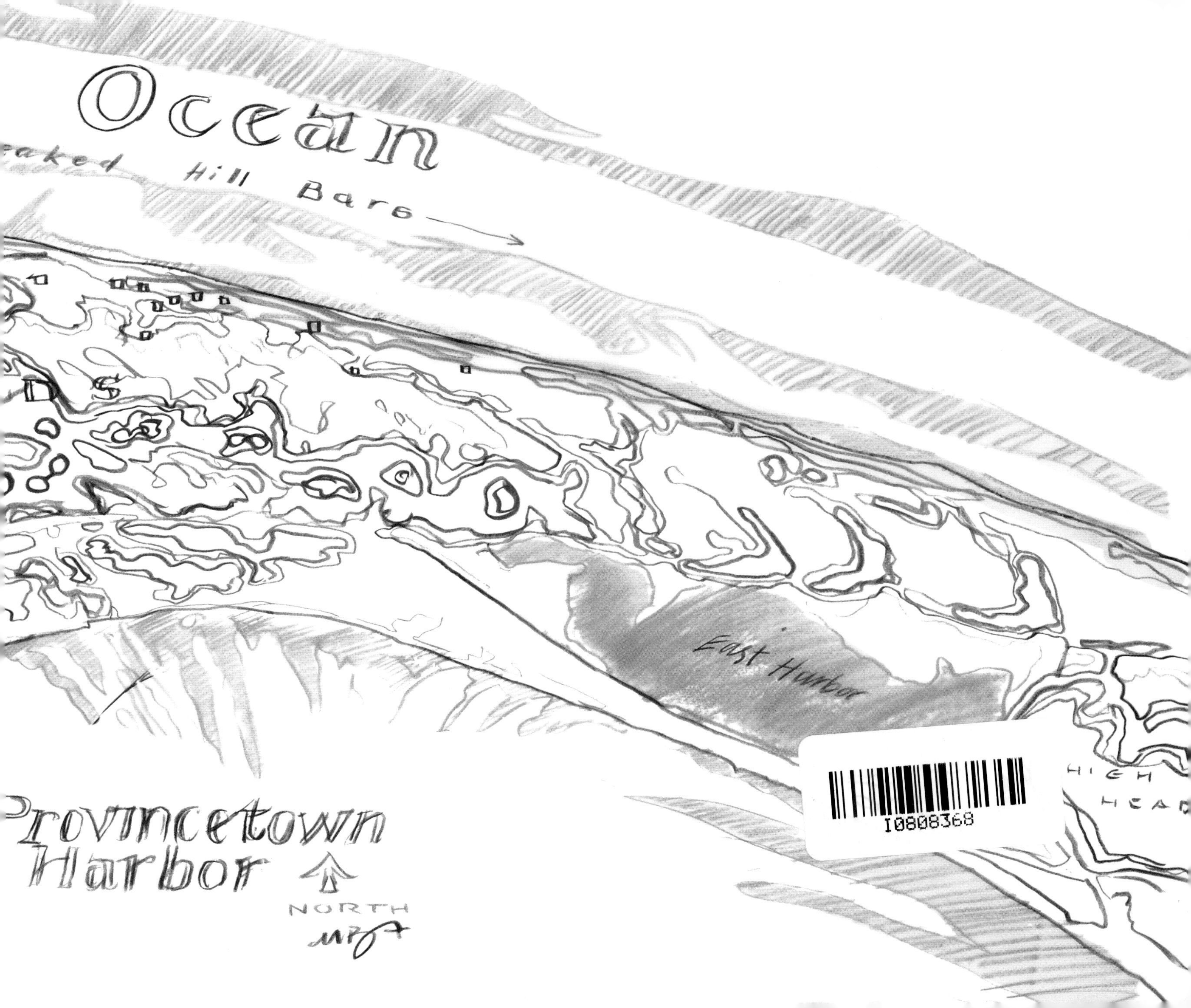
Ocean
eaked Hill Bars
East Harbor
Provincetown
Harbor
NORTH

DUNE SHACKS OF PROVINCETOWN

Jane Paradise

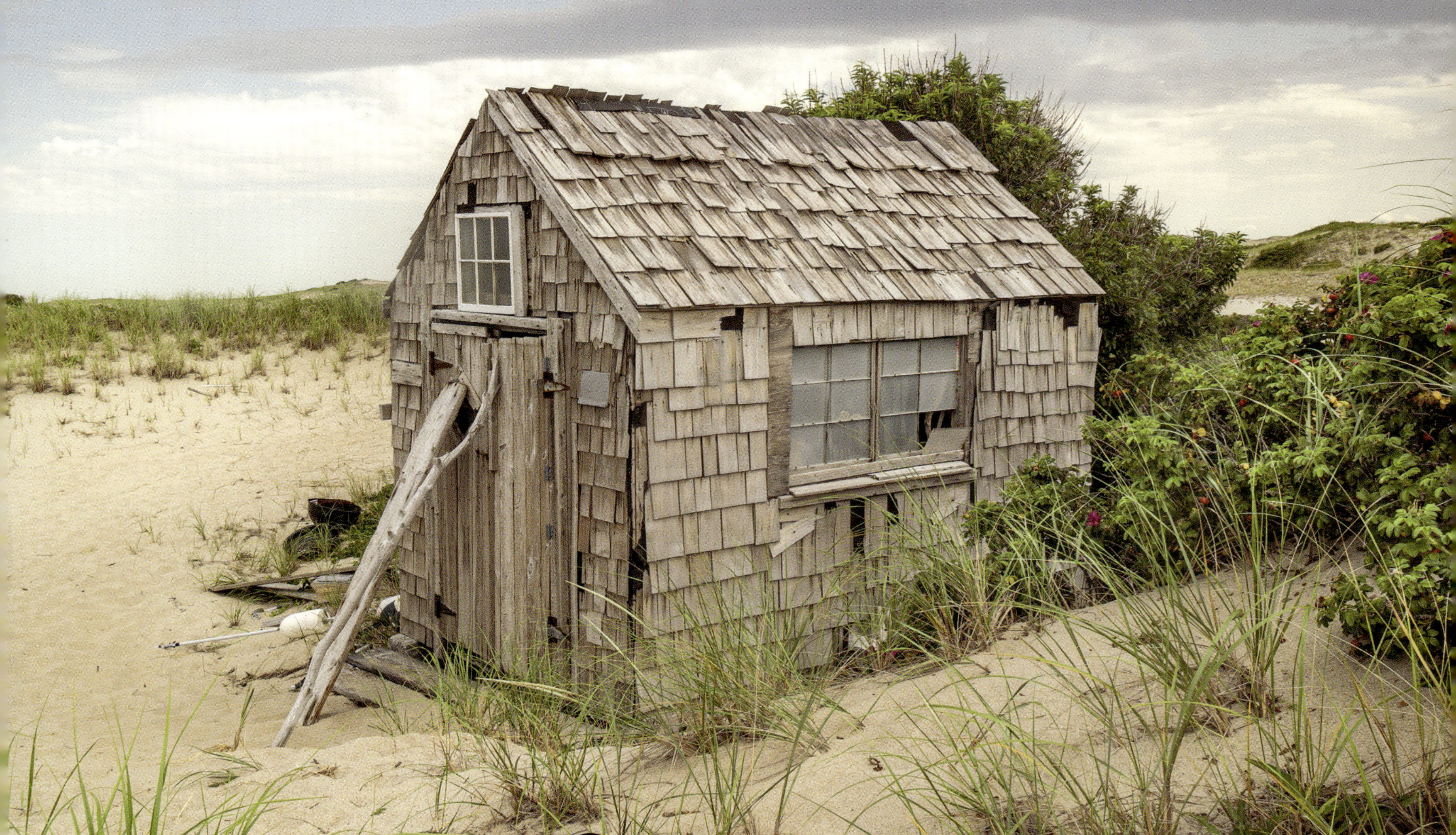

SCHIFFER PUBLISHING
4880 Lower Valley Road • Atglen, PA 19310

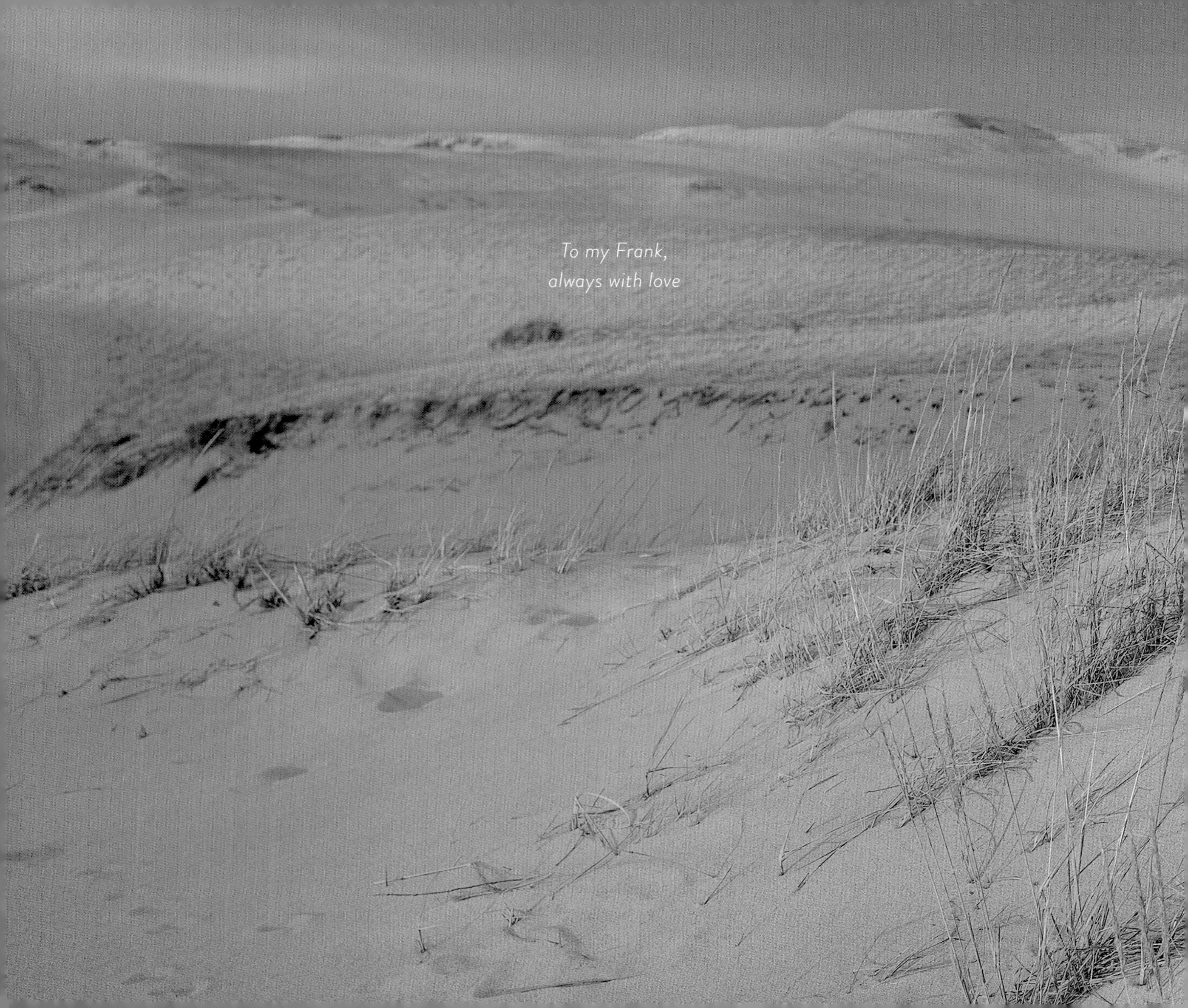

To my Frank,
always with love

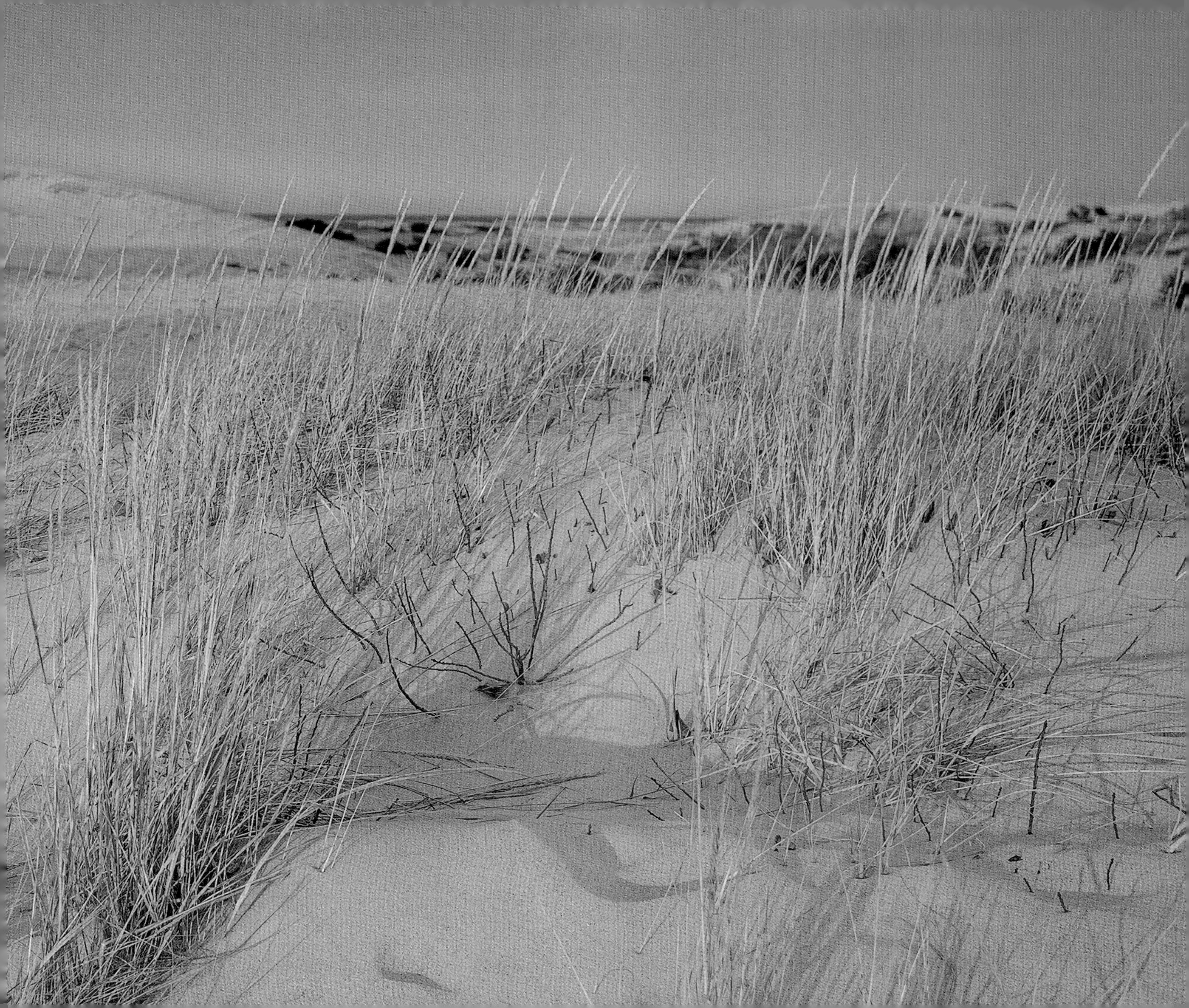

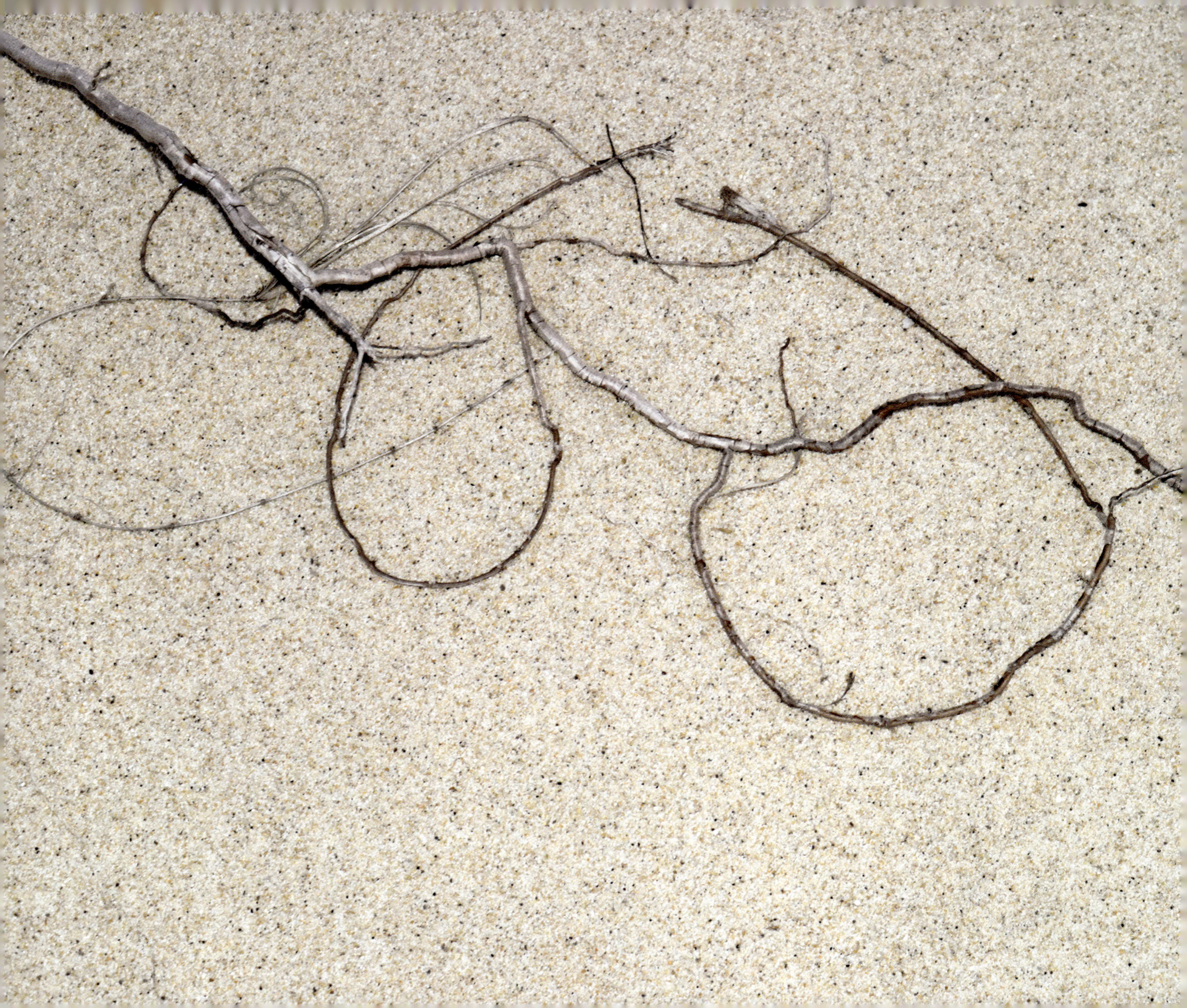

CONTENTS

FOREWORD

Looking through the extraordinary photos in Jane Paradise's book brought back a flood of childhood memories of my time spent in the dune shacks of Provincetown in the early seventies. My mother, Beverly Bentley, moved my brother Stephen and me up to Provincetown from New York City when she separated from Norman Mailer, my father, in 1969. They had a summer place on Commercial Street, the main thoroughfare in town, where I would spend the next eight years of my life living year-round. By default, I was a townie, though lacking Portuguese blood, since it was a Portuguese town back then—certainly in the off-season, I always felt as if I was on the outside looking in. Be that as it may, I had this extraordinary playground at my fingertips—the beaches and dunes of this magical place called Provincetown, a town my father often referred to as the Wild West of the East.

Every summer, usually in June, my mother would book a week in either of the dune shacks, Euphoria or Thalassa, owned by Hazel Hawthorne, one of the many distinguished writers/poets whom Provincetown tended to collect. They were friends and we would often be invited to Hazel's home for cookies and tea as a prelude to our trip. We would then pack up and load our week's worth of supplies into a friend's four-wheel-drive truck and embark on our journey across the dunes to get to our shack. Often the shortest route was dicey, for it involved traversing the highest of the sand dunes that only the sturdiest of trucks with enough speed could mount. I felt as if I were Lawrence of Arabia crossing the great and impenetrable Nefud Desert.

Once we unloaded and watched our transport disappear, I knew the three of us would be together, removed from the rest of humanity, over the next six days. The isolation yet interconnectedness with the sand, the sea, and the various living creatures created a harmony of living unlike anything I have experienced to this day. It was my Walden Pond and I often attempt to relive those moments in order to find a meditative calm when things feel particularly chaotic and out of sync in my adult years.

The dune shacks, both rickety and firm, are part of the earthly elements and speak to a gentler, holistic time. They are humble monuments of simplicity and serenity that exist outside the tumult of the modern era—a majestic counterpoint to the digital age. Jane's photography captures their simple elegance as a form of visual poetry. She brings the reader into a past lost yet still very much with us. While for me it may beckon a trip down memory lane, for the uninitiated her dune shack photos may present a glimpse of Eden as it was for the artists who created their works under the light of kerosene lamps.

Michael Mailer

INTRODUCTION

Curiosity and a sense of adventure led me to the backshore of Provincetown and the dune shacks. With the crash of ocean waves as a backdrop, I feel fully at peace here.

This is my primal landscape. I find comfort in the bare land hiding a bounty of living organisms that thrive despite harsh conditions. I spent childhood summer vacations here, running up and down the vast dunes. Later, as an adult seeking seclusion, I wandered the stark landscape, surprised to find the mirage of dune shacks seemingly appearing out of nowhere. I began to wonder about their occupants, the determined sojourners who braved the arduous, sandy trek to reach their homes. I also wondered what the shacks looked like inside. This began my dune shack journey: ten years of research, photo shoots, friendships, an artist residency, and more than a dozen overnight stays—all of which culminated in this book.

Writers, artists, and families built the makeshift summer homes on the wild backshore of Provincetown in the early 1900s. Some were originally life-saving huts in the late 1800s, but most were constructed in the 1920s through the 1950s out of debris and shipwreck ruins. Nineteen of them still survive—some restored, some bandaged, some dilapidated, and all loved. Each shack has its own name, personality, and storied history.

I learned quickly that it is not easy to live or stay in the shacks. To reach them requires a mile-plus walk through rolling, steep dunes. There is no electricity or running water. Vintage kerosene lamps provide light, and freshwater wells are a sandy walk away. Propane is used for cooking and refrigeration. Woodburning stoves are used for heat. Compost outhouses are nearby. The day gets quickly occupied by daily tasks, including foraging for kindling and chopping wood for the stove and pumping the cool, refreshing groundwater for drinking and washing.

The landscape is frequented by an abundance of wildlife. Numerous animal tracks surround the shack by morning, and I always wonder where they came from and how I never heard a sound.

I thought I'd find stillness here, but unexpectedly there is none. I did find solitude, but with the sound of the sea ever present. I found a partner in the noise of crashing waves. Coyotes howl in the night, skulk of foxes cry and scream, quarrel of sparrows argue, colonies of gulls screech, and bobs of seals leisurely track one's movements. Out of nowhere the winds moan.

Within this backshore, inspiration and creativity flowed alongside full-moon parties and drunken revelries. Literature and the arts flourished amid this simple lifestyle, as did generations of families who summered here. I feel this history every time I walk through a dune shack door.

Notable visitors to these windswept shores include Mary Oliver, Norman Mailer, Eugene O'Neill, Ann Patchett, Edmund Wilson, e.e. cummings, Jackson Pollock, Tennessee Williams, and Jack Kerouac, who wrote part of *On the Road* here.

Modern-day writers, artists, poets, dancers, and scientists still apply for residencies and are drawn here for the spirit of the place, the love of the land, and the creativity that it inspires. Families continue to raise their children, grandchildren, and great-grandchildren here. Memories are created and recalled.

Writer Mary Heaton Vorse (1874–1966) wrote in her historic memoir *Time and the Town*, "I do not know of any country which is so wild and so diverse within so small a compass. This little piece of land, small when you measure it in square miles, is unlike any other place; nor have I found anyone who has seen anything like it."

The shacks will outlive us. They have so far. We must believe that.

DUNE SHACK HISTORY

The Dune Shacks of Peaked Hill Bars Historic District is an approximately 1,960-acre, oceanfront cultural landscape that emerged as an isolated and informal seasonal retreat sought for recreation and creative expression during the twentieth century. The district encompasses more than 5 miles of undeveloped coastline. The district includes 18 contributing buildings and one contributing site, comprised of wood shacks and the surrounding dune landscape. All of the shacks were initially built between the 1920s and early 1950s, but some were rebuilt and moved back from the shoreline during the late twentieth century.

The Peaked Hill Bars Historic District is eligible for listing in the National Register of Historic Places . . . for its twentieth-century growth as an isolated, coastal retreat developed with distinct, rustic shelters that attracted a creative seasonal colony of summer recreationists and prominent American art, theater, and literary figures, many of whom had strong connections to the Provincetown art community. The district meets designation criteria at the national level in the areas of art and literature for its historical significance as a scenic destination sought by intellectuals, writers, painters, and other artists who found its dramatic landscape and solitary experience with nature inspirational to their work.

Several influential American creative figures are directly associated with the area, such as playwrights Susan Glaspell and Eugene O'Neill; writers Mabel Dodge, Harry Kemp, Mary Heaton Vorse, Hazel Hawthorne

Werner, and Edmund Wilson; and artist Boris Margo. The dune shacks community thrived within an innovative atmosphere where members' social and intellectual interaction in the district during their productive lives resulted in work that impacted American culture.

The backshore's strikingly scenic, wild natural landscape, spartan lifestyle, and amusing maritime folklore is perpetuated throughout plays, poetry, novels, and paintings that reached a popular audience. Interaction between select dune shack occupants and visitors continued year-round in the radical Bohemian intellectual society of Greenwich Village in New York City, and extended into downtown Provincetown, which was already an established arts center by 1920. These layered social circles enhanced the summer art colony's sphere of influence and cultivated the area's identity as an unconventional creative society whose members shared appreciation for the simplistic, freethinking lifestyle and experience of solace with nature found in the dunes.

Excerpted from the **National Register of Historic Places** Registration Form, 2012

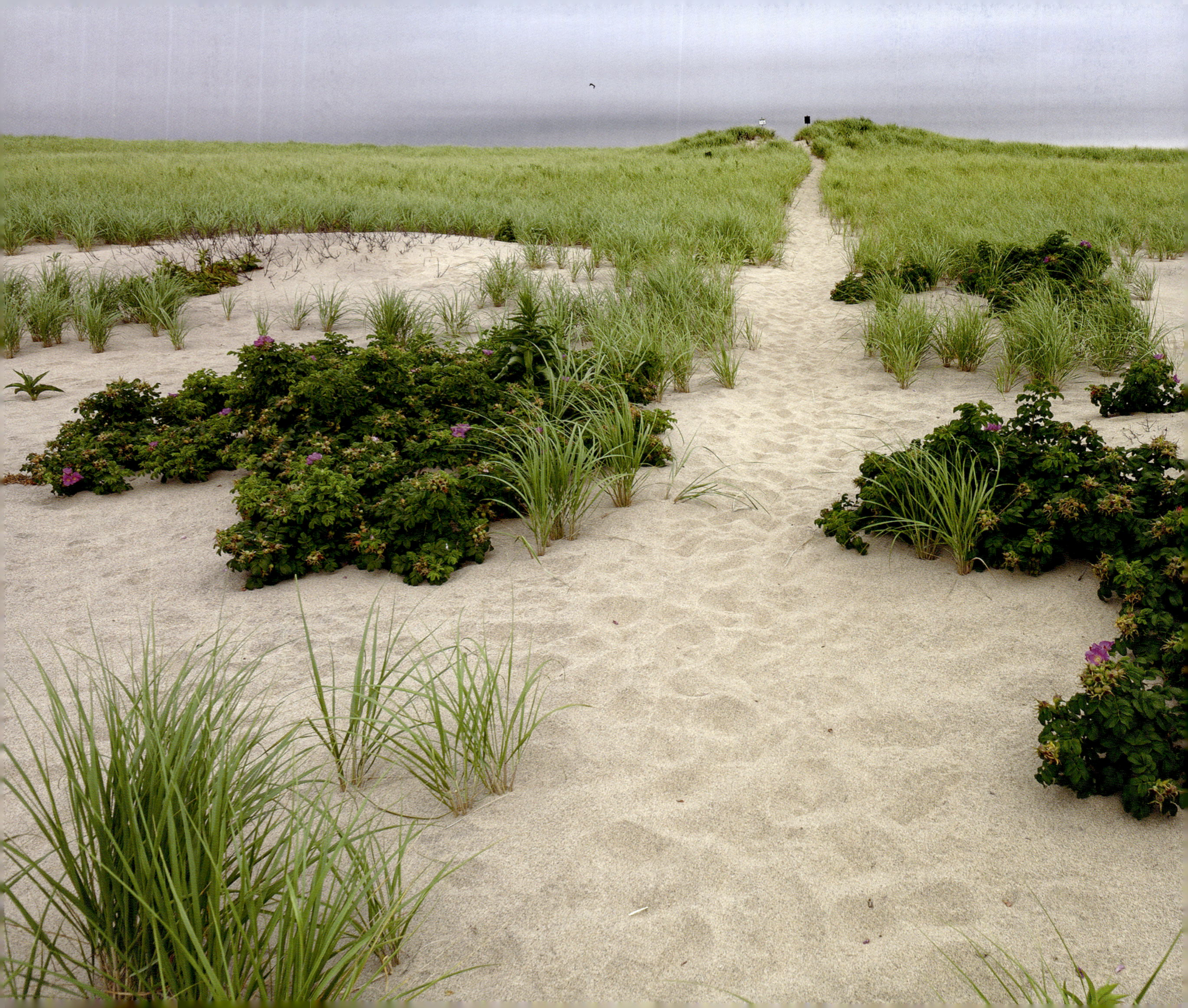

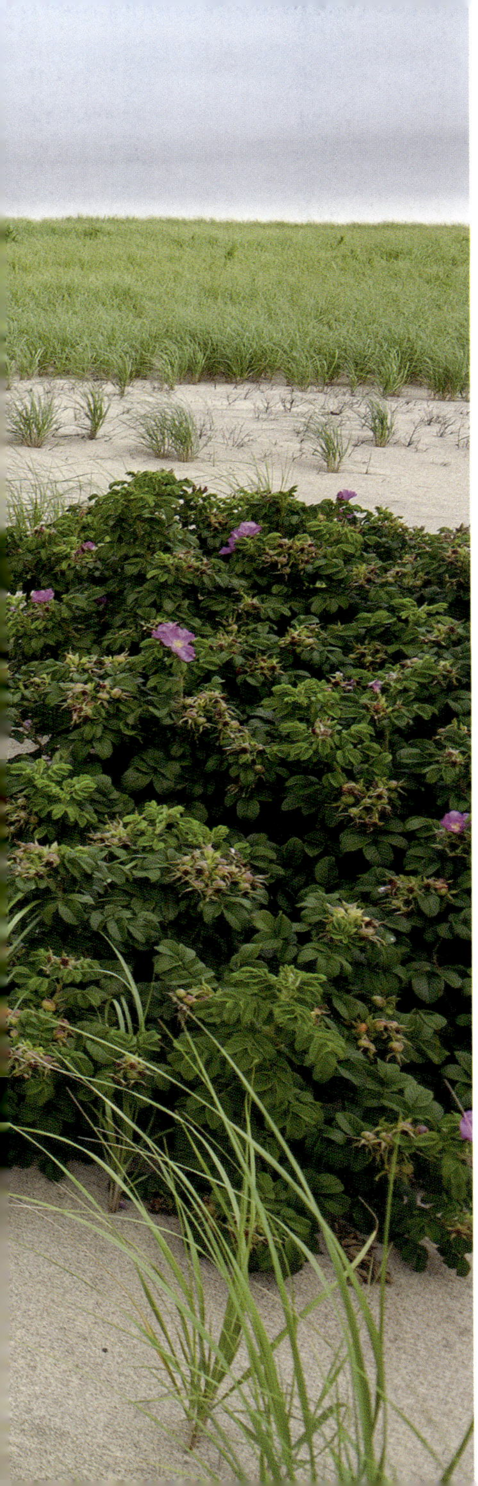

DUNE SHACKS OF PROVINCETOWN

Once across the dunes we live in an exquisite unreality.

HAZEL HAWTHORNE

author, dune shack dweller and doyenne

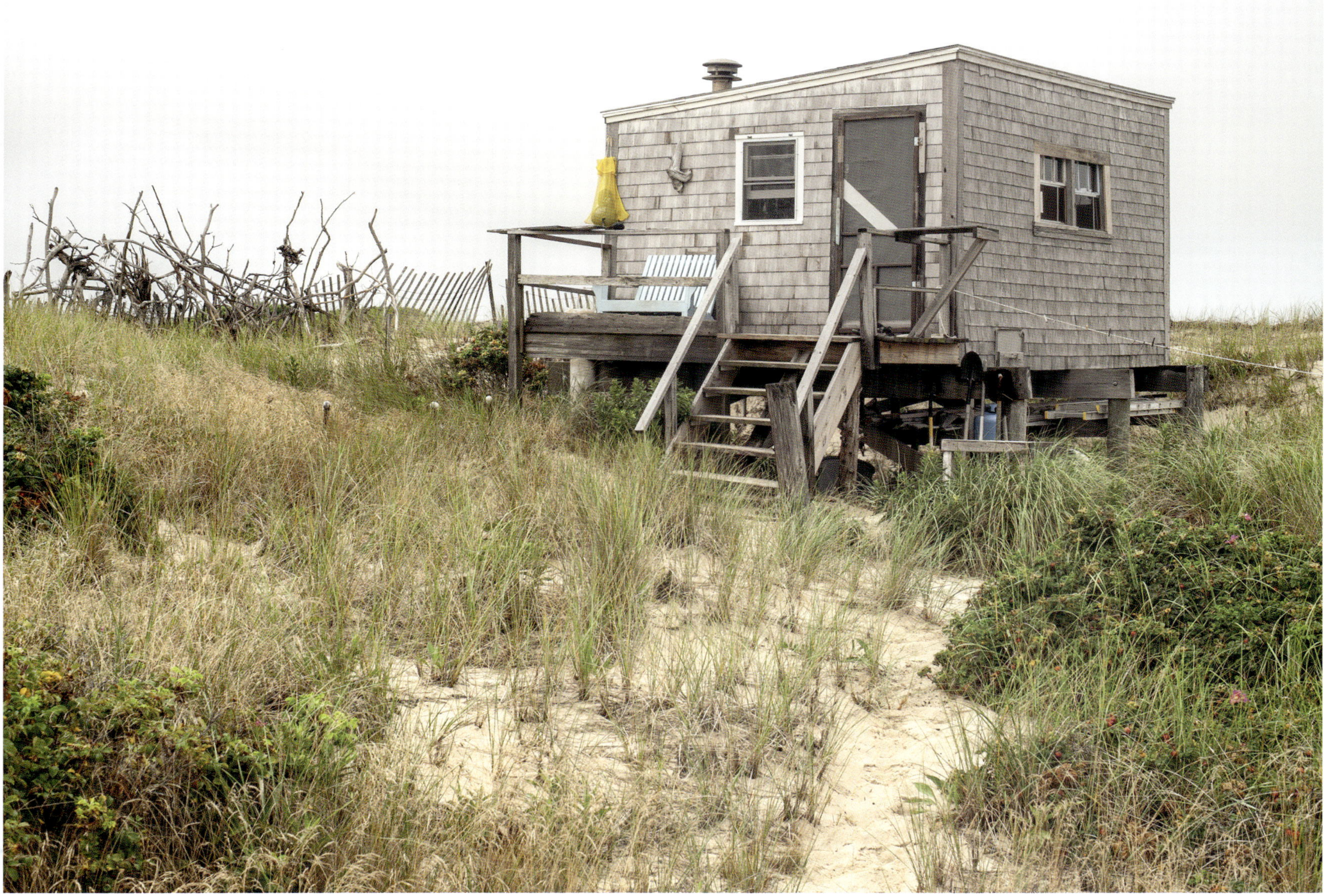

The dunes walk. A great wind will lift them bodily.
A vast crater appears where last year there was none.

MARY HEATON VORSE

labor activist, journalist, author

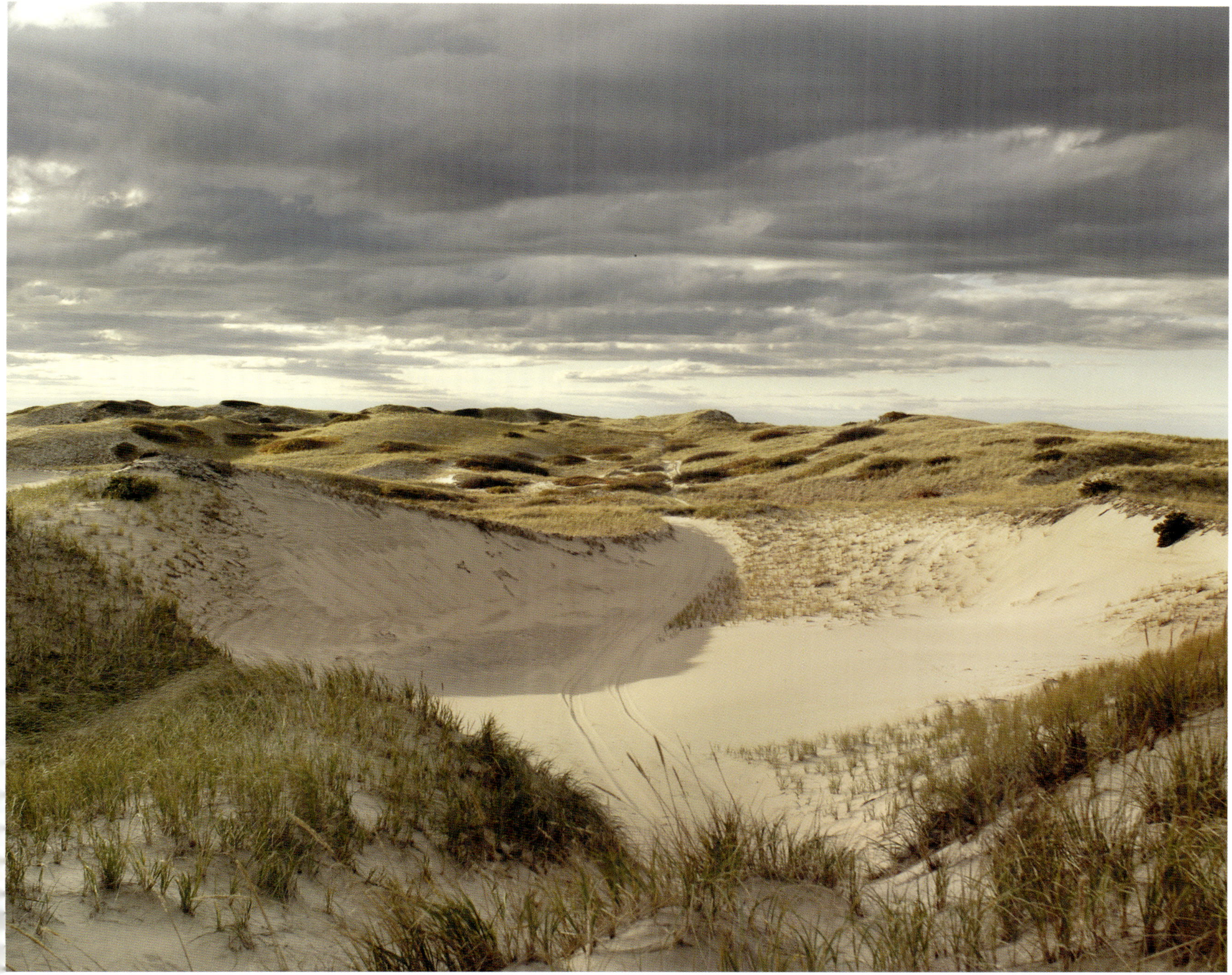

Indeed, it was the wreck of all cosmical beauty there within.

HENRY DAVID THOREAU

essayist, philosopher

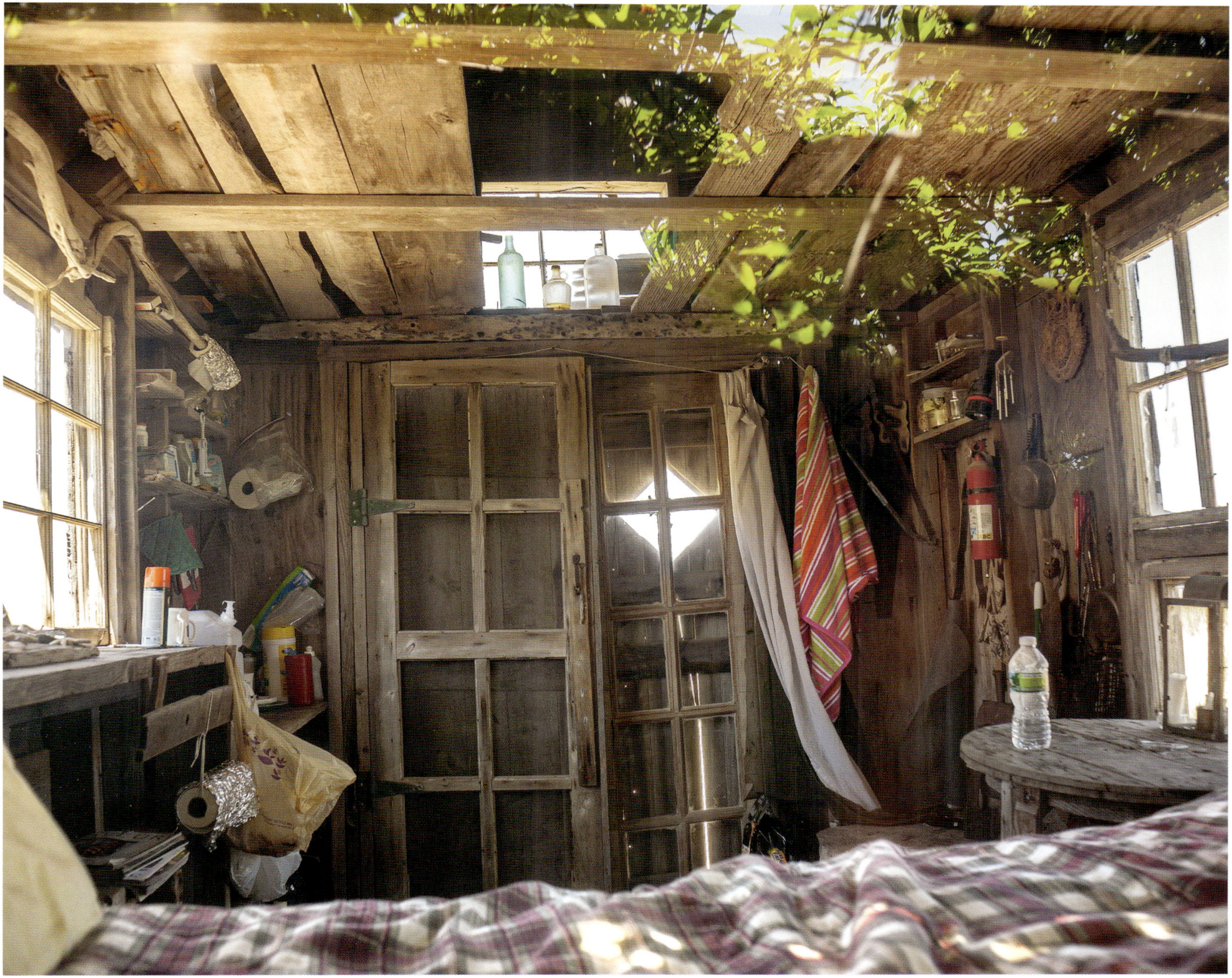

The Dune Shacks of Peaked Hill Bars represent a rare, regional beachside expression of a basic shelter constructed to provide human protection in the wilderness and designed in response to place-specific environmental conditions. The wilderness shelter architectural type defined here is a broad classification of small-scale, often fragile, function-based survivalist buildings that historically enabled people to interact with the natural landscape.

US DEPARTMENT OF THE INTERIOR

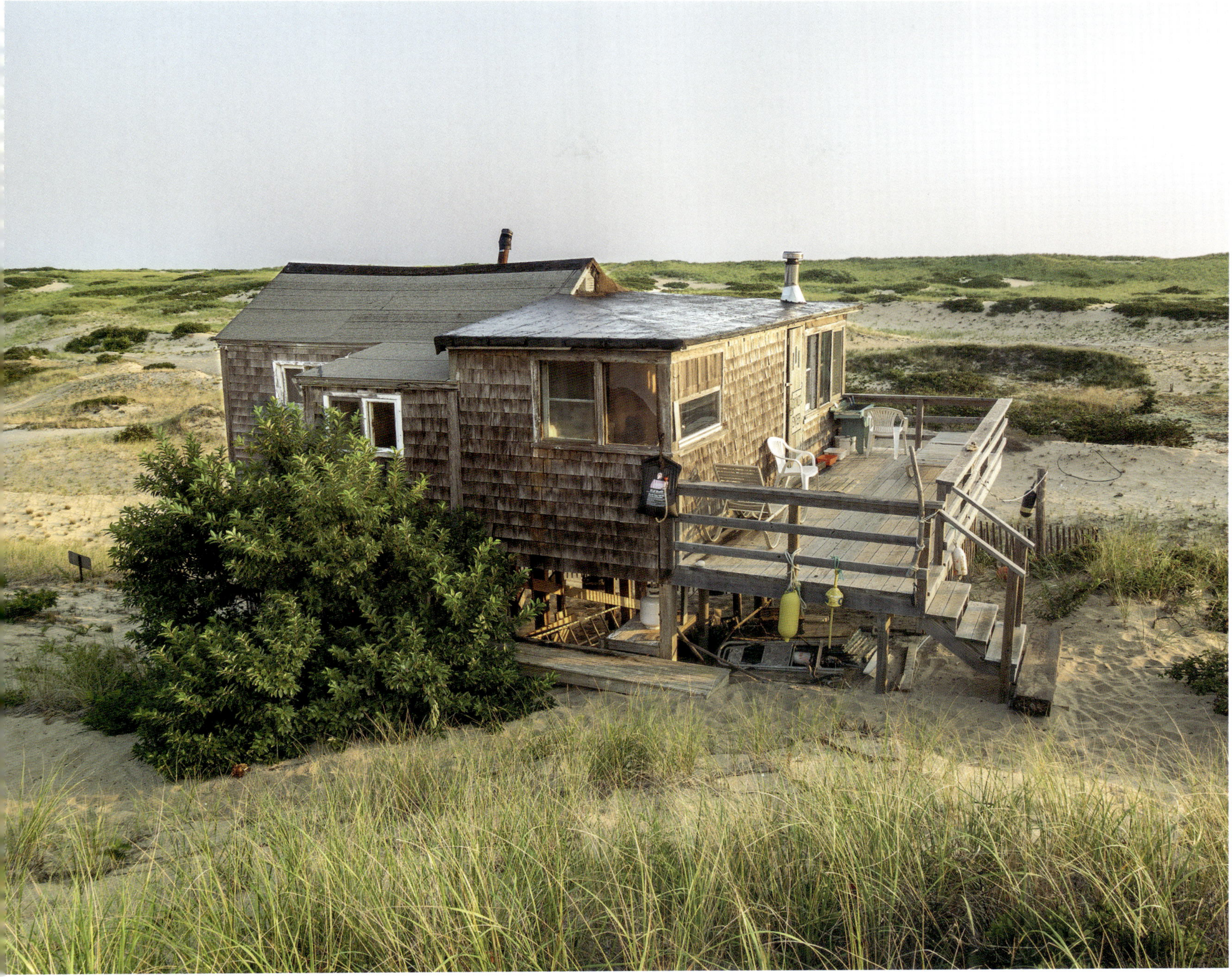

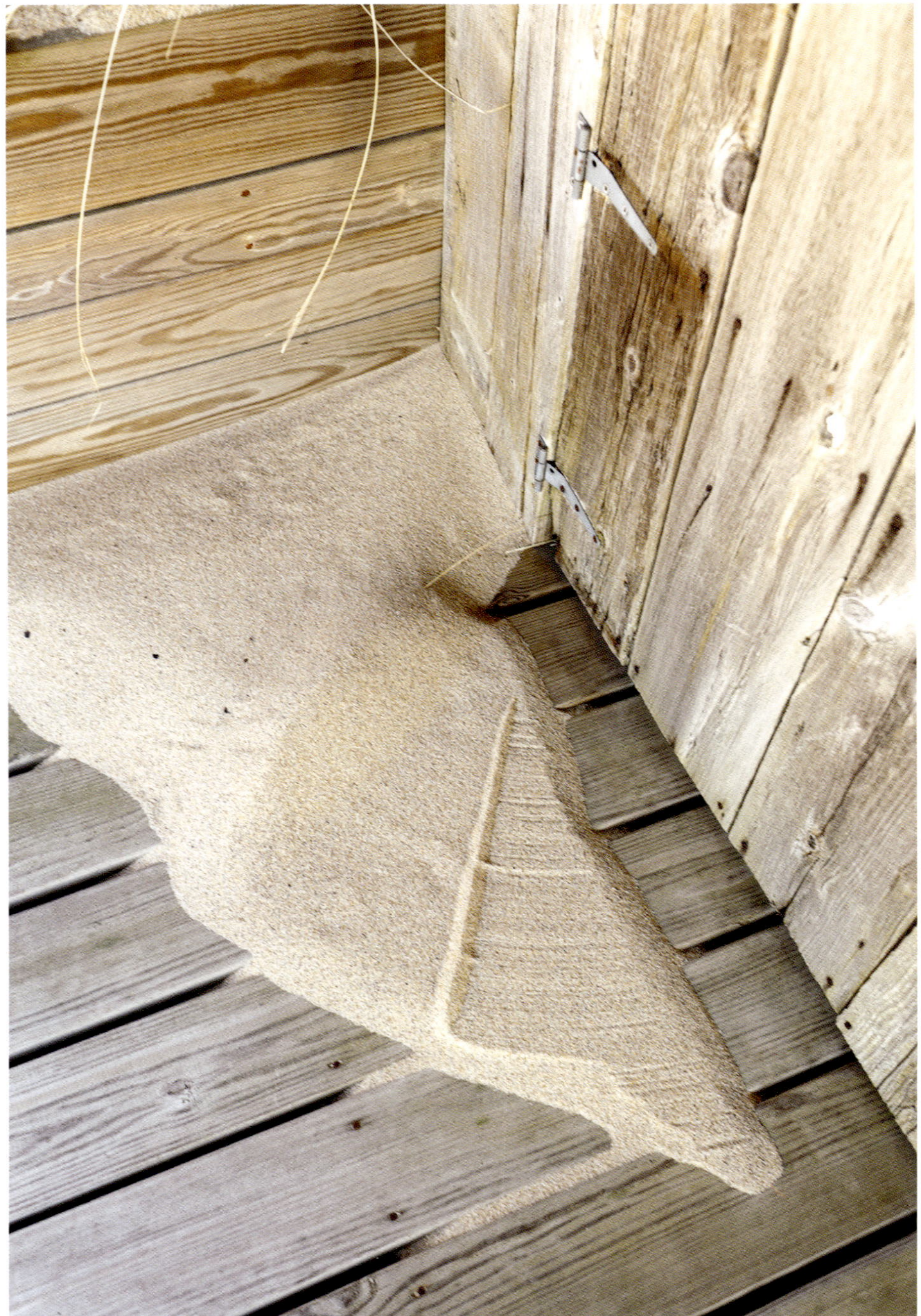

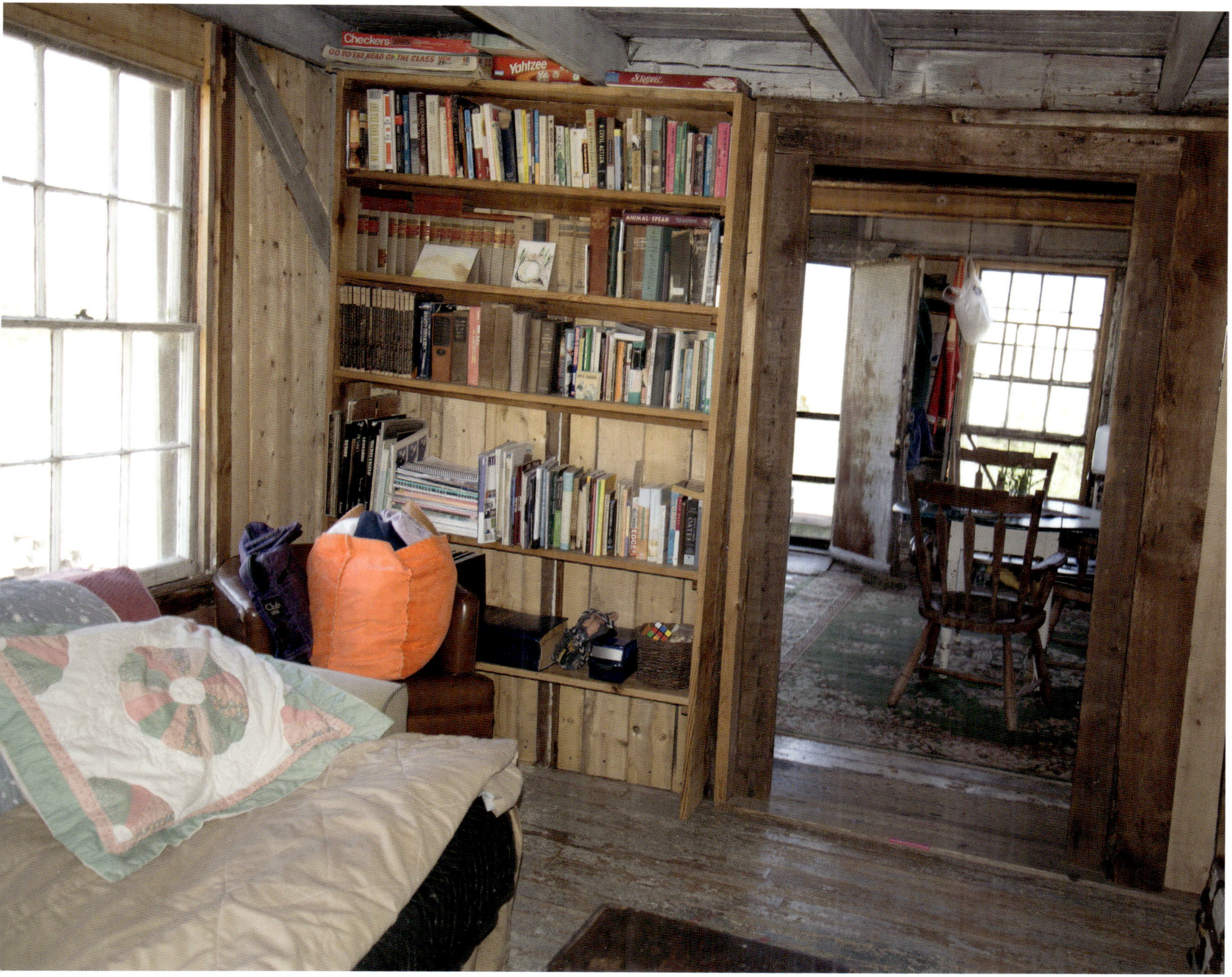
Checkers
GO TO THE HEAD OF THE CLASS
Yahtzee
A CIVIL ACTION
ANIMAL-SPEAK

We must all teach ourselves to be fine, to be poets.
Spend a lifetime in hard work with a humble mind. In his attempt
to develop the beauty he sees, the artist develops himself.

CHARLES HAWTHORNE

artist, founder of the Cape Cod School of Art

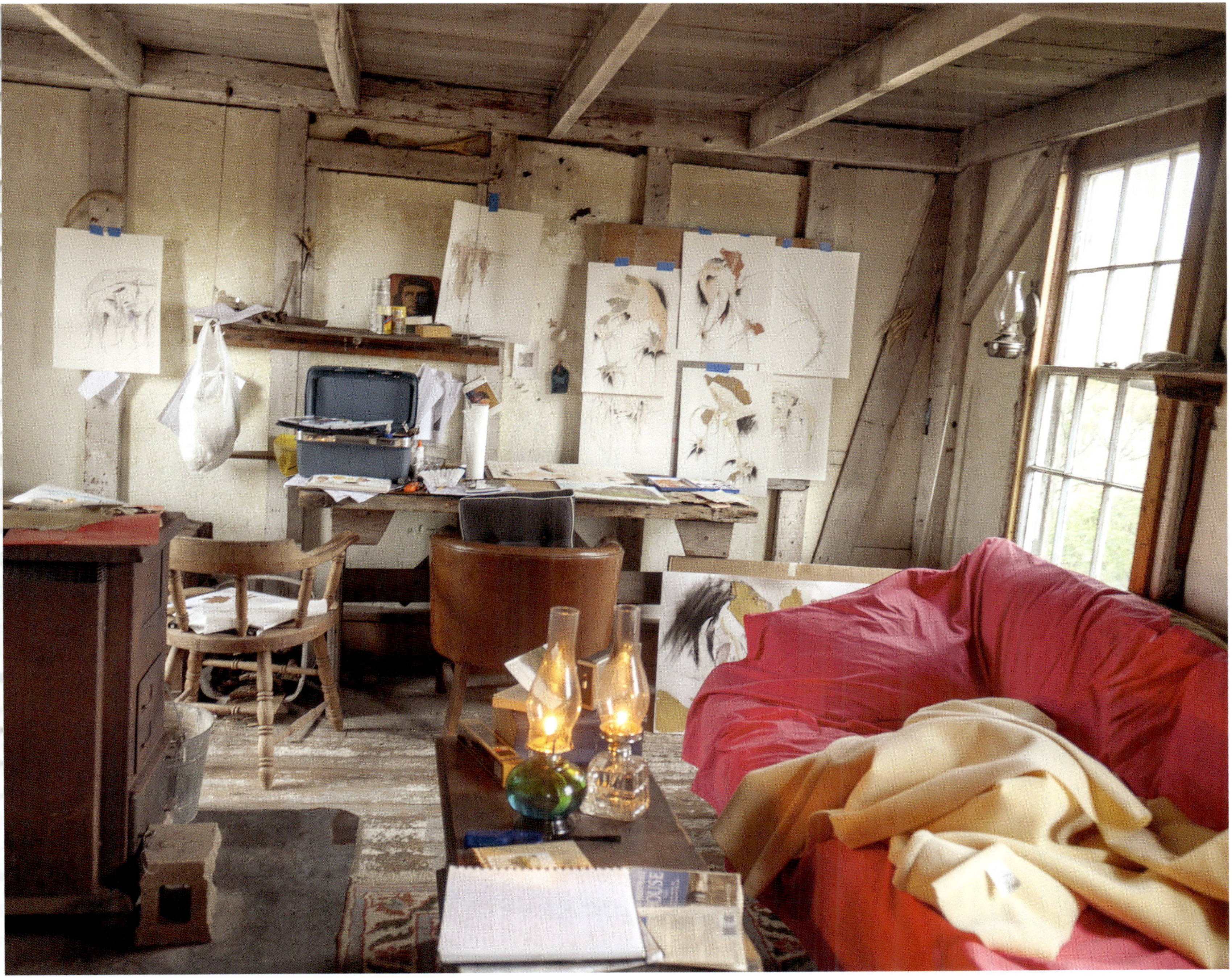

The way of the artist is curious and can never be determined, but . . . it is a fact that many need solitude, and some of the greatest work done in America, notably the early plays of Eugene O'Neill, have come from living in solitude in the dunes and shacks on the Back Shore of Cape Cod.

NORMAN MAILER

novelist, playwright, Pulitzer Prize winner

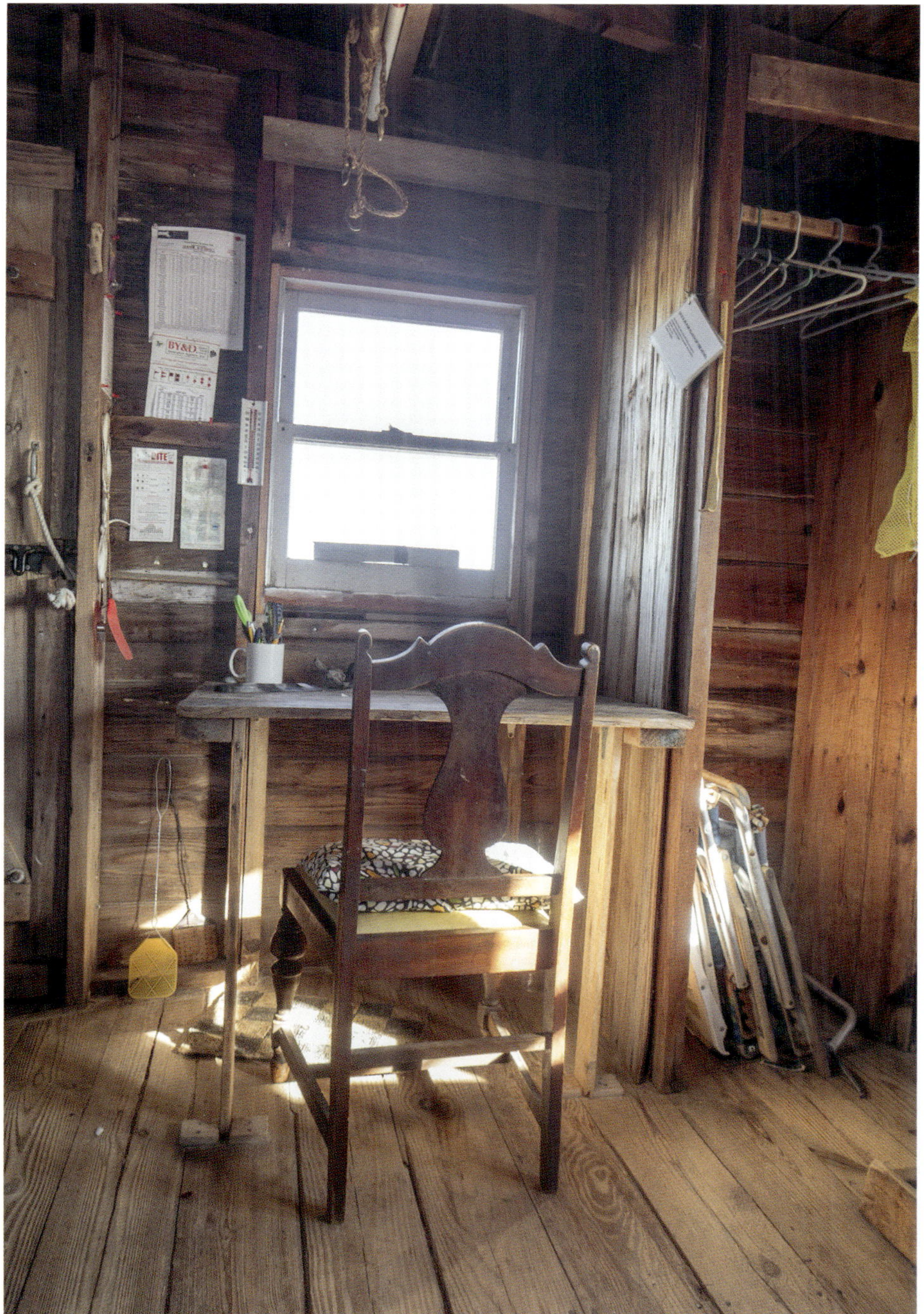

The shacks shouldn't be torn down,
any more than old adobe dwellings from a park in the Southwest.

JACK KEROUAC

author, pioneer of the Beat generation

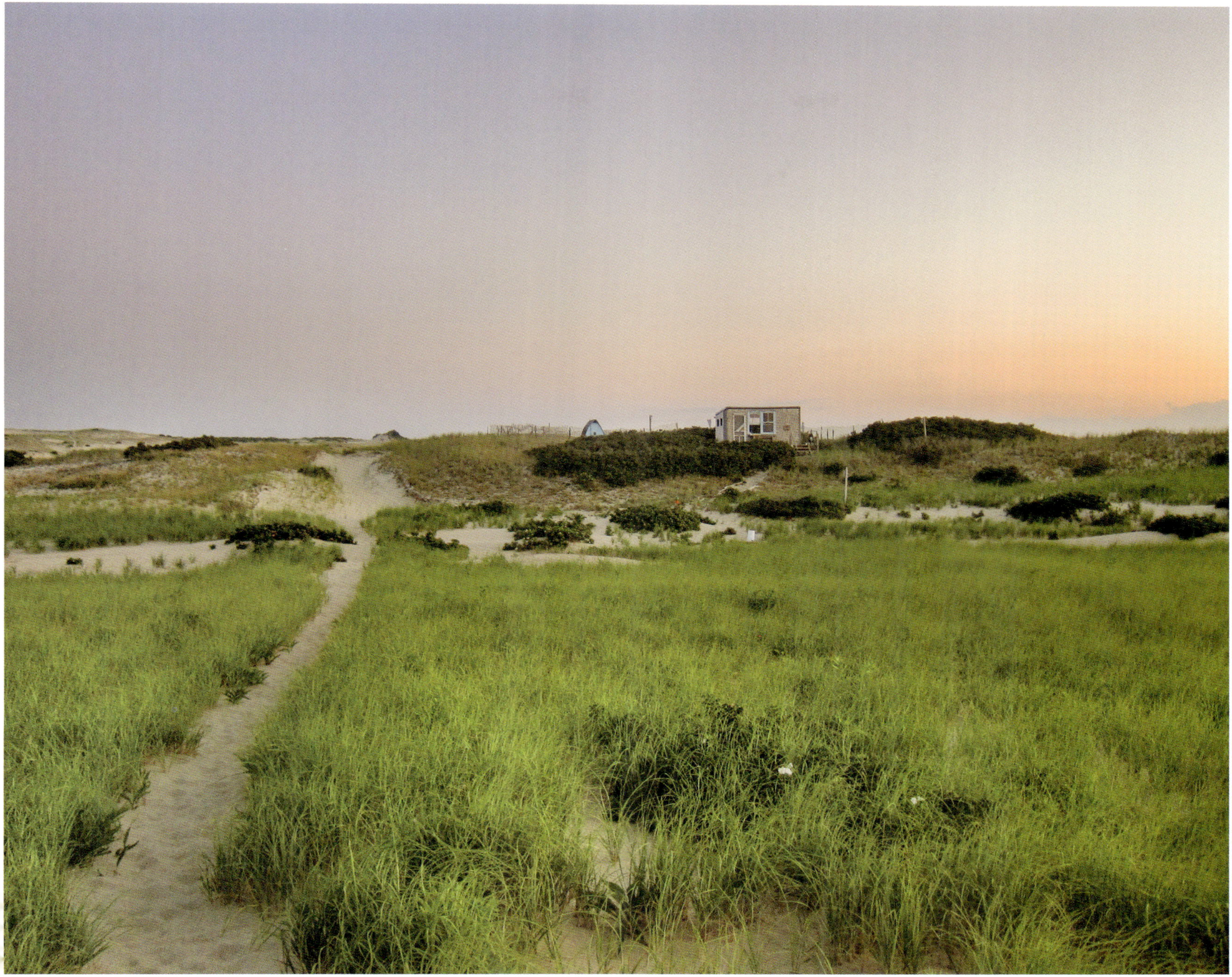

Eugene O'Neill boasted of having the Atlantic as his front lawn and miles of sand dunes as his back yard. He didn't have to wear clothes, as there were no houses within sight and there were none of "the unrefined refinements of civilization." He described the three-mile walk to town, up and down over sand dunes, as the penalty one paid for communication with the world of people.

CROSWELL BOWEN

author, journalist

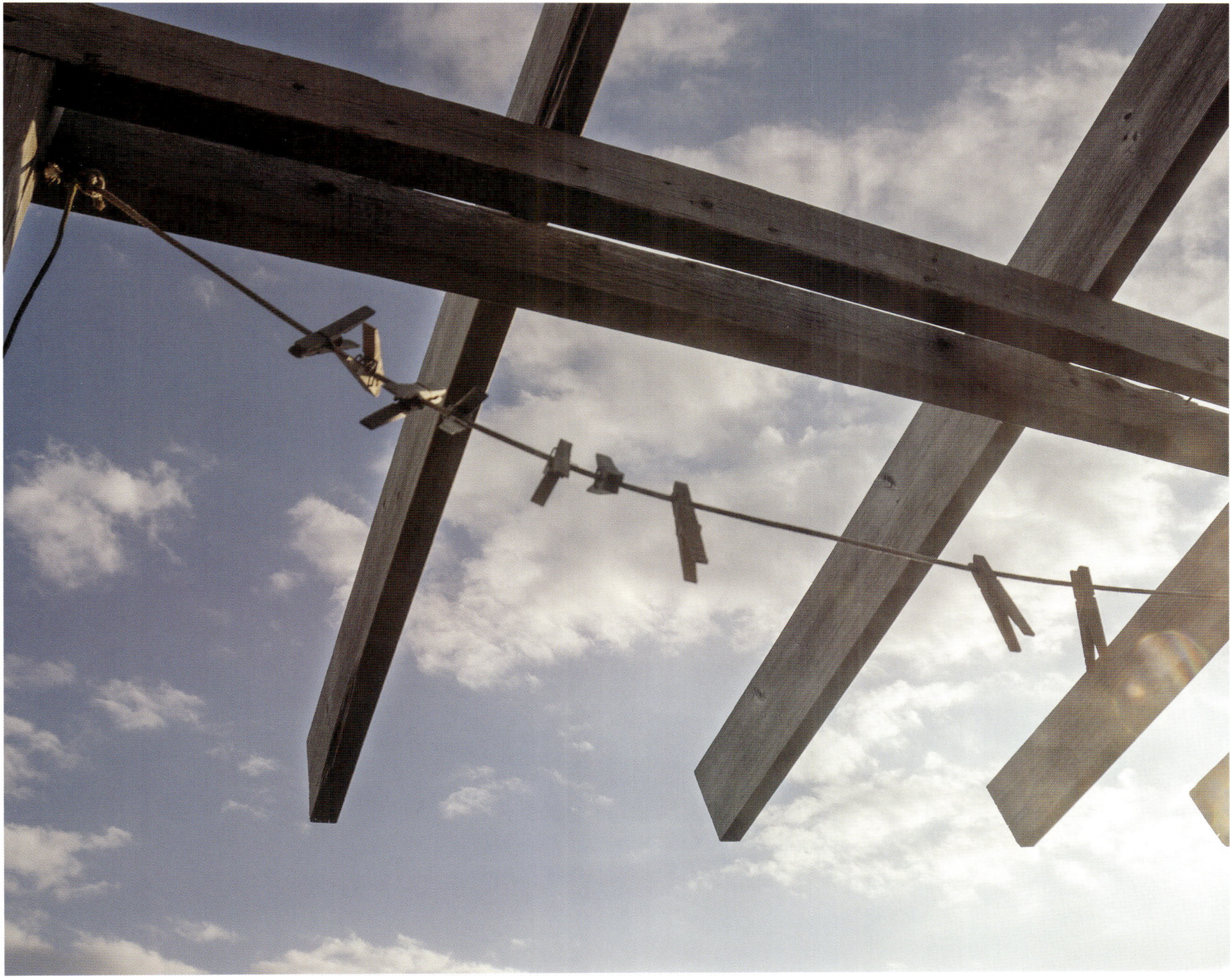

On the dunes when the grass bends in complaisance to the wind,
it sweeps a design at the same time.
Thus in still weather you will find a perfect circle lying upon the ground.

HAZEL HAWTHORNE

dune shack dweller and doyenne, author

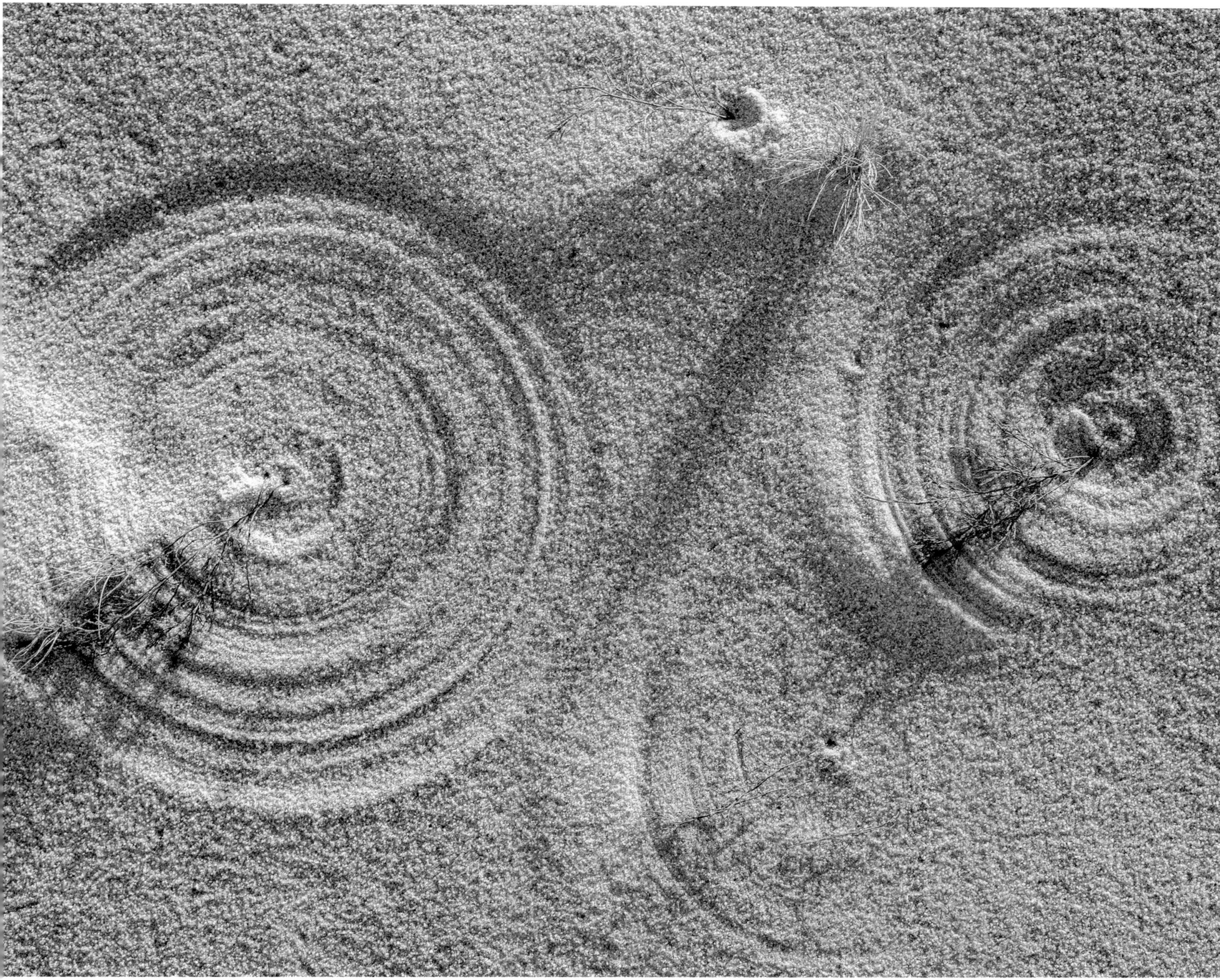

The dunescape is simultaneously verdant and lunar. It is dotted with brush and scrubby, stunted pine. It has a smell: pine and salt, with an undercurrent of something I can only describe as dusty and green.

MICHAEL CUNNINGHAM

novelist, screenwriter, Pulitzer Prize winner

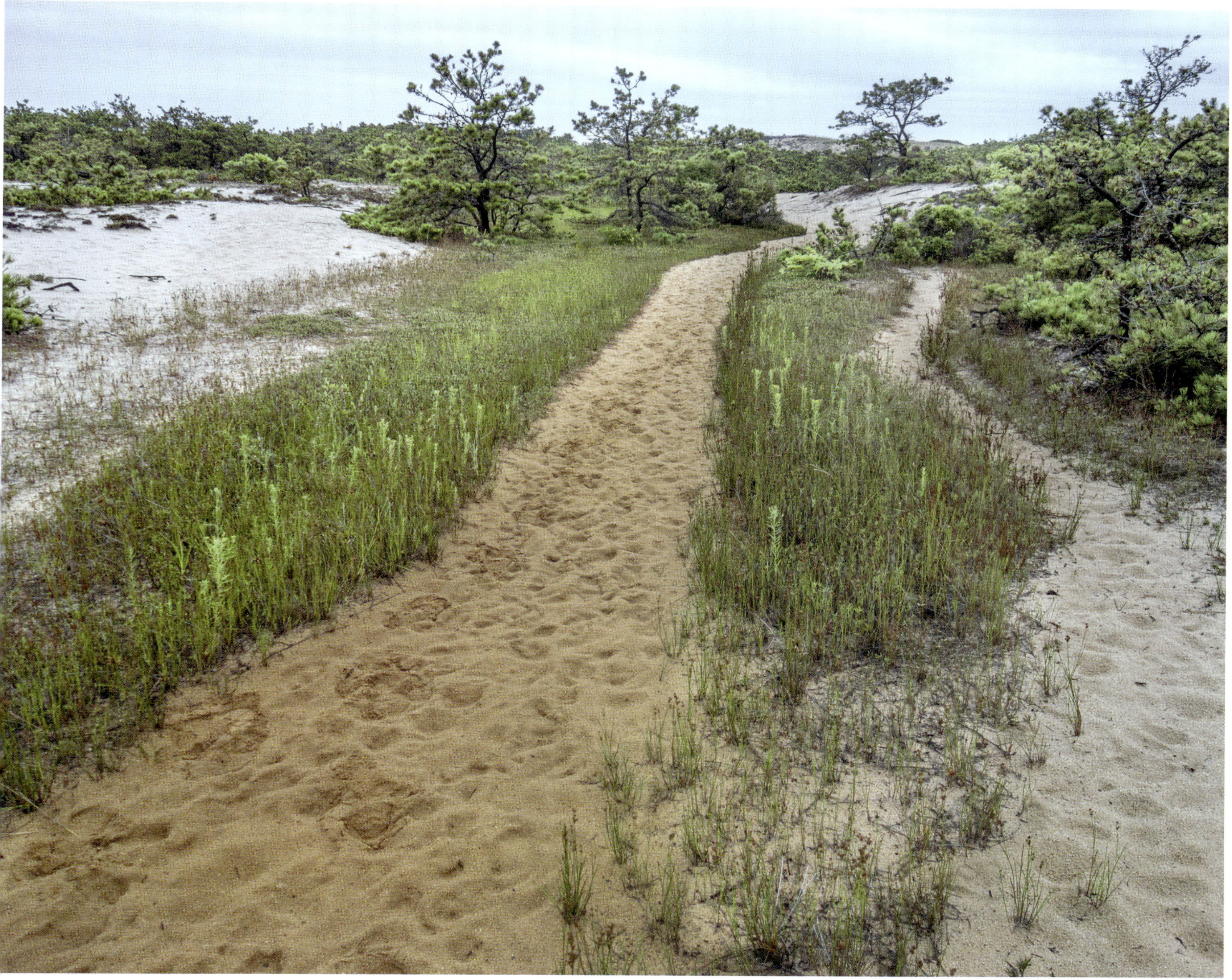

My shack standing in the middle
Of all this, in the midmost
Of the leagues of sand, of the long, rolling leagues,
Next door to heaven and close on the gates of sunset,
The opening doors of dawn:
I've got what few have, I've got the life I want!

HARRY KEMP

dune shack dweller, poet, author of *Poet of the Dunes*

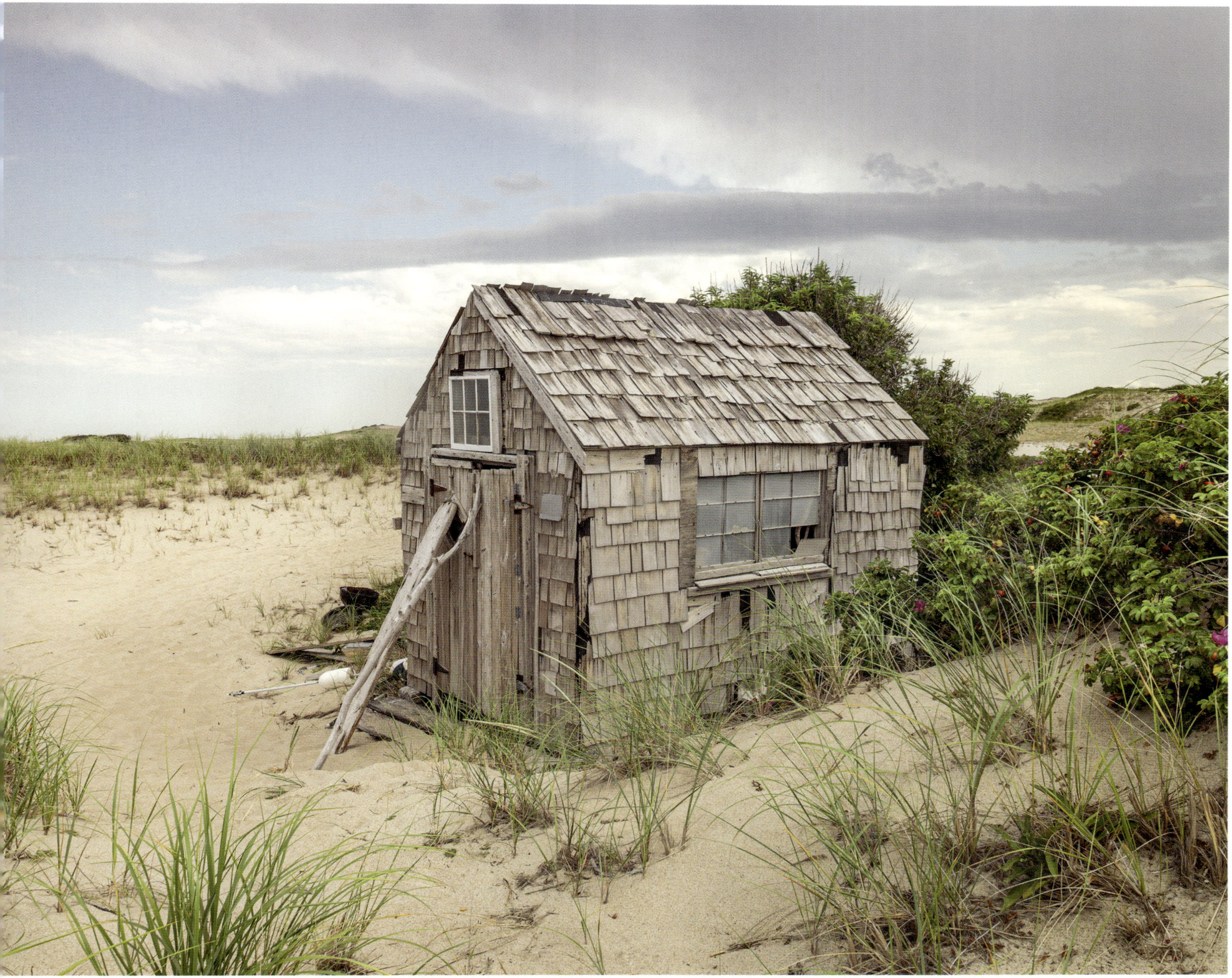

It was the peace and rest for which I have been longing,
rest more exquisite perhaps than we shall ever know together again.

HAZEL HAWTHORNE

dune shack dweller and doyenne, author

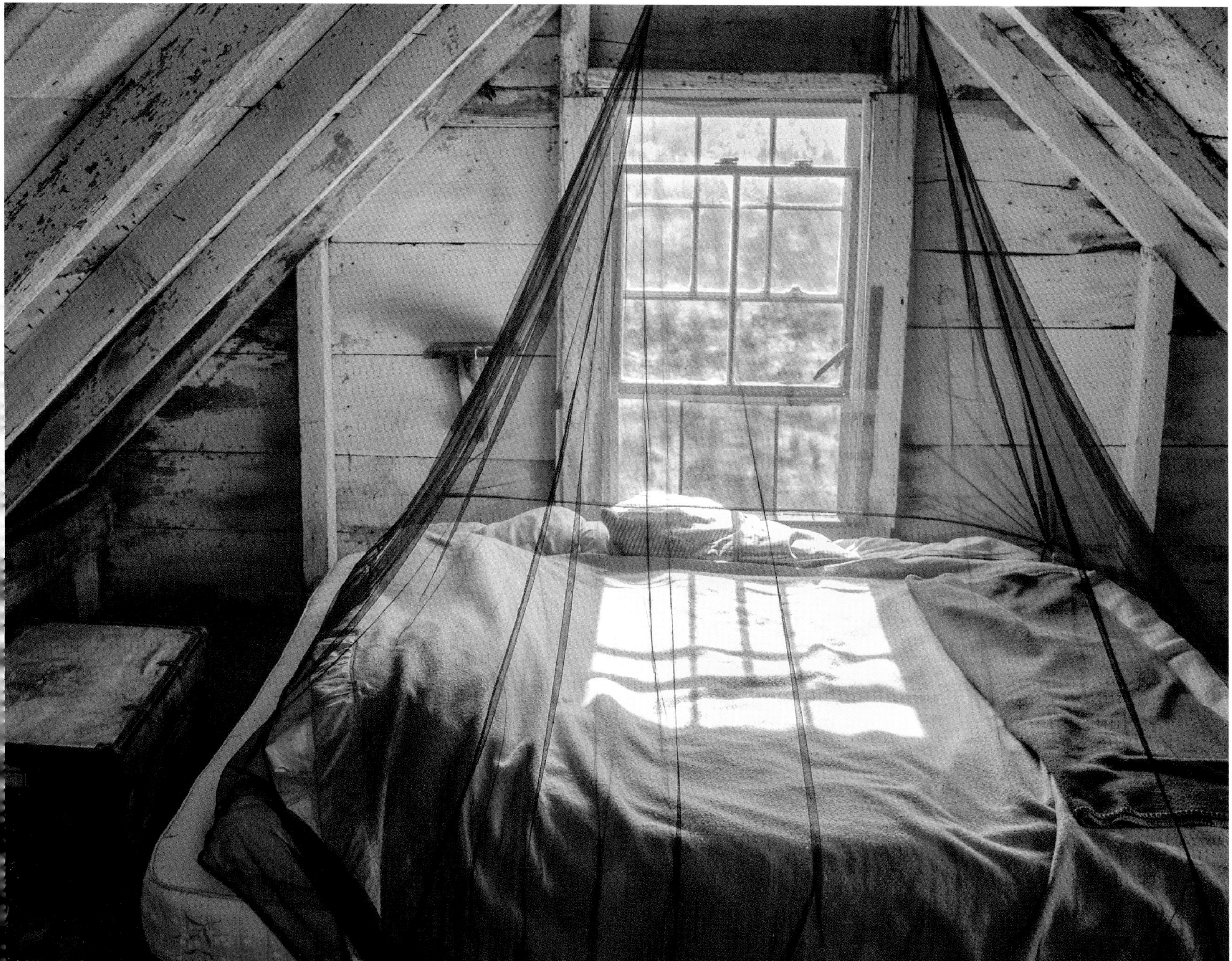

I feel more myself here than anywhere else.

ZEHRA KHAN

artist, artist-in-residence

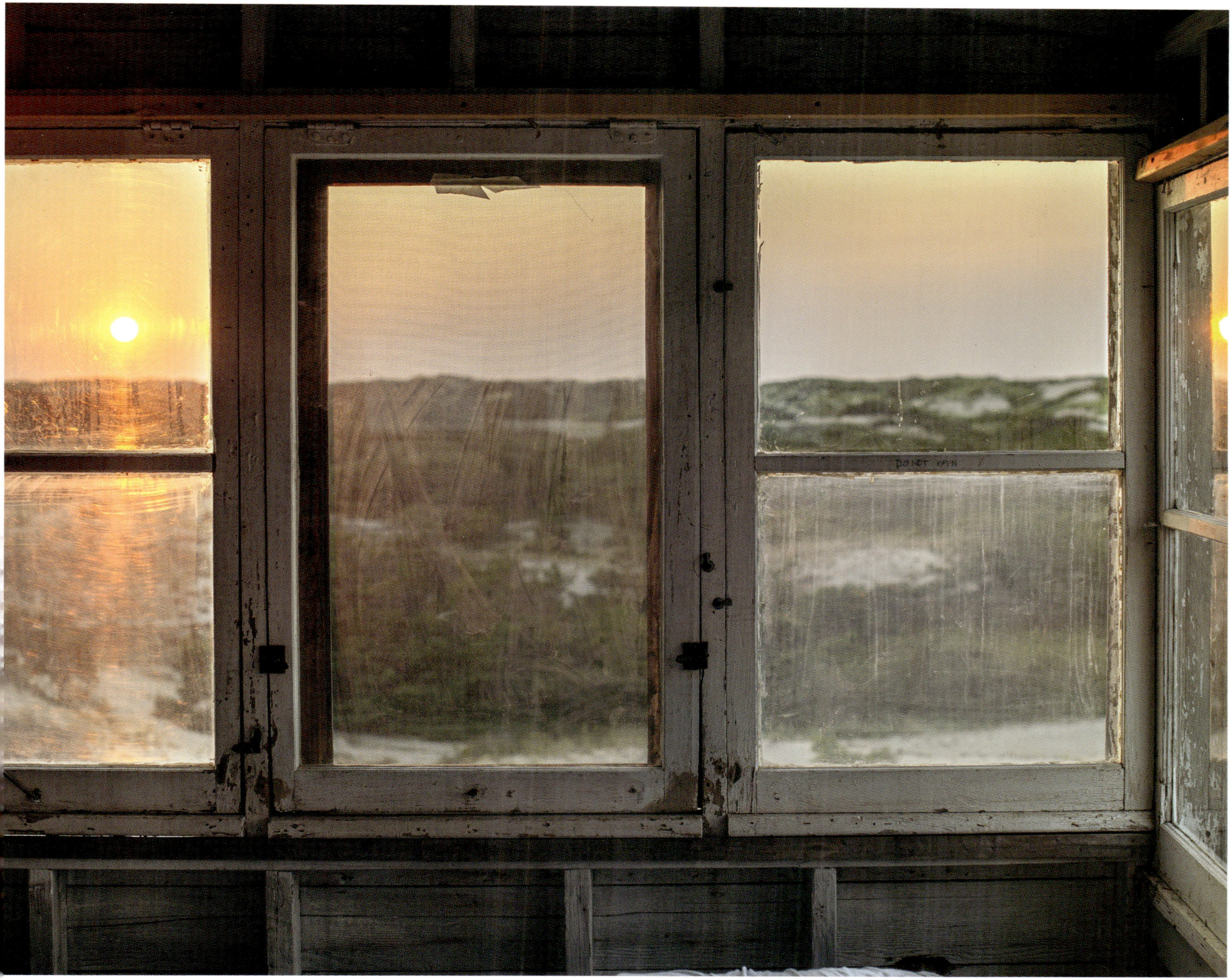

When I set out to draw the shape of the glass of the oil lamp,
it is not just its breathtaking shape against the windowpane.
It is all the color of the grasses, sky, ocean trapped in its glass.

ELLEN LEBOW

artist

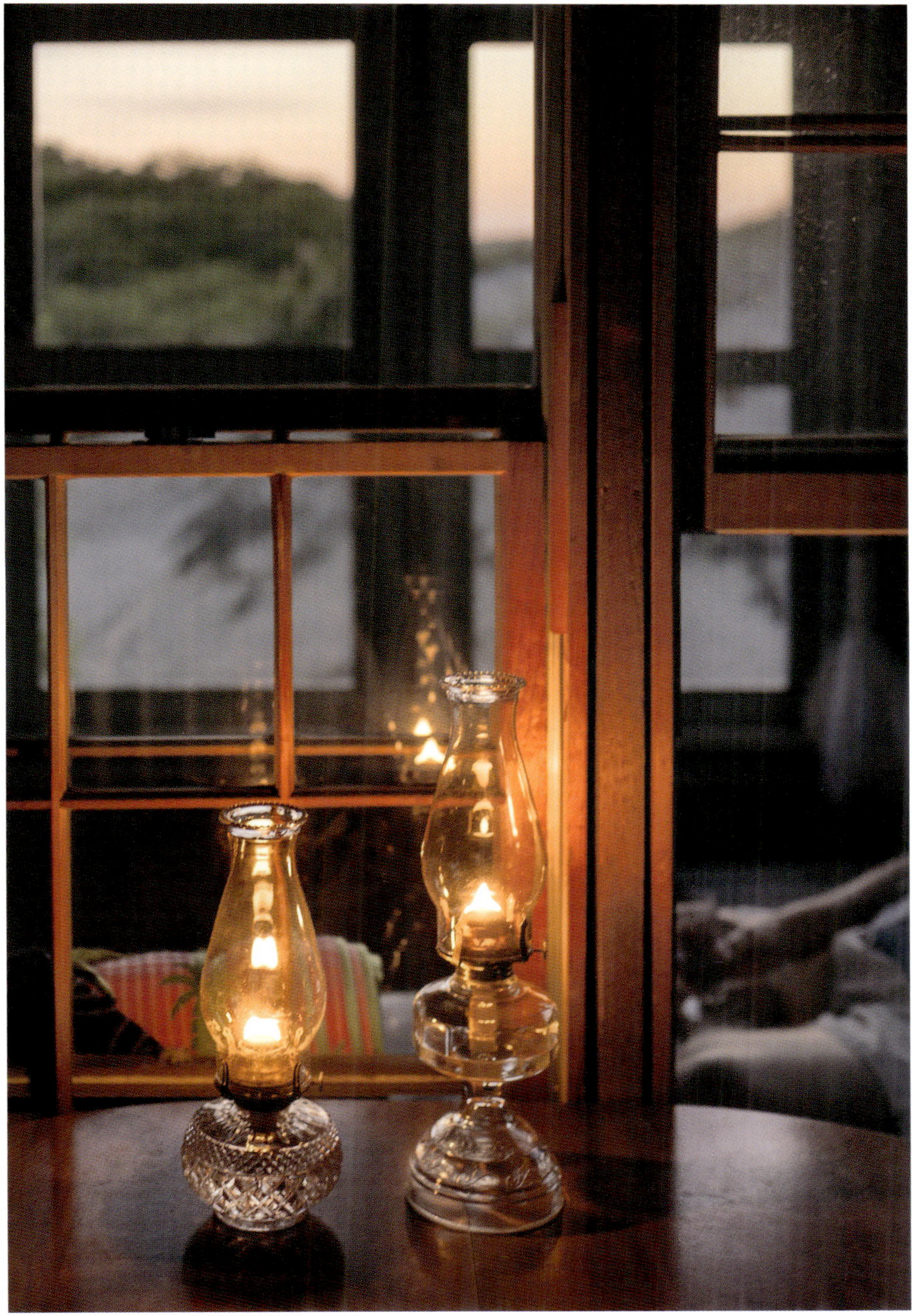

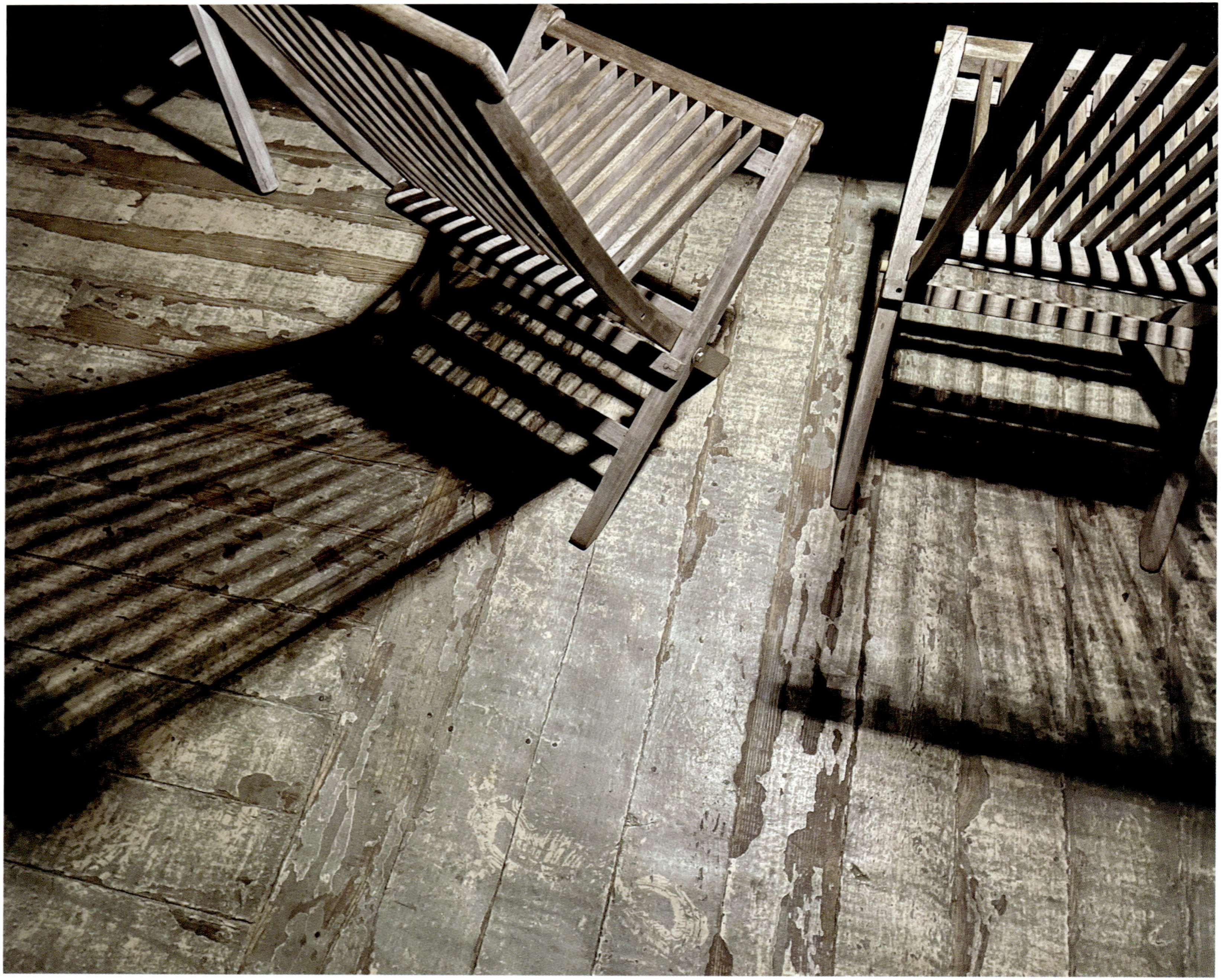

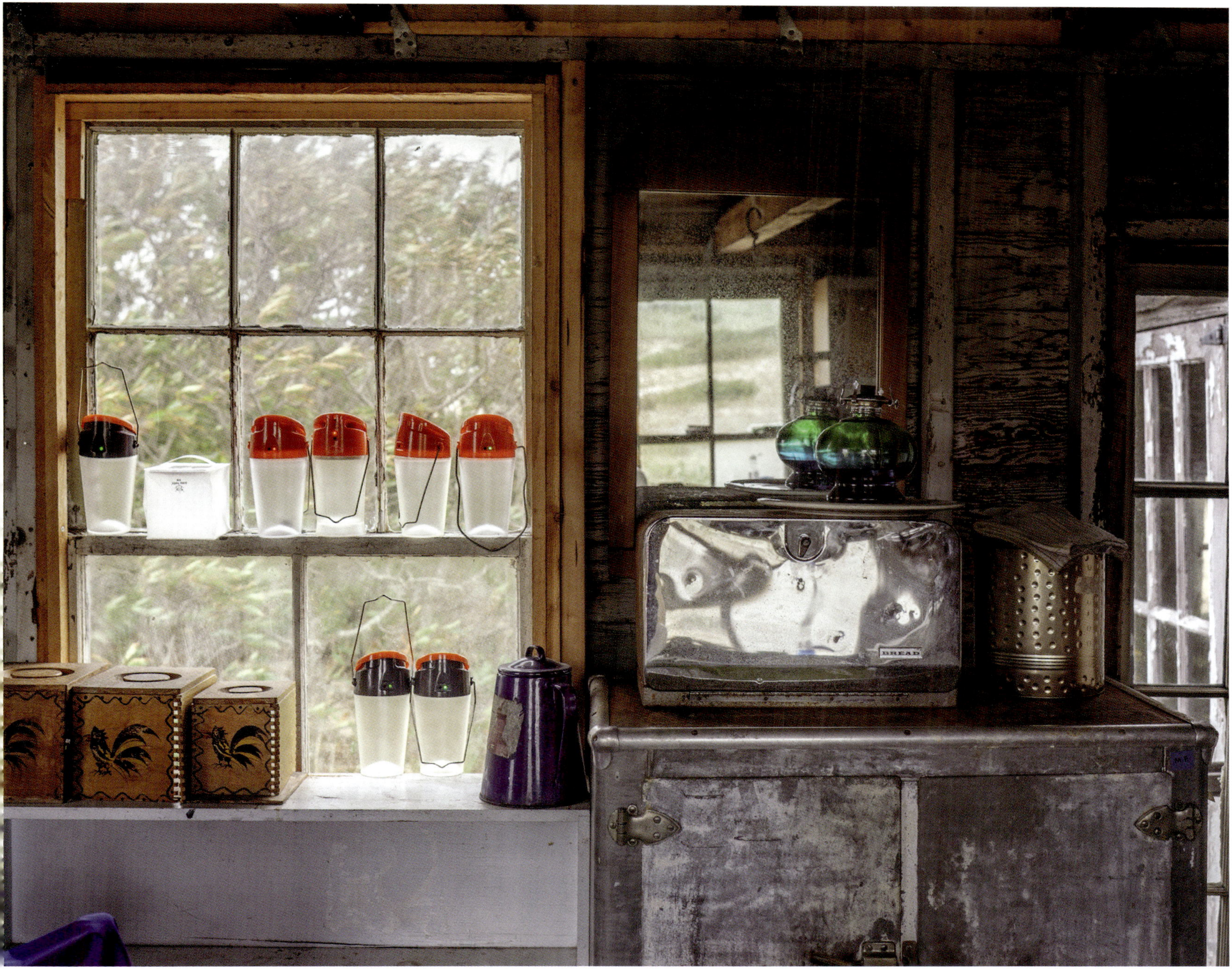
BREAD

I love rainy days when nobody comes.

GENEVIEVE MARTIN

dune shack dweller

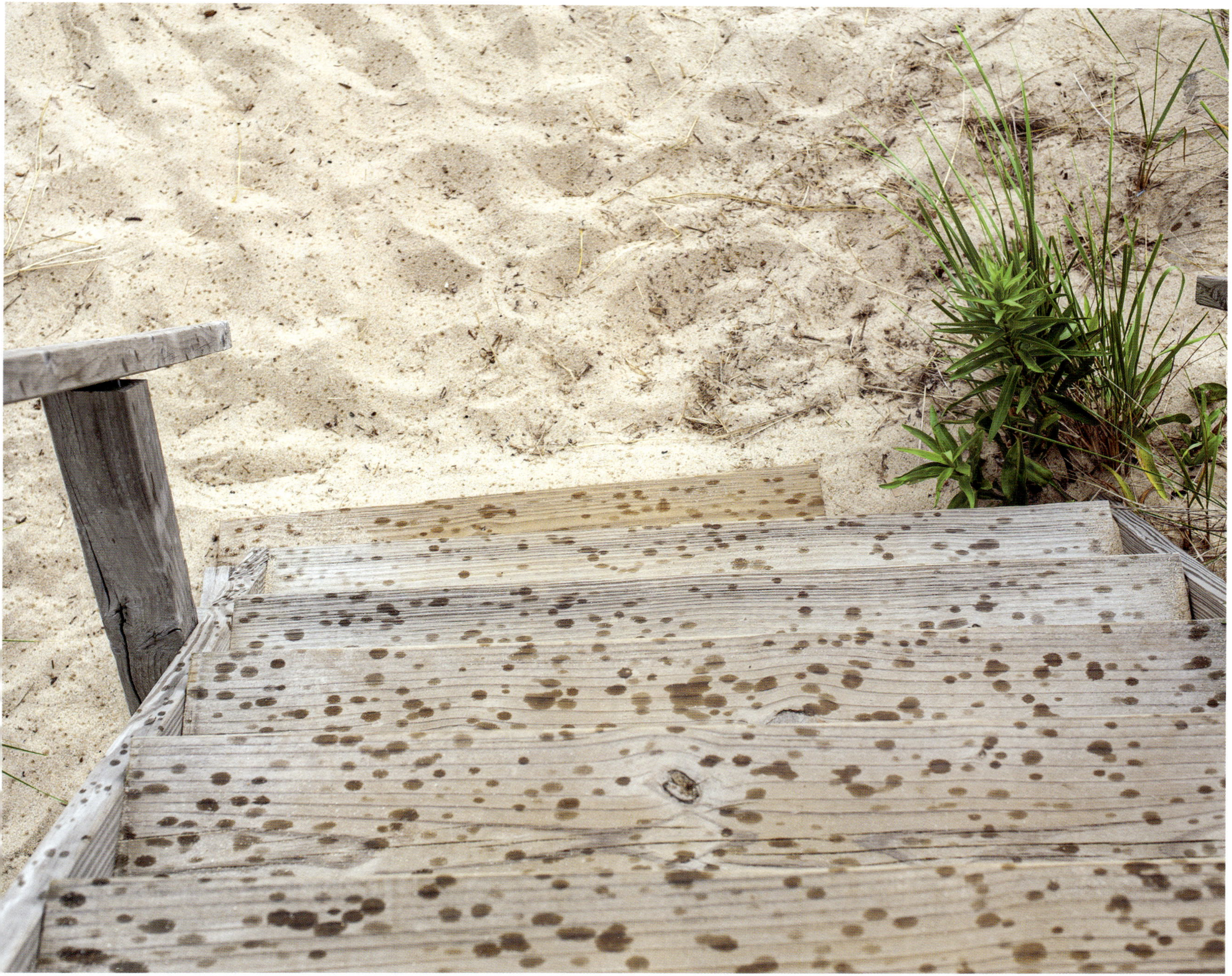

Here we come to the end of things, standing at its tip and staring back to where we have come from, discovering that place anew.

ROBERT FINCH

essayist, radio commentator, Edward R. Murrow award winner, Guggenheim Fellow

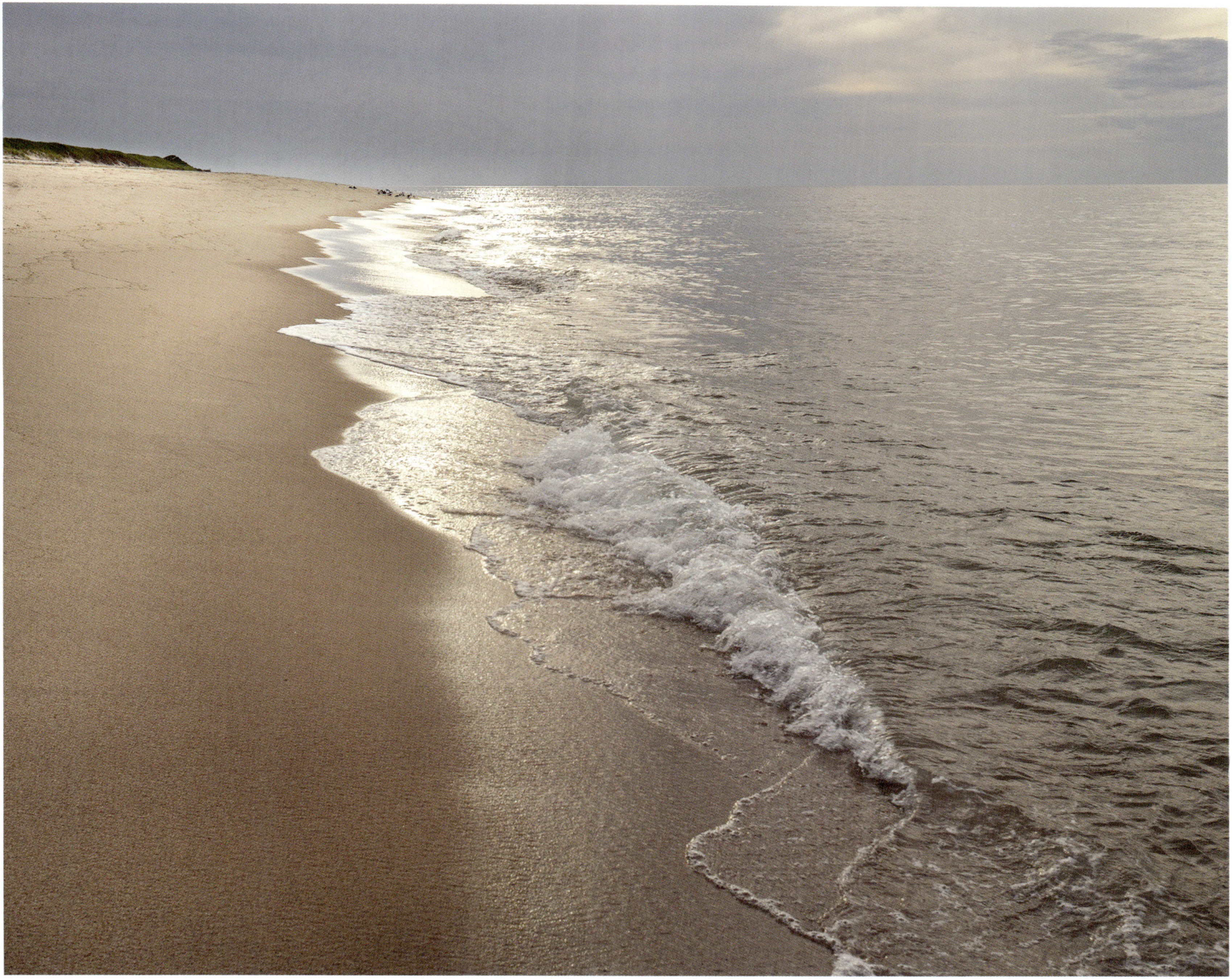

They [the shacks] survive. They're out there watching the ocean every day, every day, just collecting all the energy. They're little churches, each one of them. It's just phenomenal . . .

EMILY BEEBE

dune shack dweller

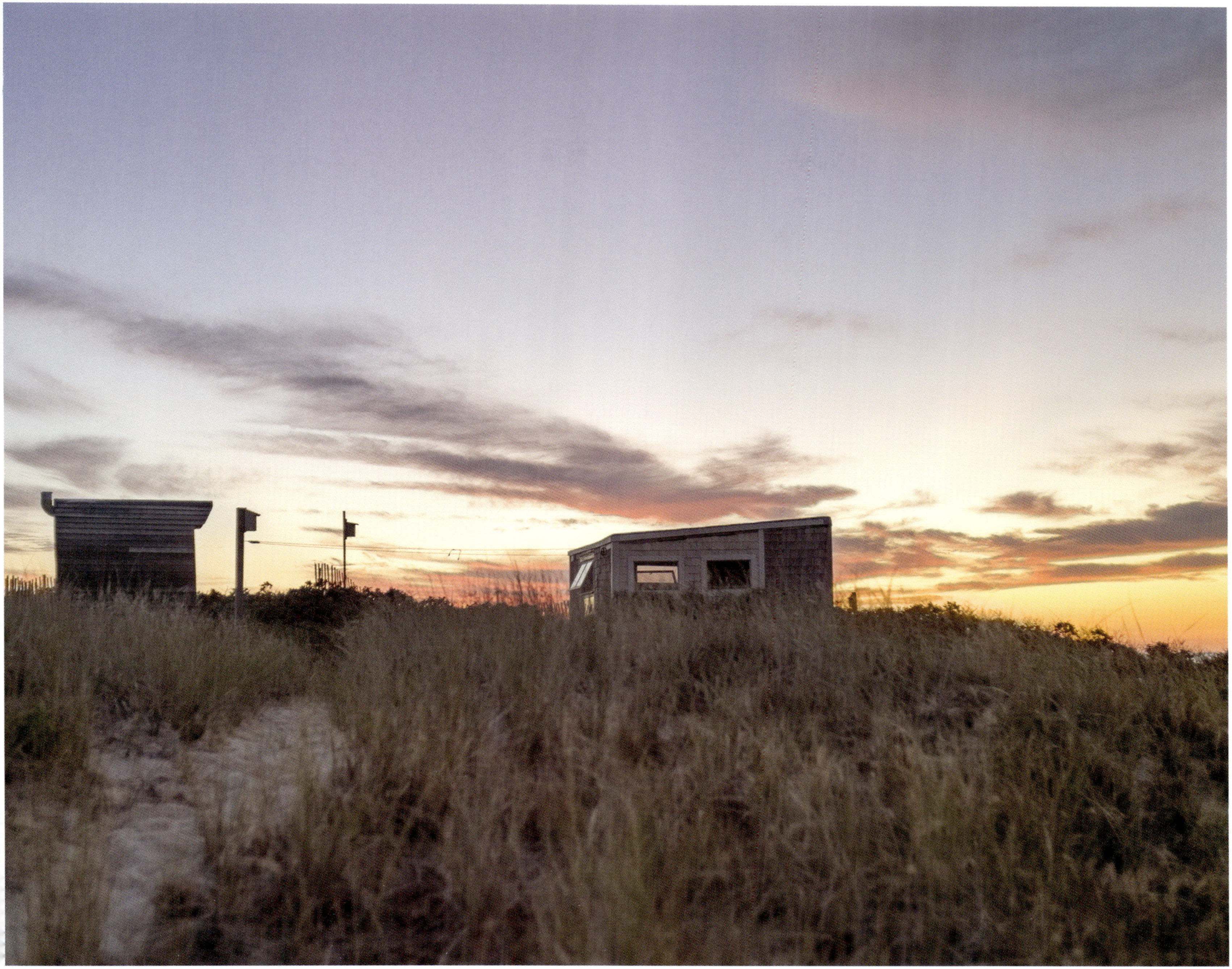

To say the shacks are basic is an understatement. But I felt like I was living at the intersection of sea and land in a way I've never experienced before.

DANIEL RANALLI

visual artist, artist-in-residence

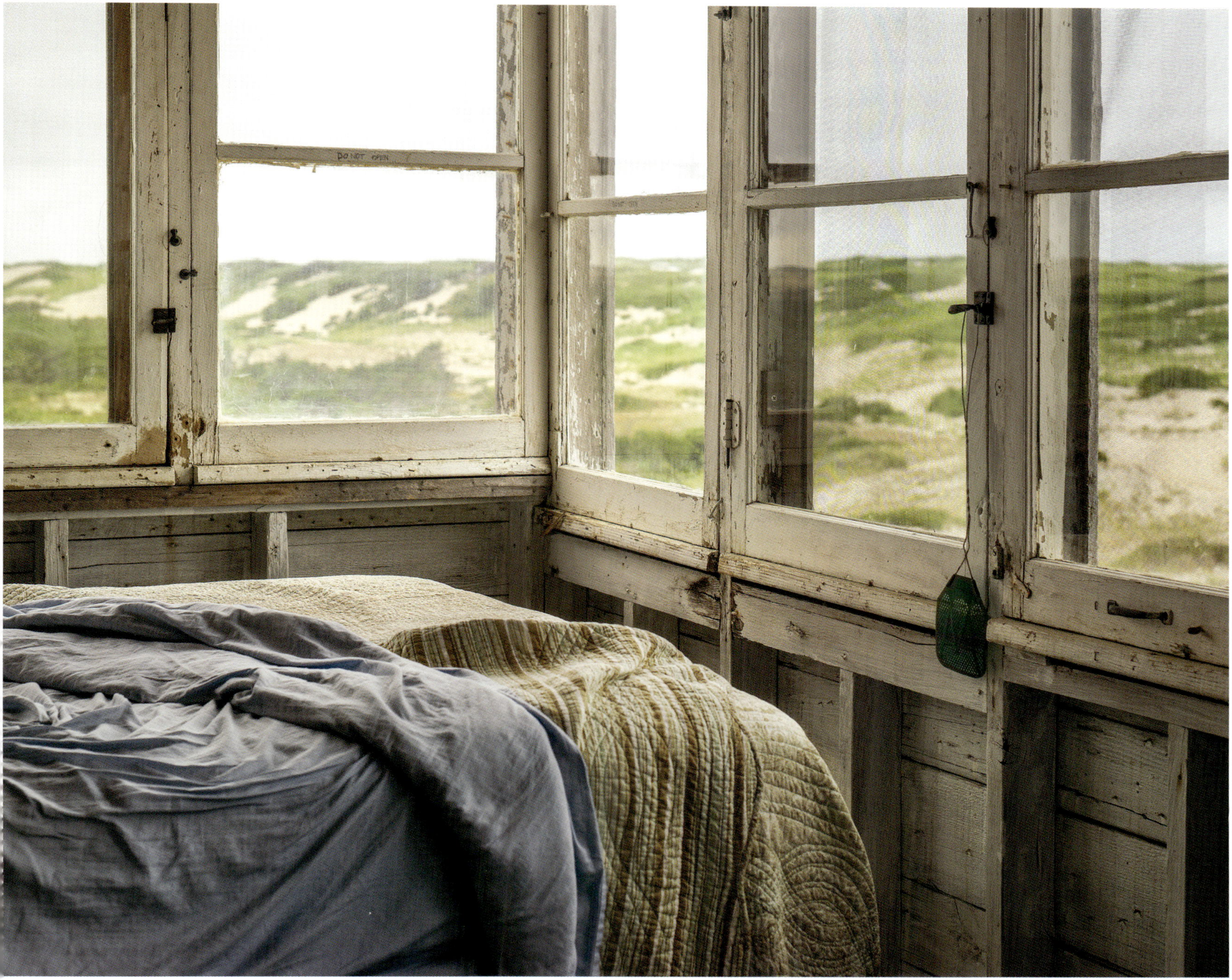

I have early but vivid memories of going out to the family shack as a toddler with my sister and my parents, who carried all of our food and their art supplies on their backs. . . . I remember once trying to eat sand—an endless supply of food! It felt like a great discovery, and I was quite upset at being told not to eat it.

TABITHA VEVERS

dune shack dweller, artist

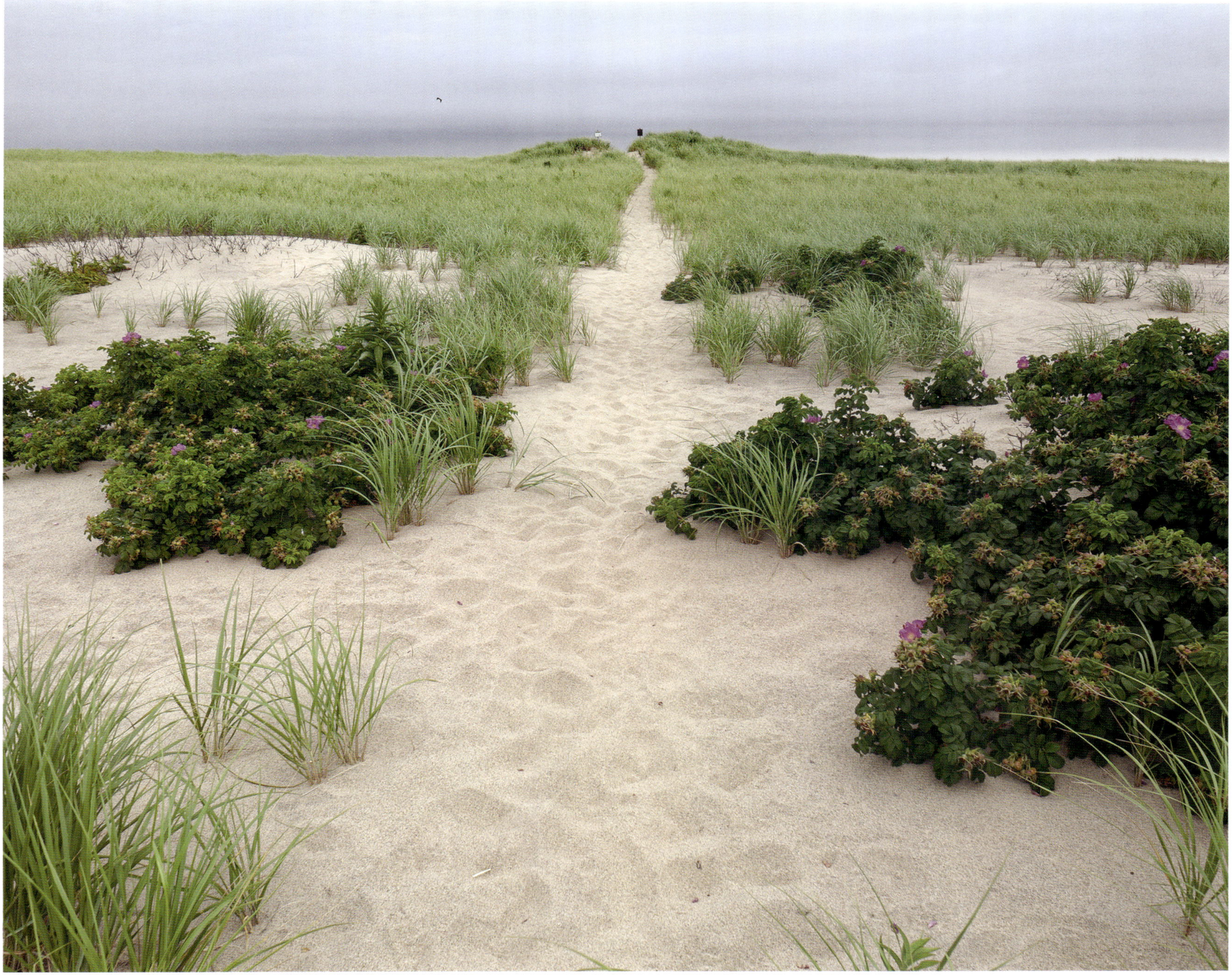

I may only go in for a minute or two, but I go in. And I open my eyes to let the salt water in them. It's good for my eyesight.

HARRY KEMP

dune shack dweller, poet, author of *Poet of the Dunes*

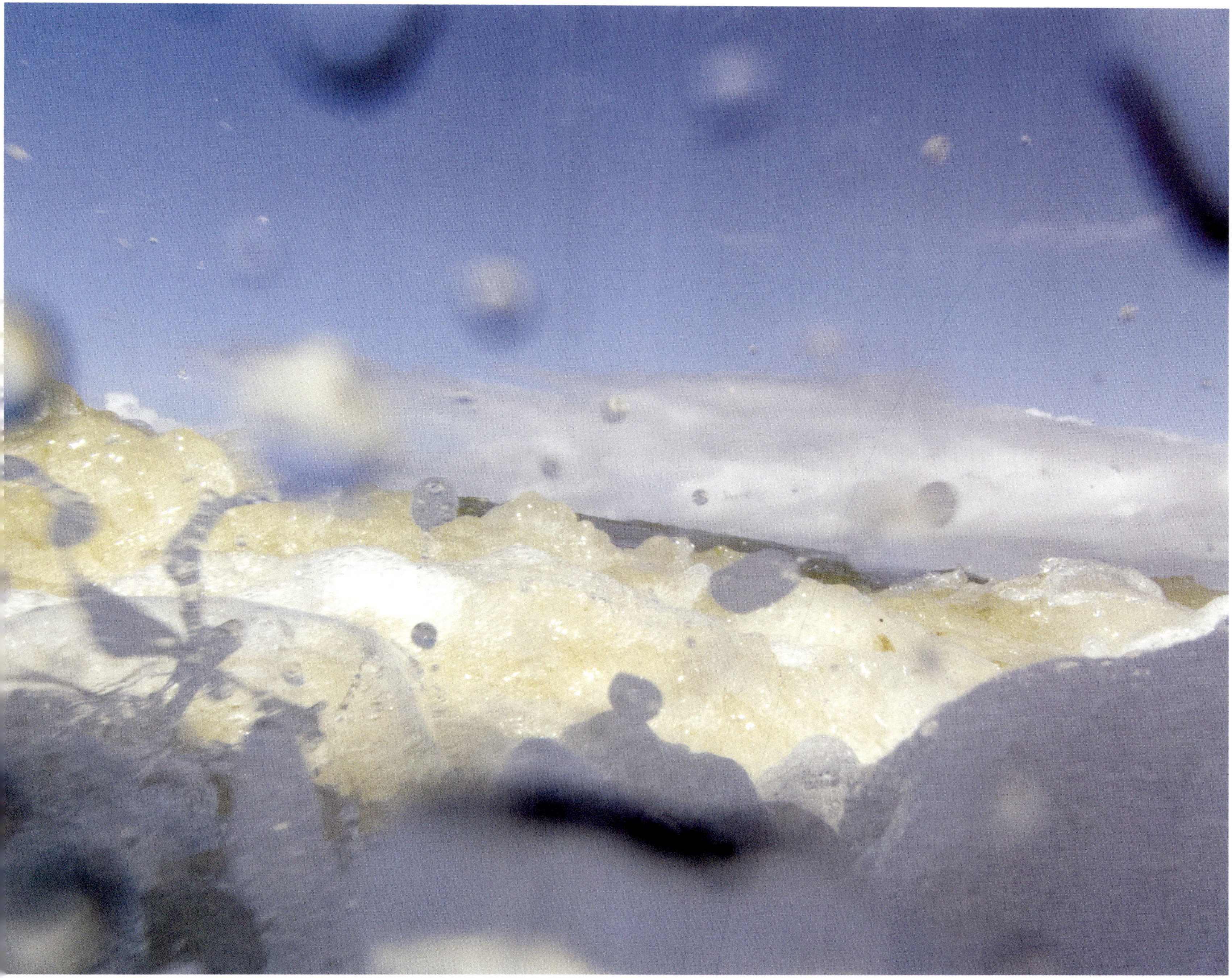

Scrub the bottom of your pots with sand before final washing, as sand is the perfect abrasive.

JEANNE “FRENCHIE” CHANEL

dune shack dweller, artist

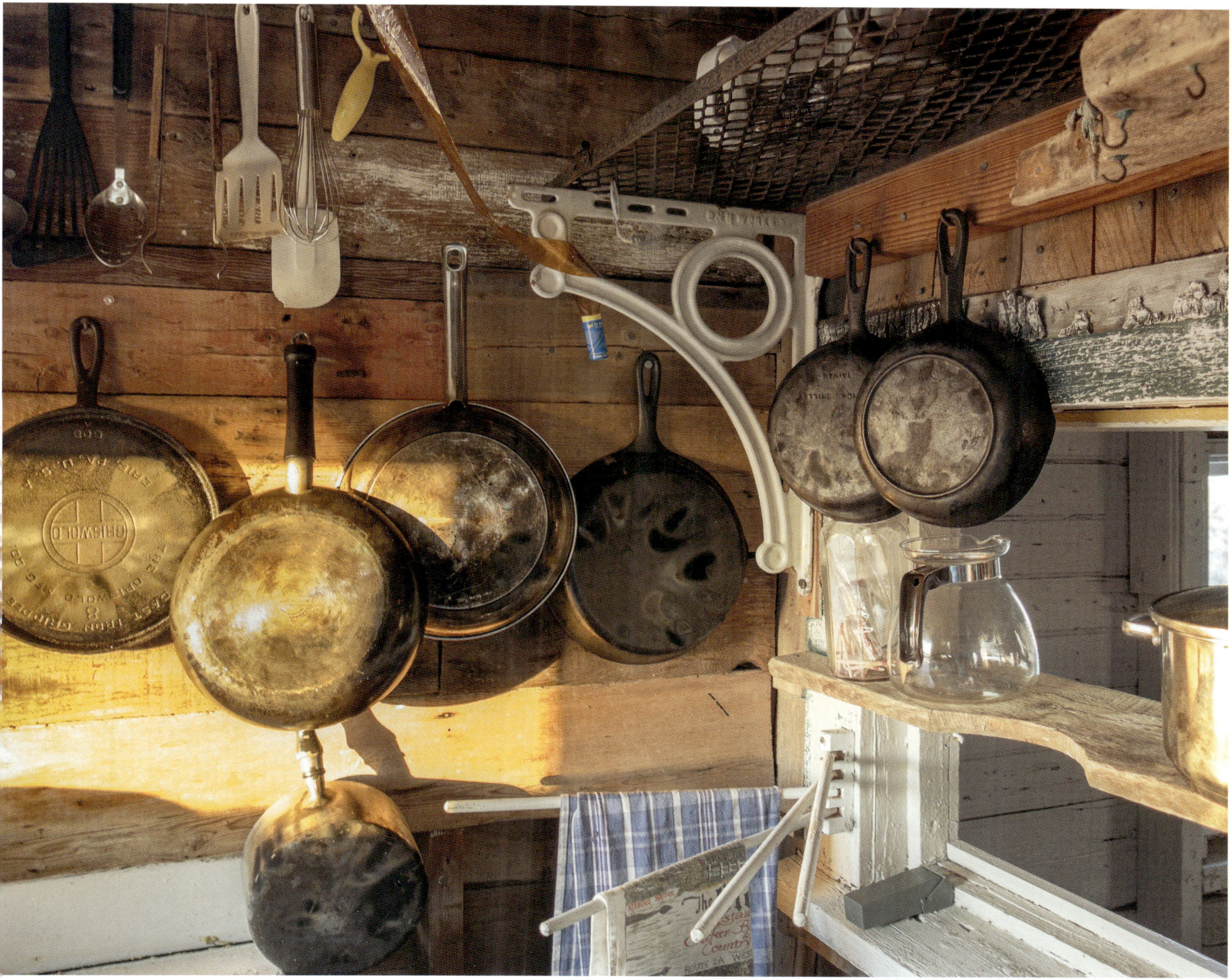
GRISWOLD

Flies. They've been coming in through the pane that I had to smash. Martin speared at them with scissors, taking the postures of a fencer, and Rake snapped his fists on them. I sat on the windowsill, laughing at these antics, and the sun flooded in richly.

HAZEL HAWTHORNE

dune shack dweller and doyenne, author

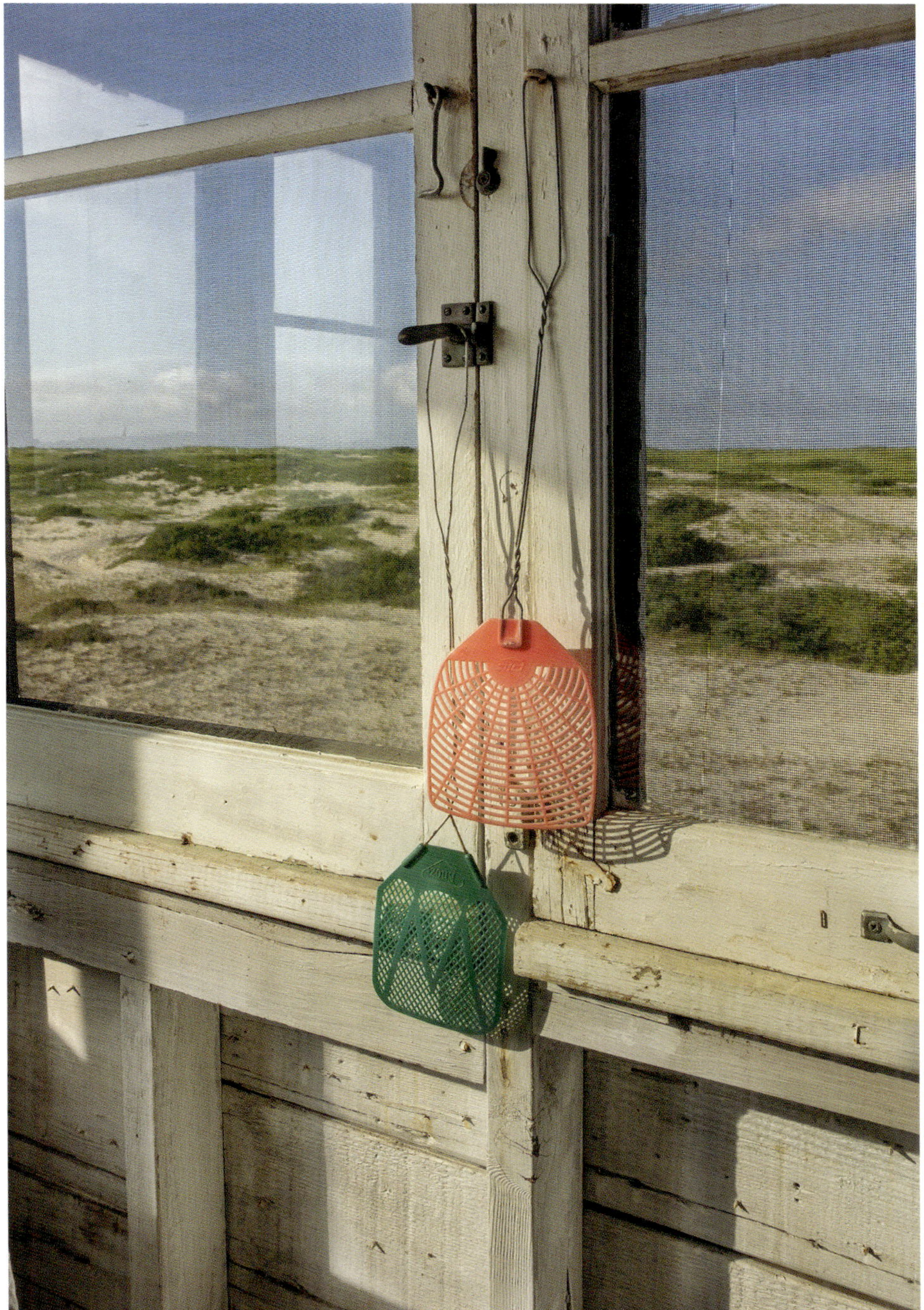

It is a home we want, not some ordinary house and lawn but a house on the earth: we want to belong here, not simply to visit.

CYNTHIA HUNTINGTON

poet, memoirist, author of *The Salt House*

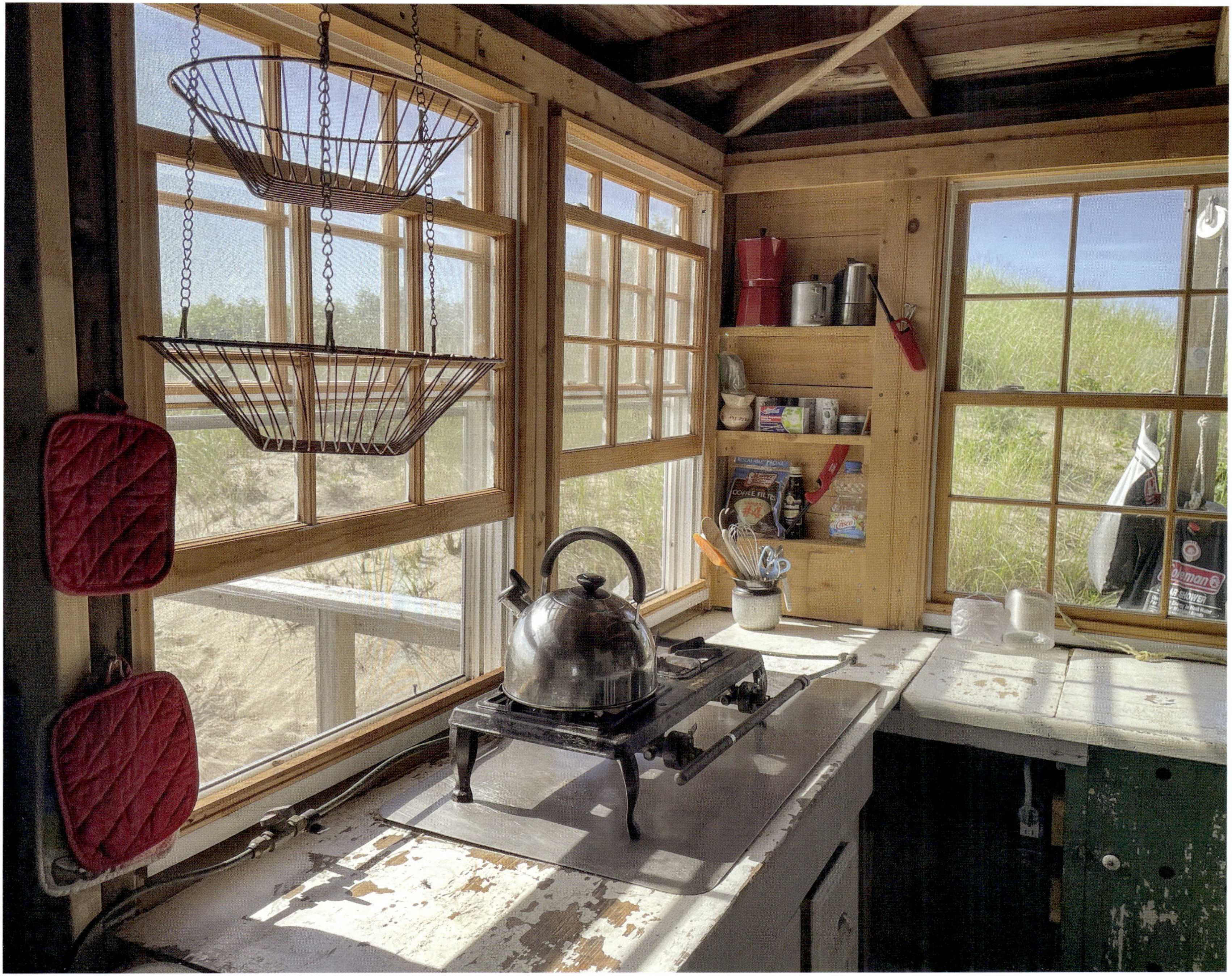
#4
Crisco

The Tibetans have a word that describes my feelings here: *stong-pa-nyid*, "emptiness," which strangely is a very full feeling here on the edge of our world, where we may be closer to life and so much closer to its impermanence.

ELIA SINAIKO

dune shack user, romantic empiricist

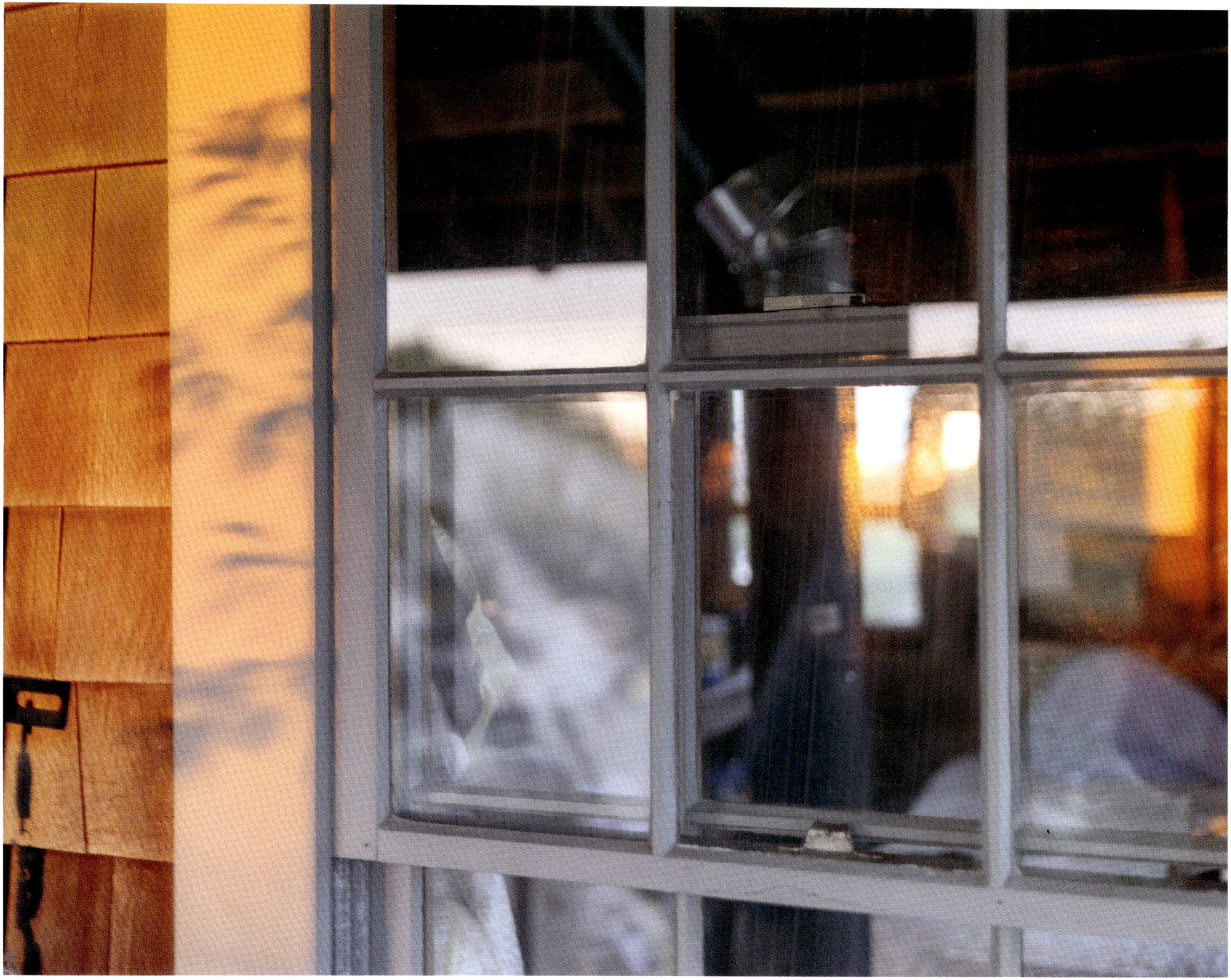

The great rolling sand dunes on the Cape are the most beautiful
I have ever seen, and to go out there and come back
in the moonlight was a thrilling experience.

HOUGHTON CRANFORD SMITH

artist

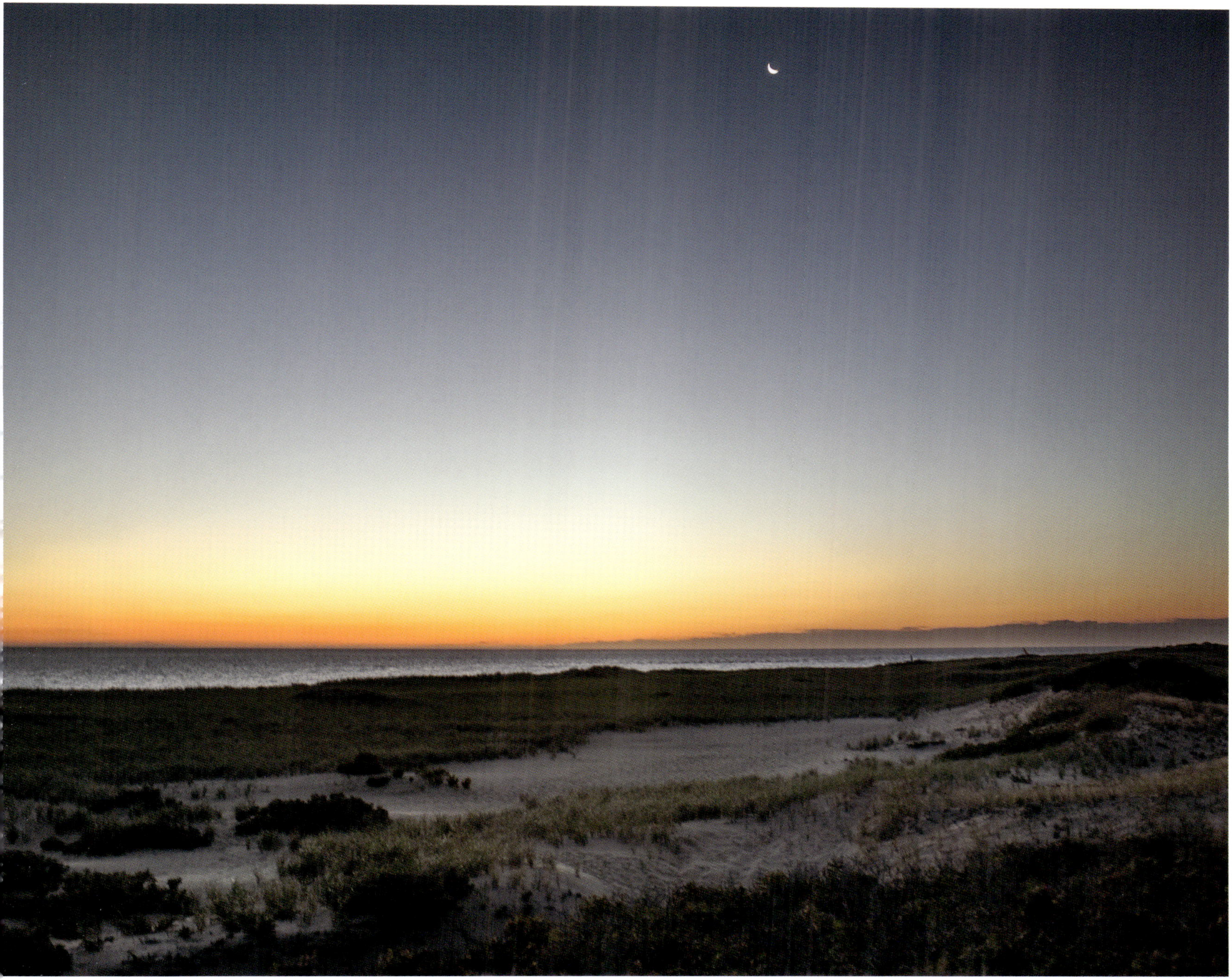

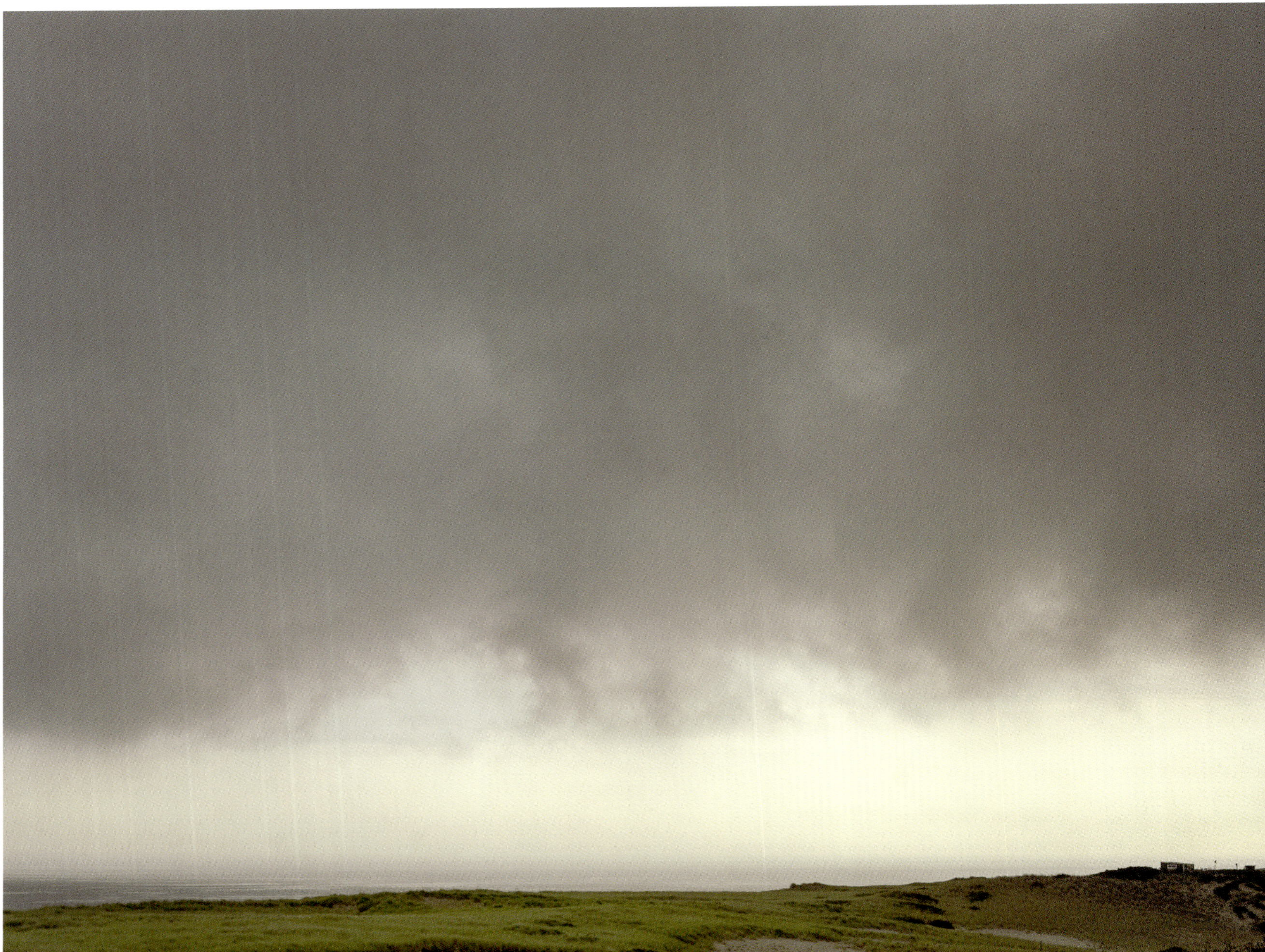

The back country is like a wild little animal that crouches under the hand of man but is never tamed.

MARY HEATON VORSE

labor activist, journalist, author

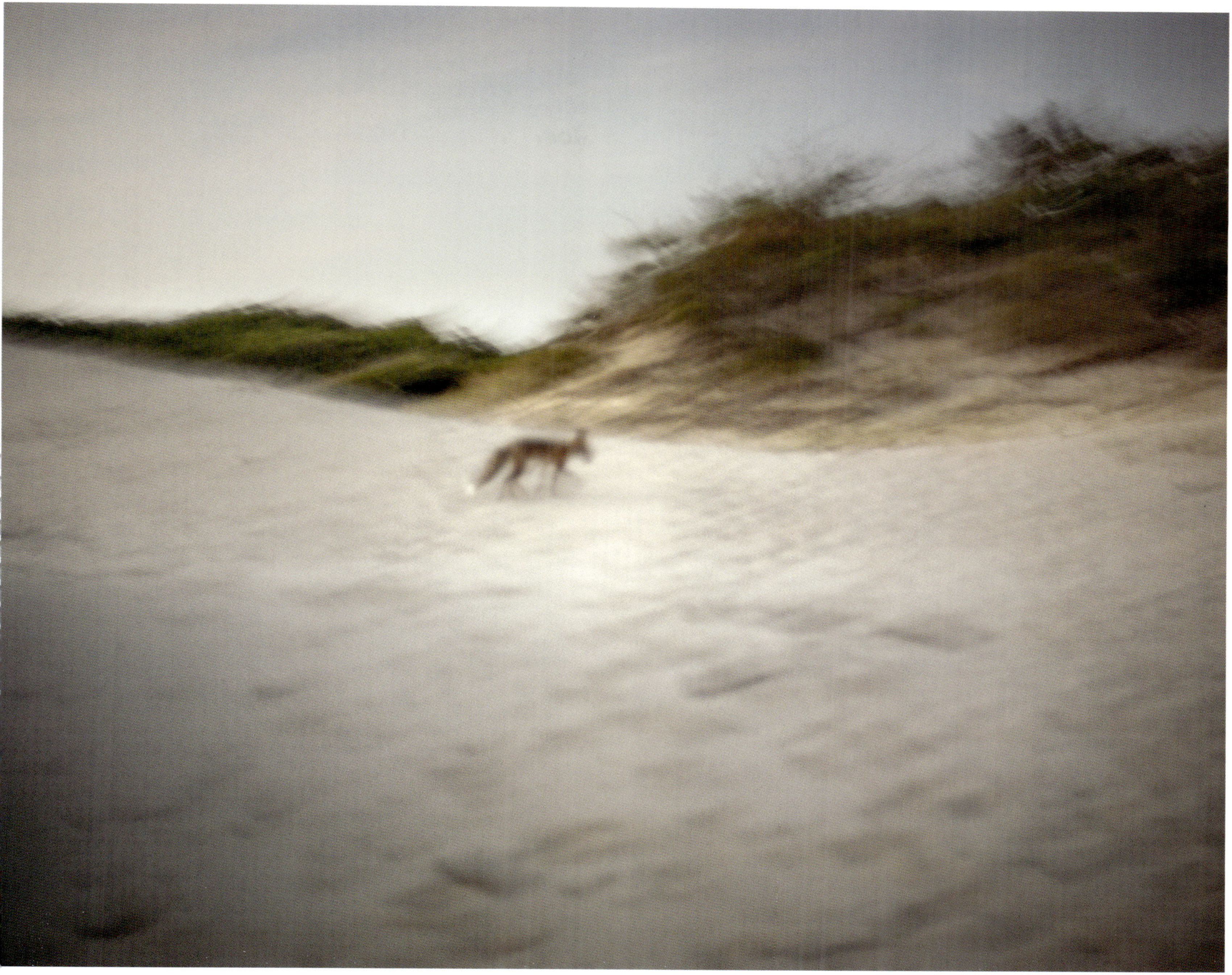

Everything is so spare. Nothing gets in the way of the creative process; it is speeded up. As both a sculptor and a writer, I have often wakened after a day or night in my shack and seen clearly that which was muddled or confused.

JOYCE JOHNSON

sculptor, writer, a founder of Peaked Hill Trust

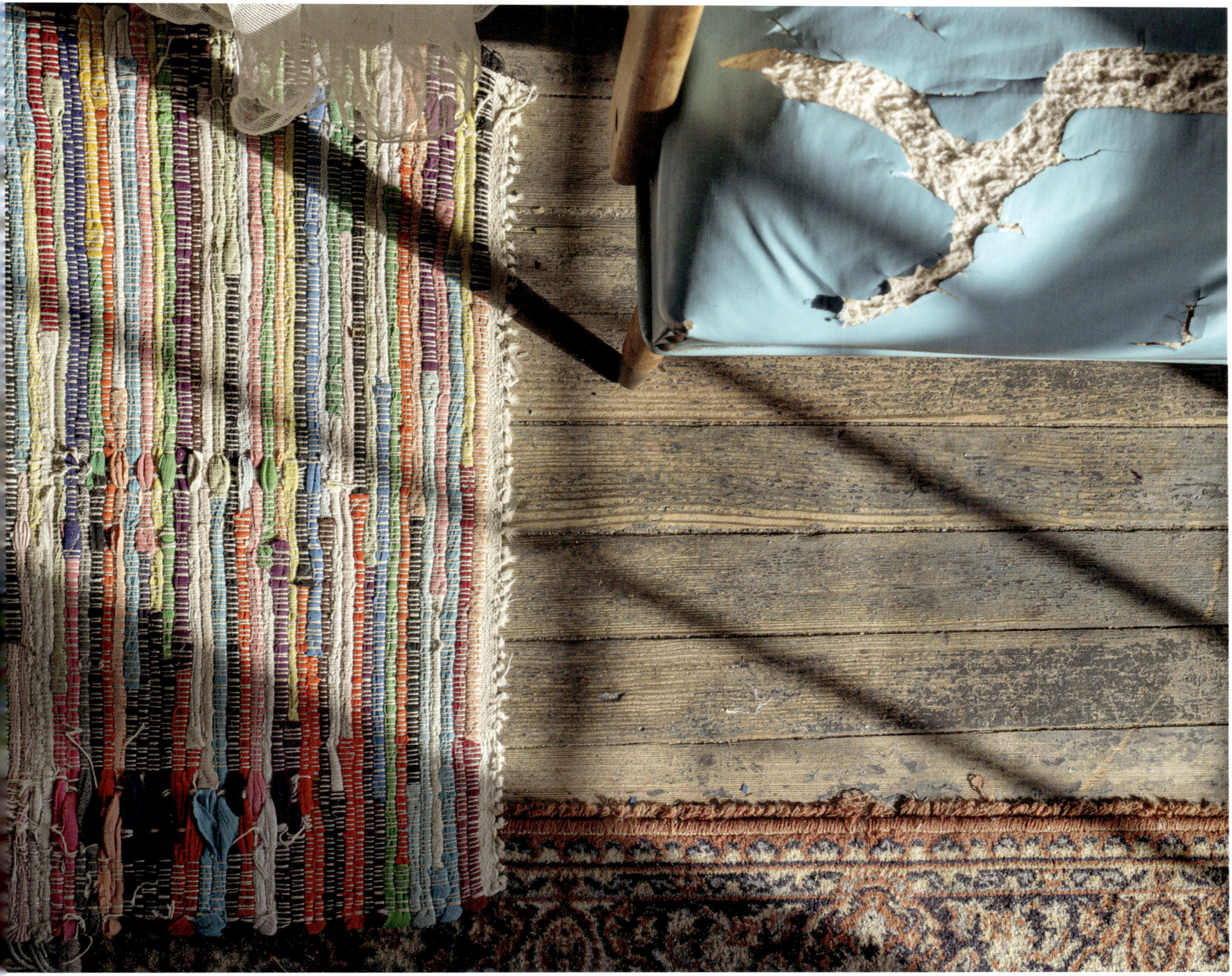

It was just the sort of the natural place to go
to start the rest of our lives together.

PAUL CHAMPLIN

dune shack dweller

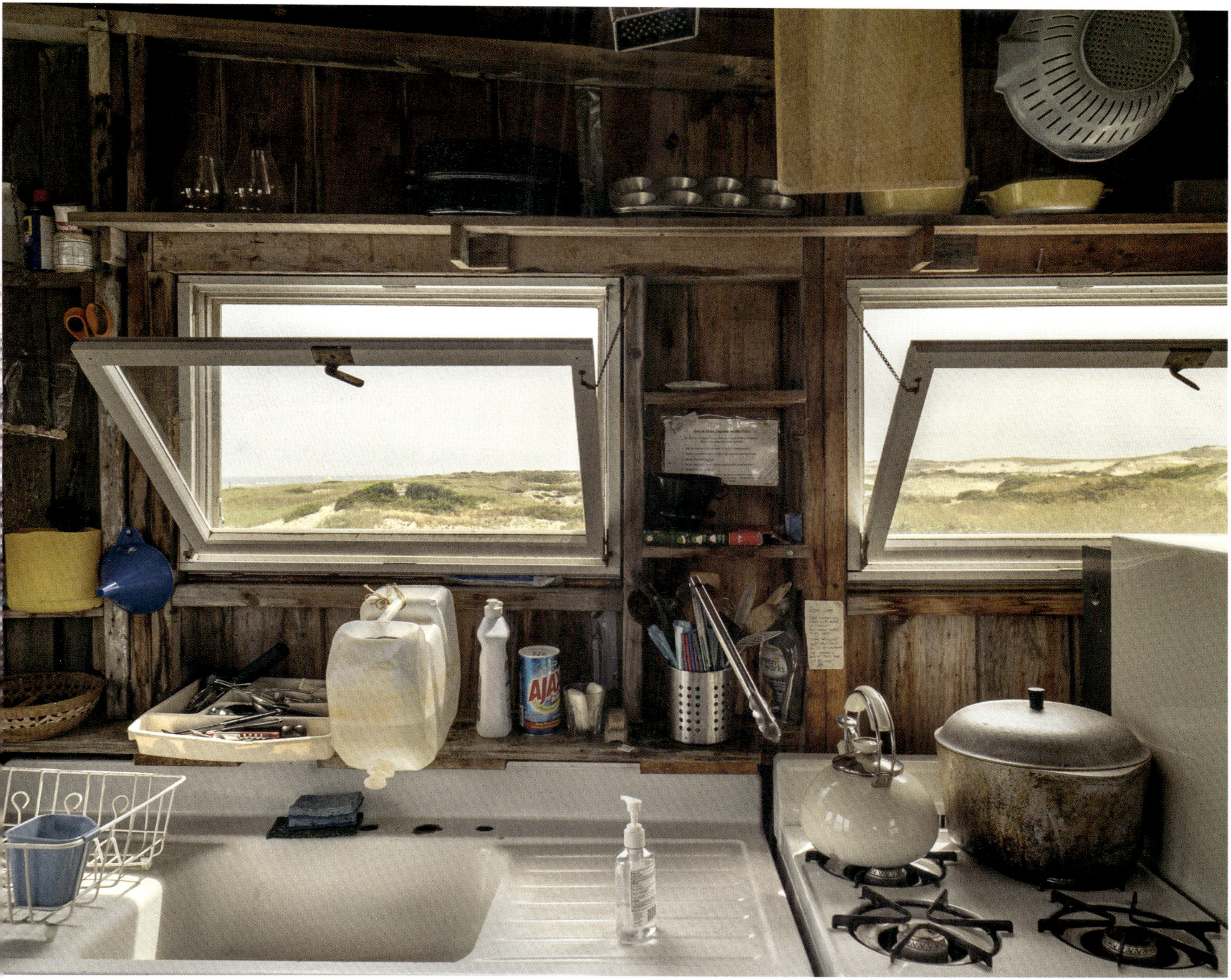
AJAX

Everything changes. Nothing stays the same.
The liquid aspect of it all is very profound.

CONRAD MALICOAT

backshore connoisseur, artist

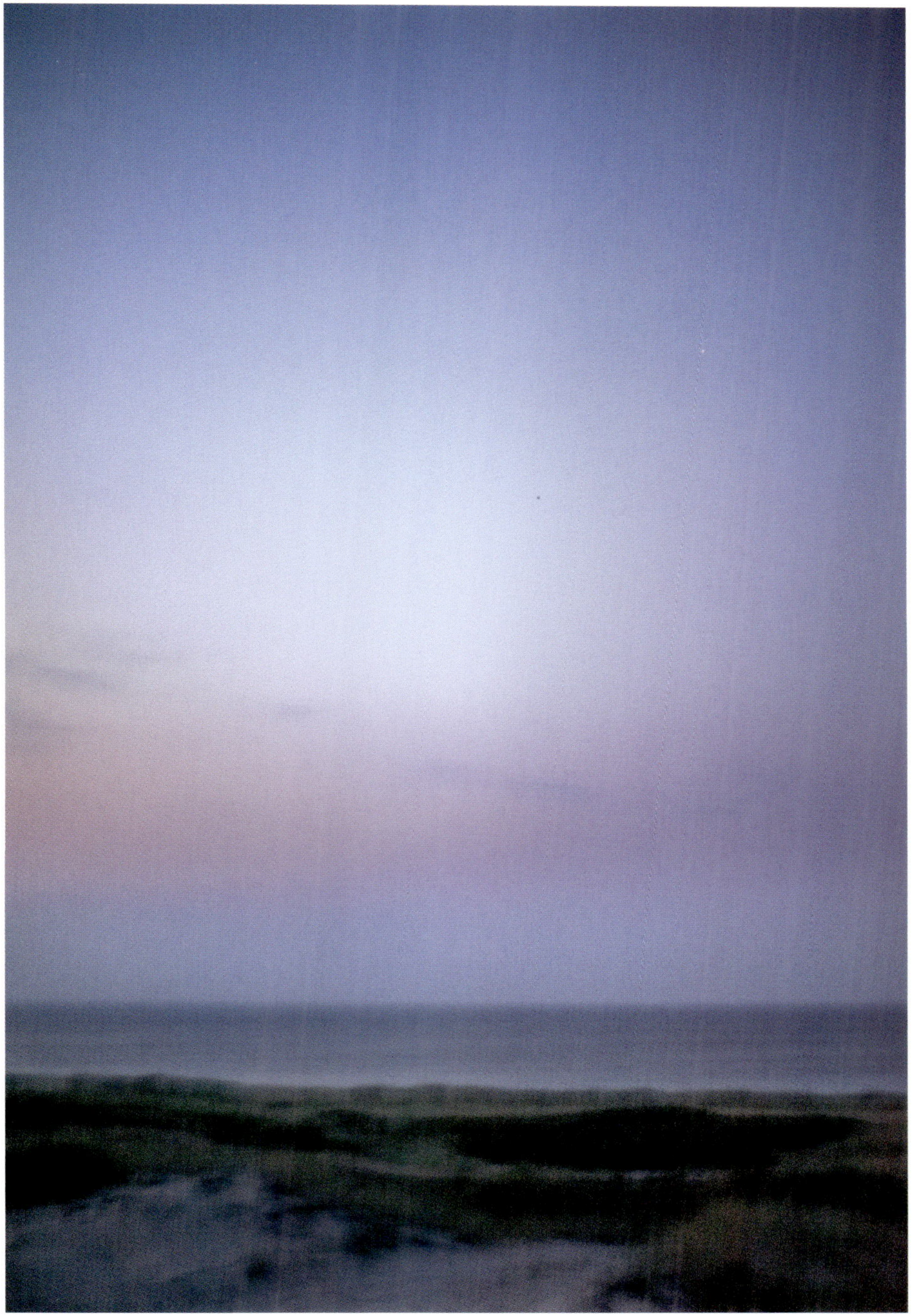

A house on the dunes—as if it were truly ours. Shack, shelter, hut, hull, or shell of boards, it is ours if anything is. No less borrowed than our bones, it holds our lives and we call it home, returning at night out of the wide dark world.

CYNTHIA HUNTINGTON

poet, memoirist, author of *The Salt House*

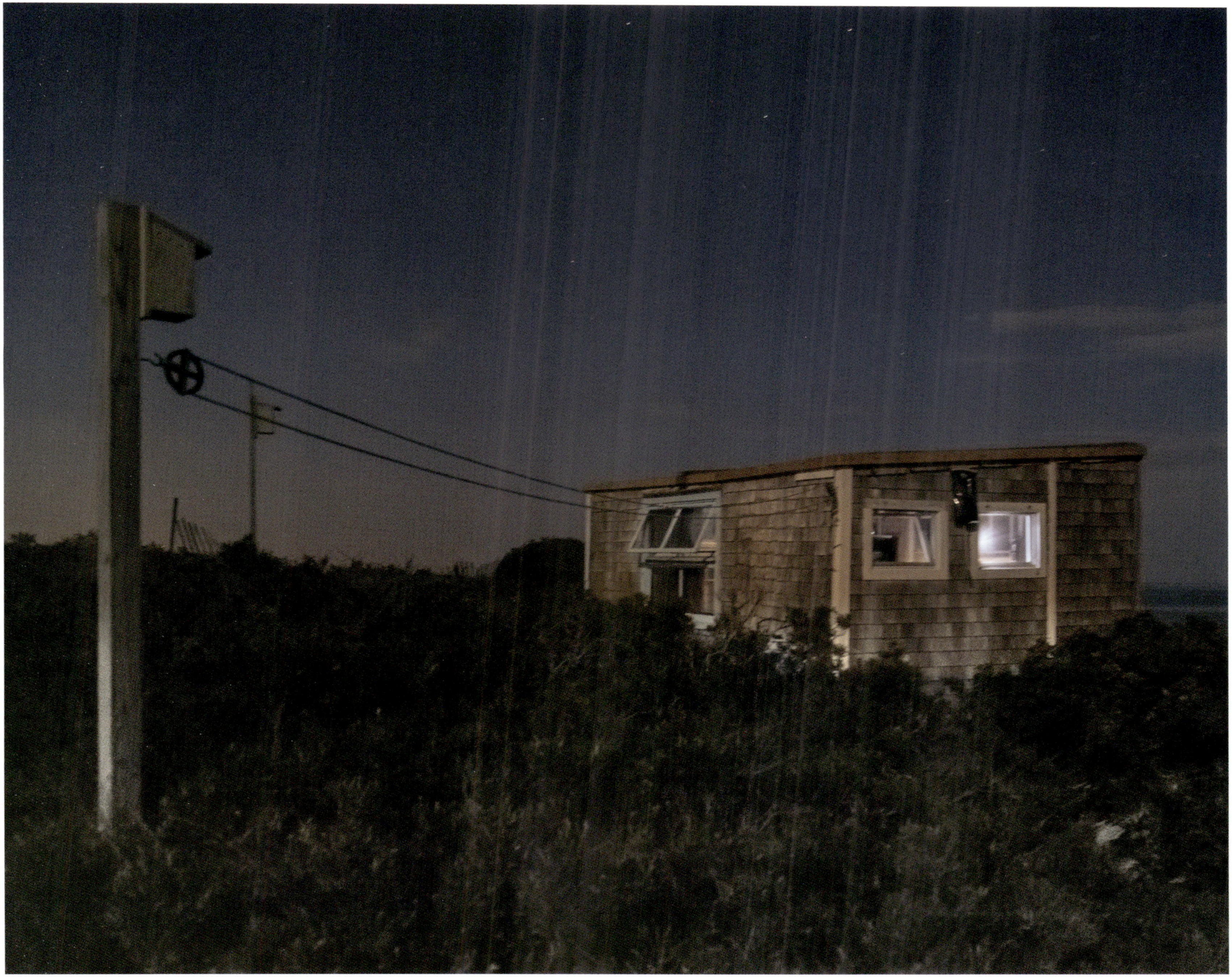

The privilege of a private room in Frenchie's shack was based on her romantic credo, which honored lovers above all other earthly creatures. It was enough for her that we were in love and, therefore, the whole of the universe between the sand and the stars was turned over to us . . .

JOSEPHINE DEL DEO

dune shack dweller, writer, historian, author of *The Watch at Peaked Hill*

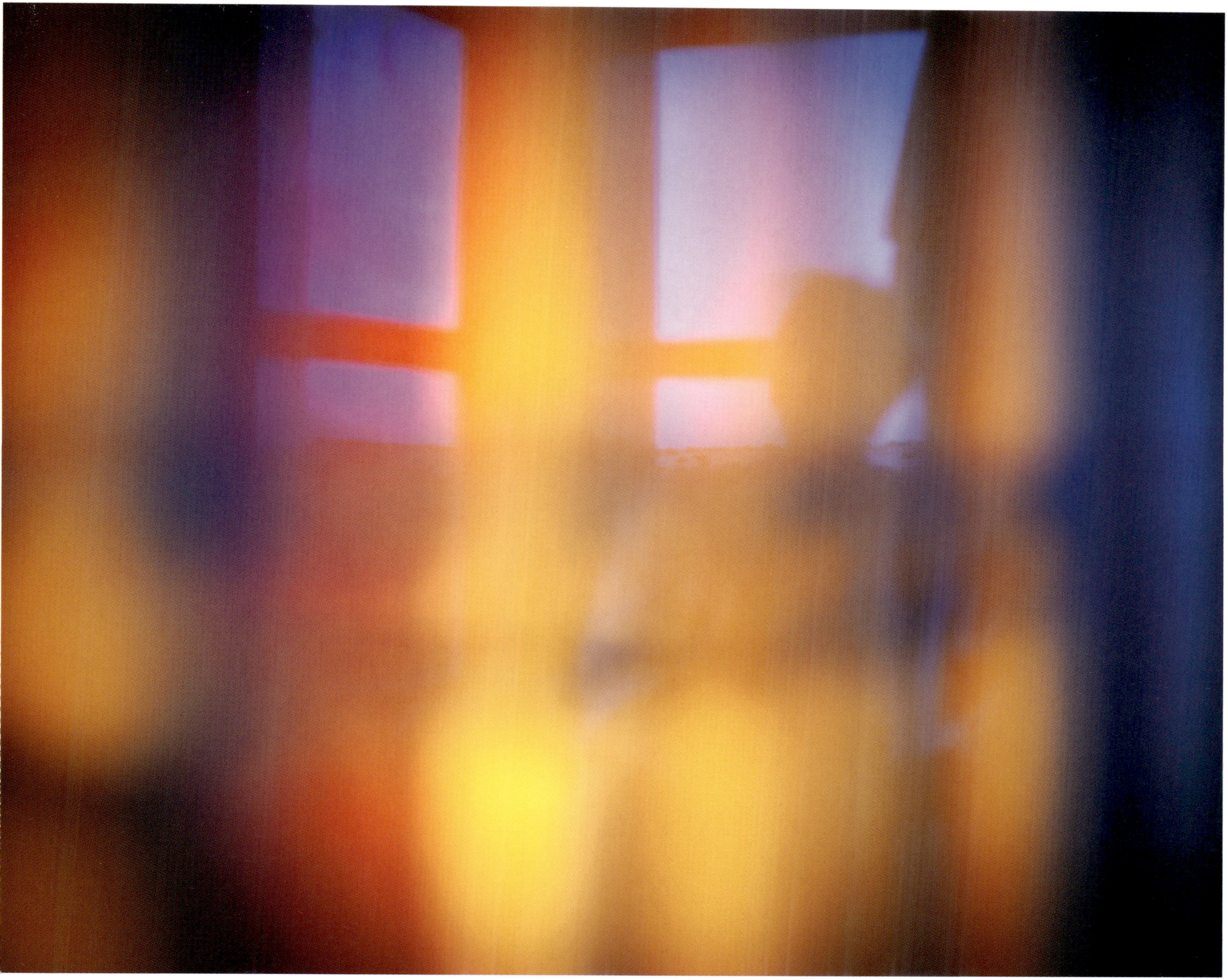

Harry Kemp had over his shack's door a little sign that said, "This house is occupied, please do not break in, nothing of value here except solitude."

DAVID ARMSTRONG

dune shack dweller

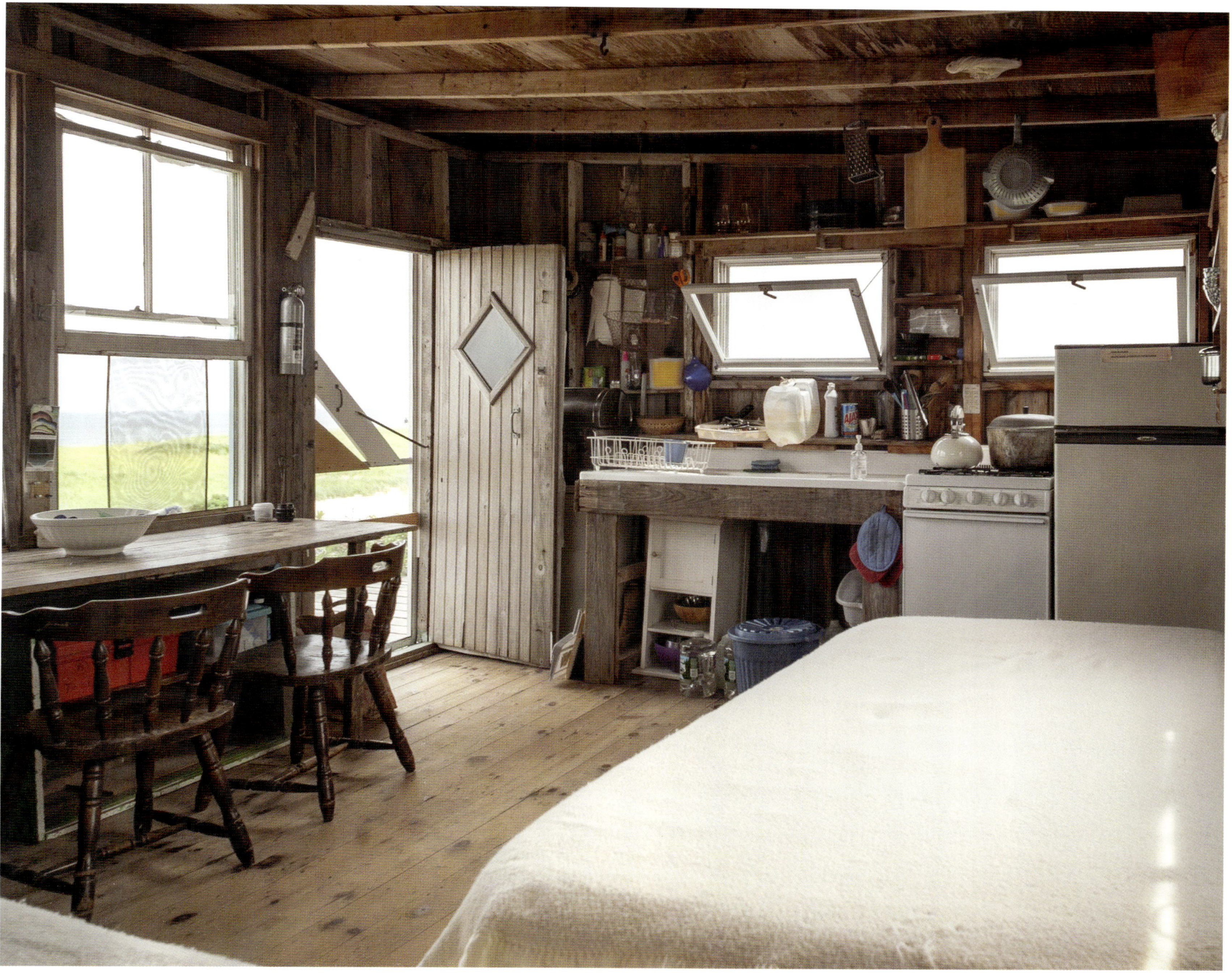

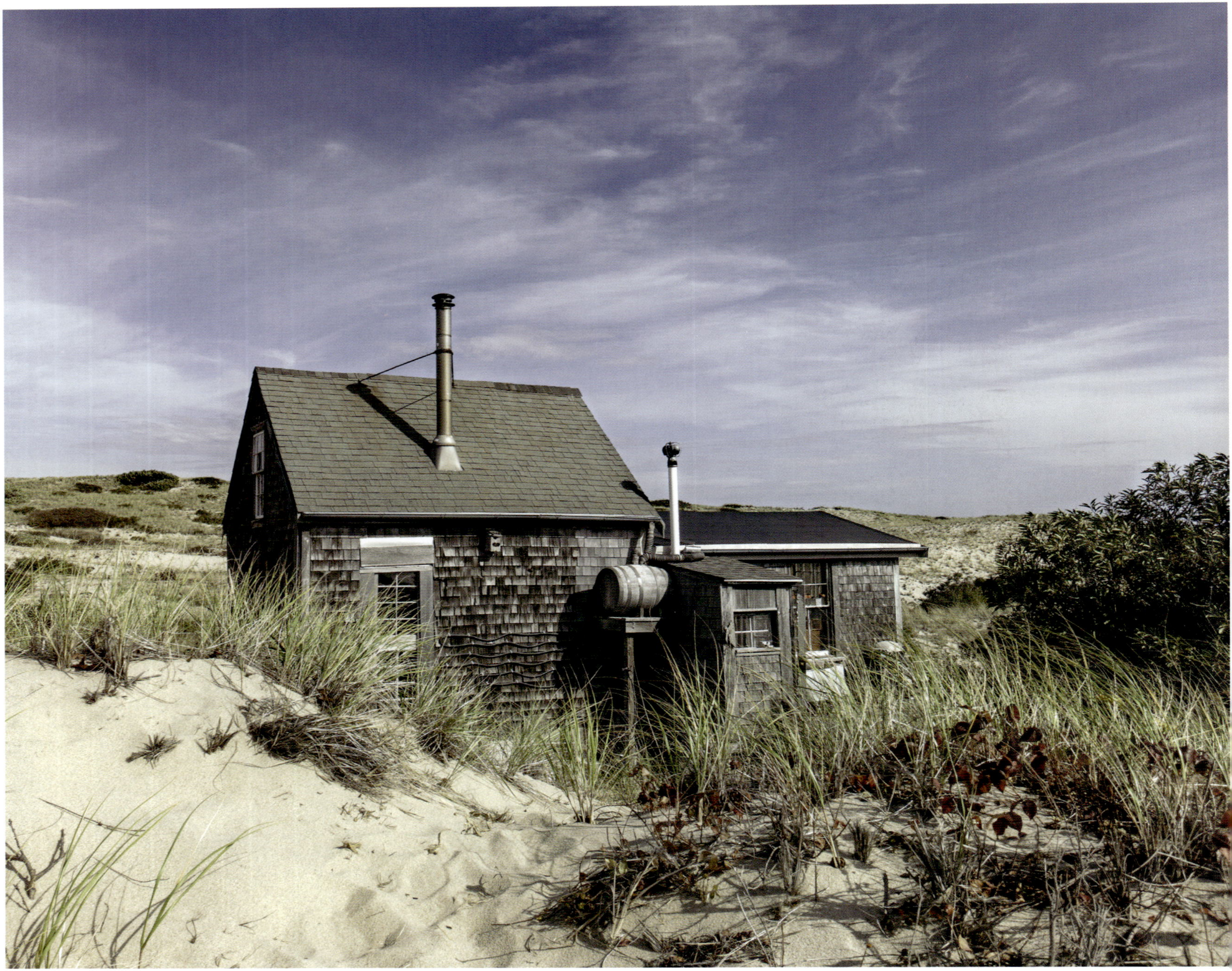

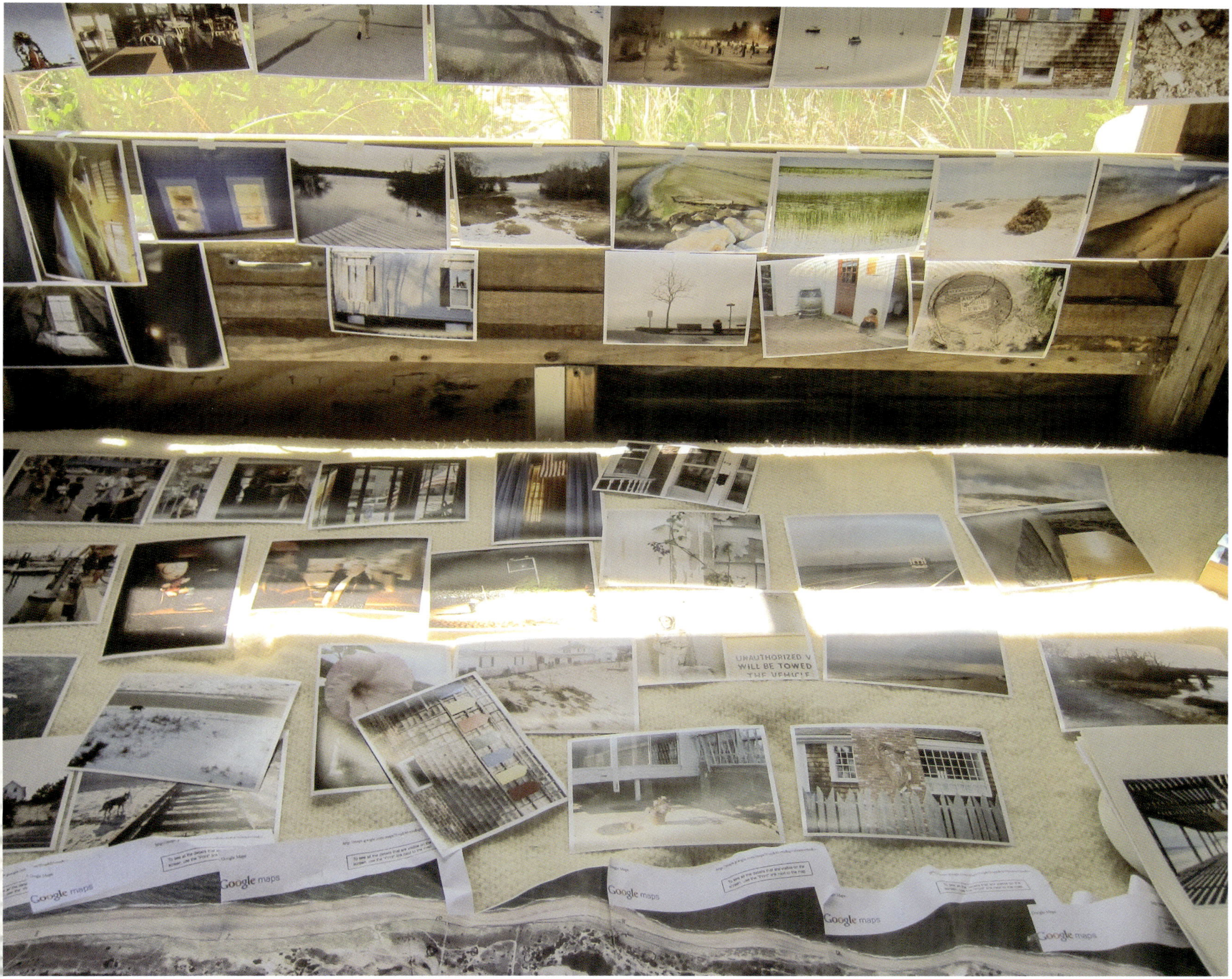
UNAUTHORIZED V
WILL BE TOWED
Google maps

Everybody has connections to everybody else. And that's how people got out on the dunes in the first place. It was because of these connections. They are very strong connections, very tight friendships that have gone on generation to generation.

HATTY WALKER FITTS

philanthropist

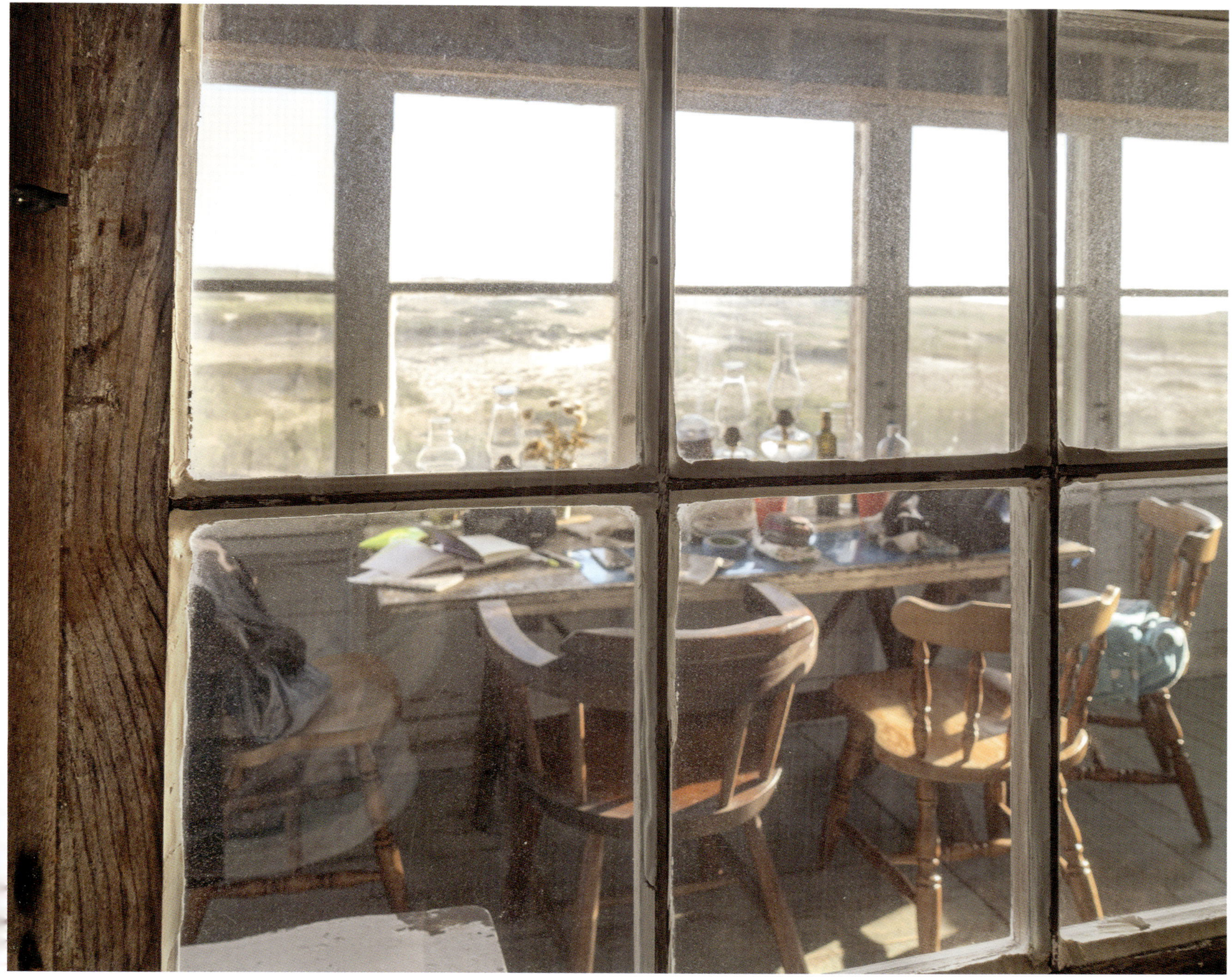

I think the dune shack provides an outpost, an anchoring of relationship with the park and the natural world around it, for me as an artist.

JAY CRITCHLEY

artist, wanderer, founder of the Provincetown Community Compact

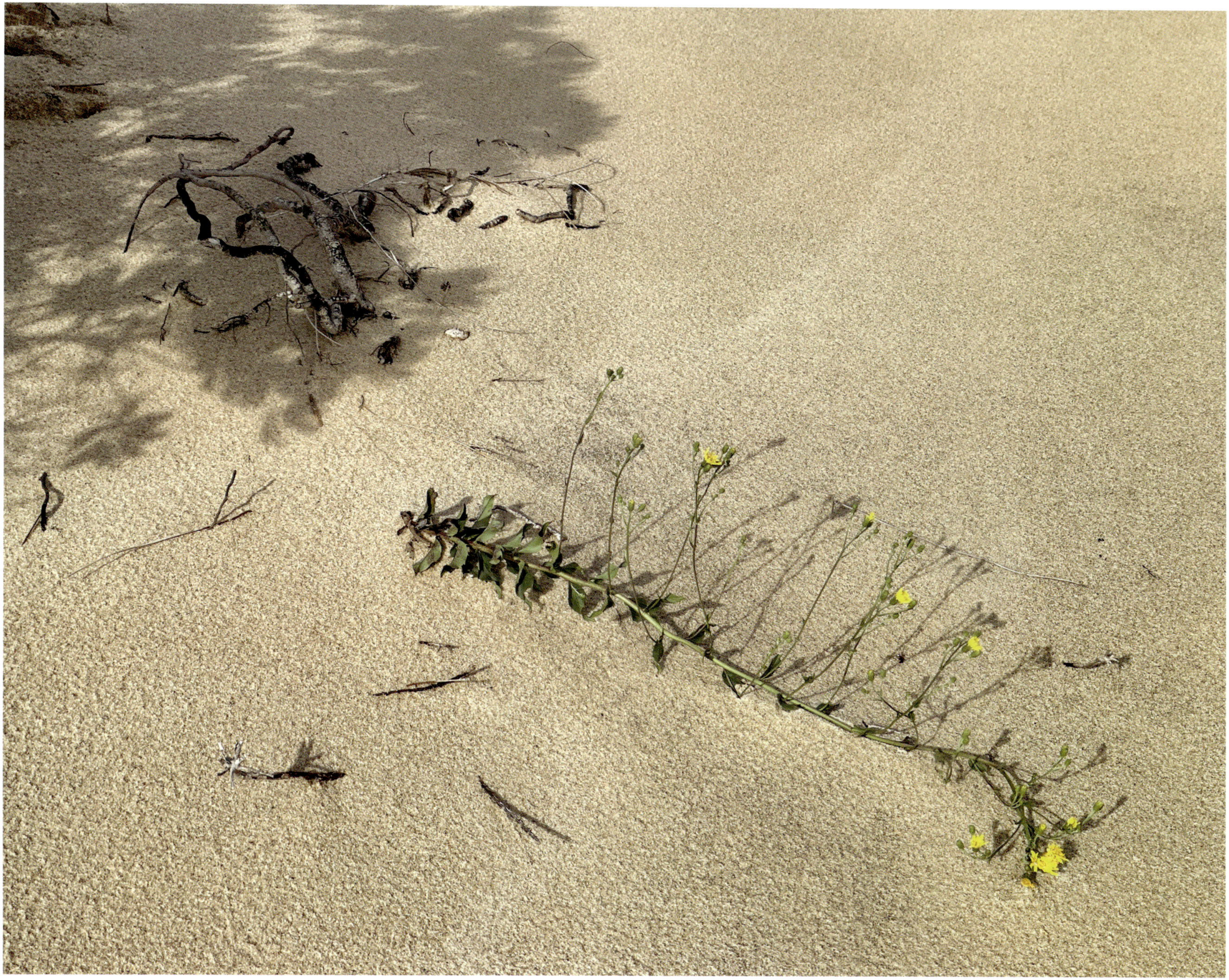

If you make your home in the dunes,
you have to become friends with the sand.

CONNIE ARMSTRONG

dune shack dweller

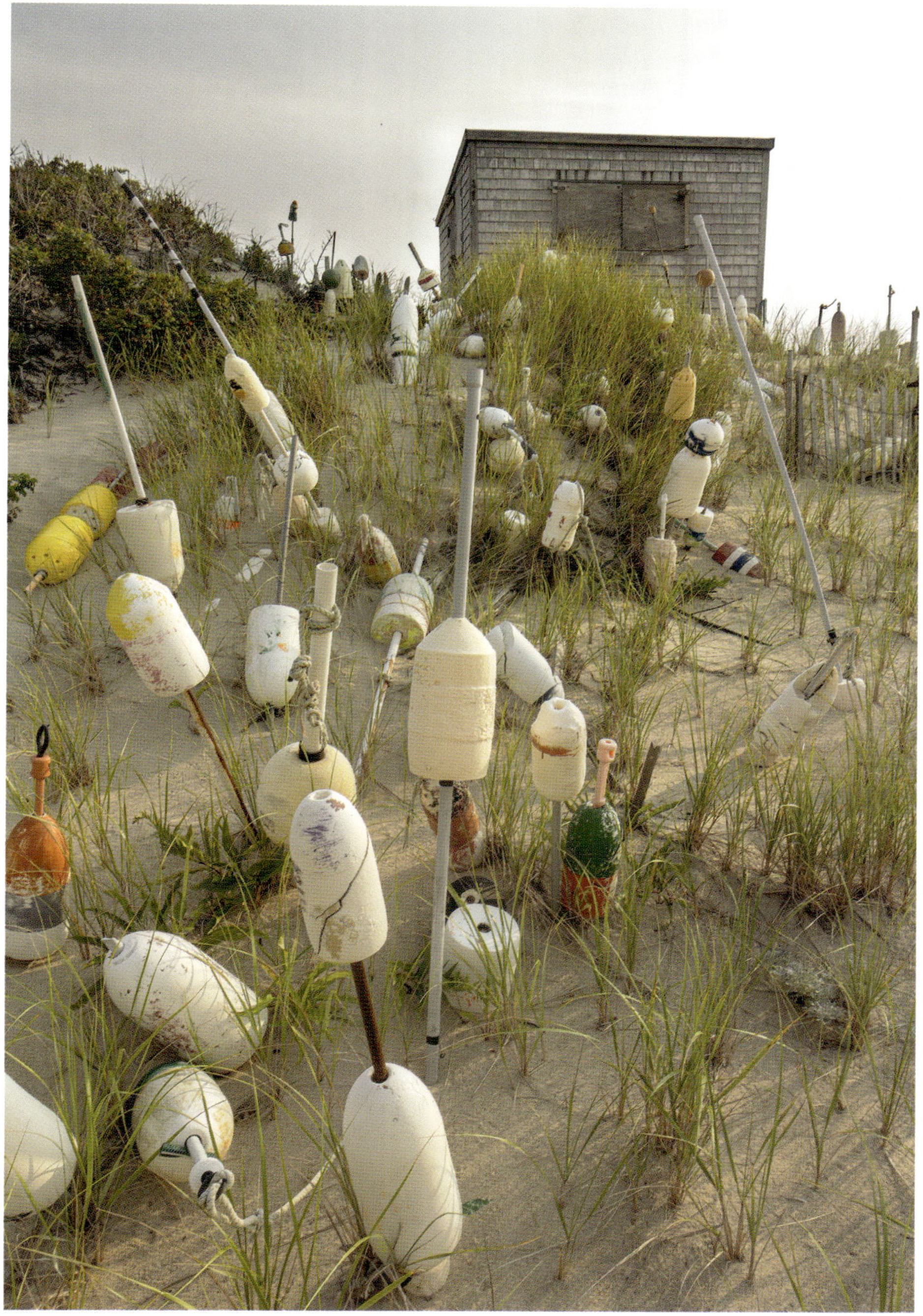

Many years ago there was a vessel bound for Nova Scotia, with a cargo of fine horses and cattle, wrecked off Peaked Hill Bars. All were drowned but a beautiful white stallion, who swam ashore. For a year he ran wild up and down the dunes, the most beautiful creature that one could imagine . . . Then, as a man with a rope approached him, he reared his head and plunged into the sea. They could see his white mane tossing above the water as he swam on out and out, defying them to capture him and preferring death to captivity. When I first came here, the old coast guard still spoke of the waves as white horses.

MARY HEATON VORSE

labor activist, journalist, author

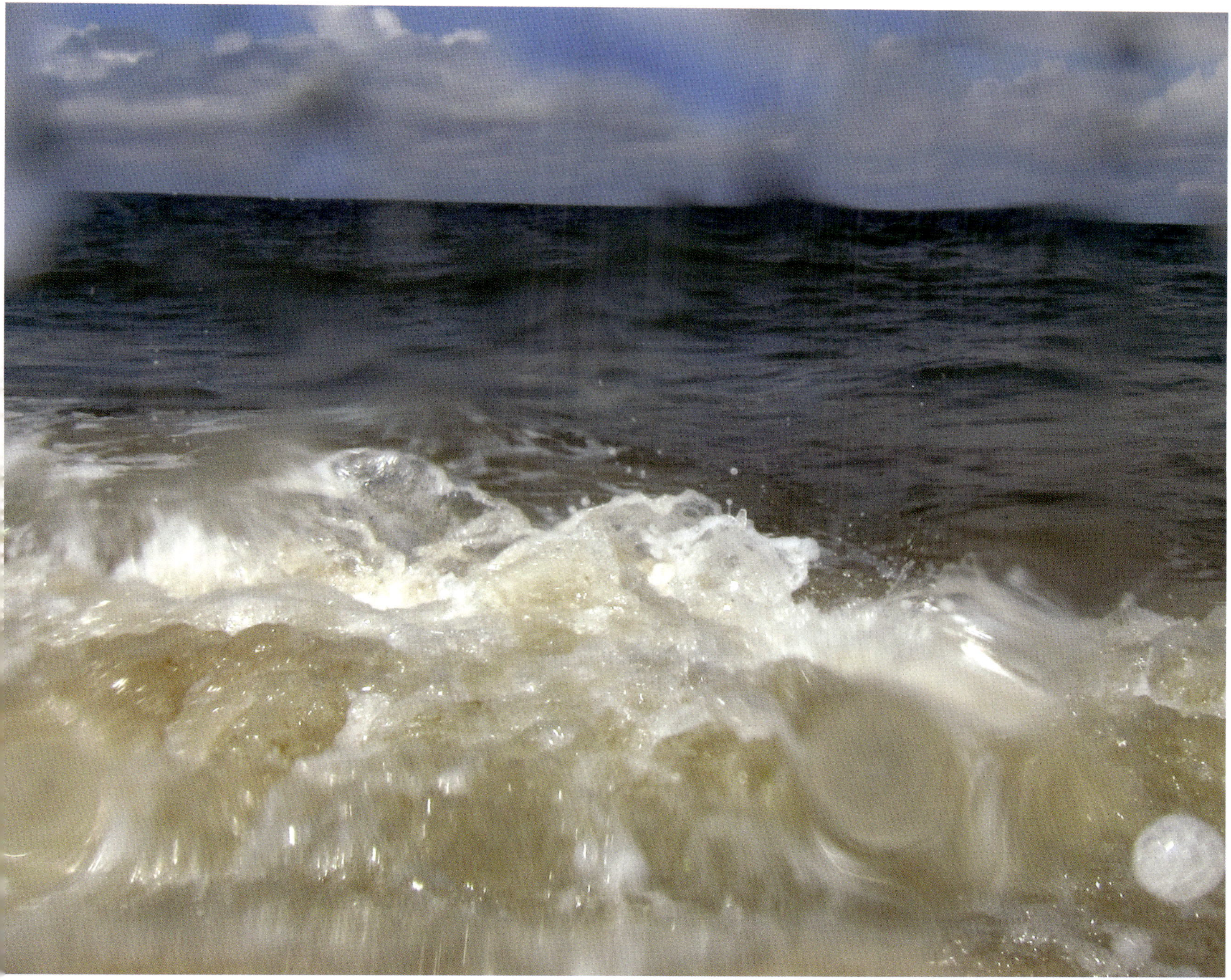

Whenever I needed to get away I'd come up through that little wooded area and go up on the big dune, and here I would have this horizon of shacks and I would see Euphoria.

IRENE BRIGA

naturalist

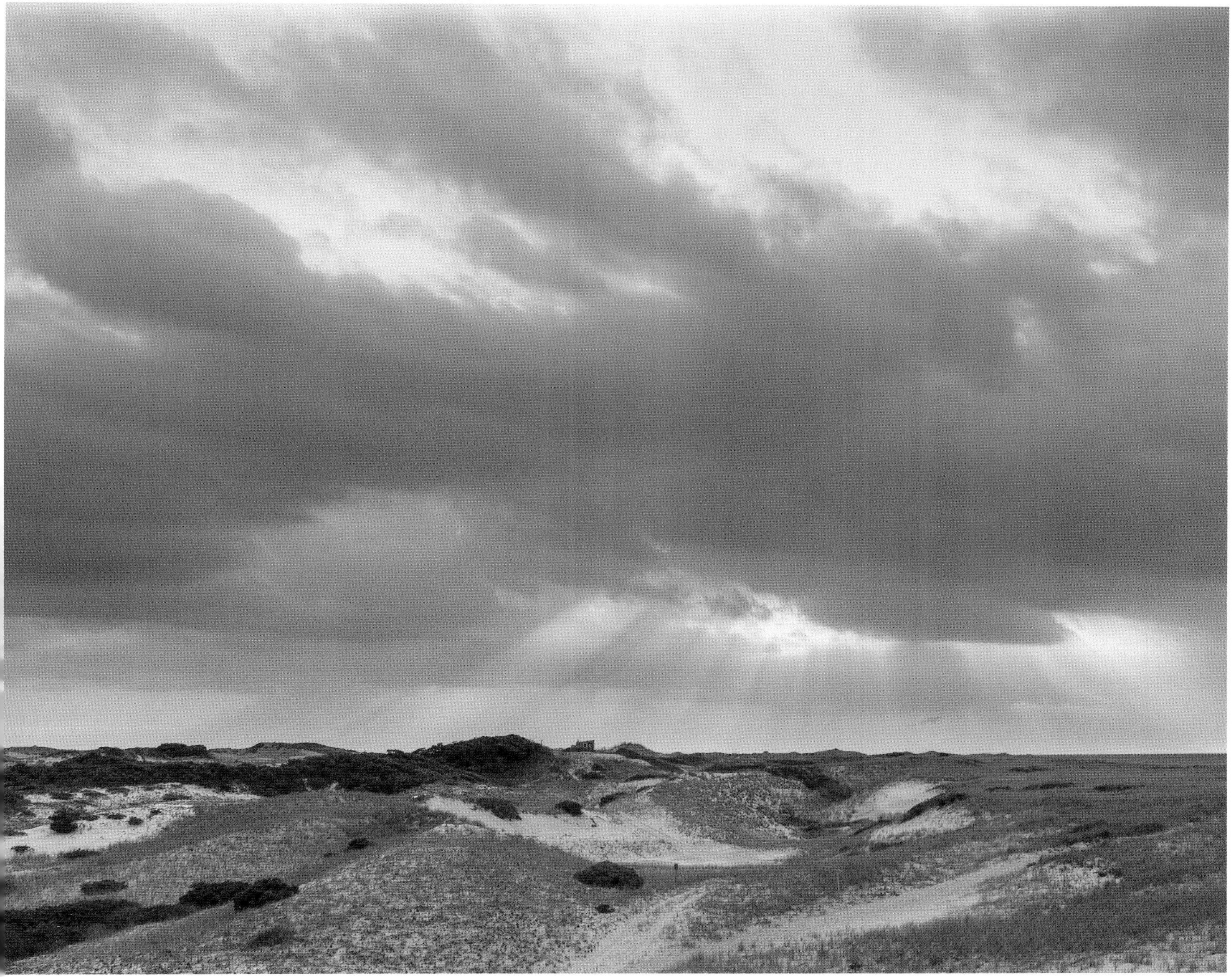

Go about in the cottages, and you may sit in a chair taken from one great wreck and at a table taken from another.

HENRY BESTON

writer, naturalist, author of *The Outermost House*

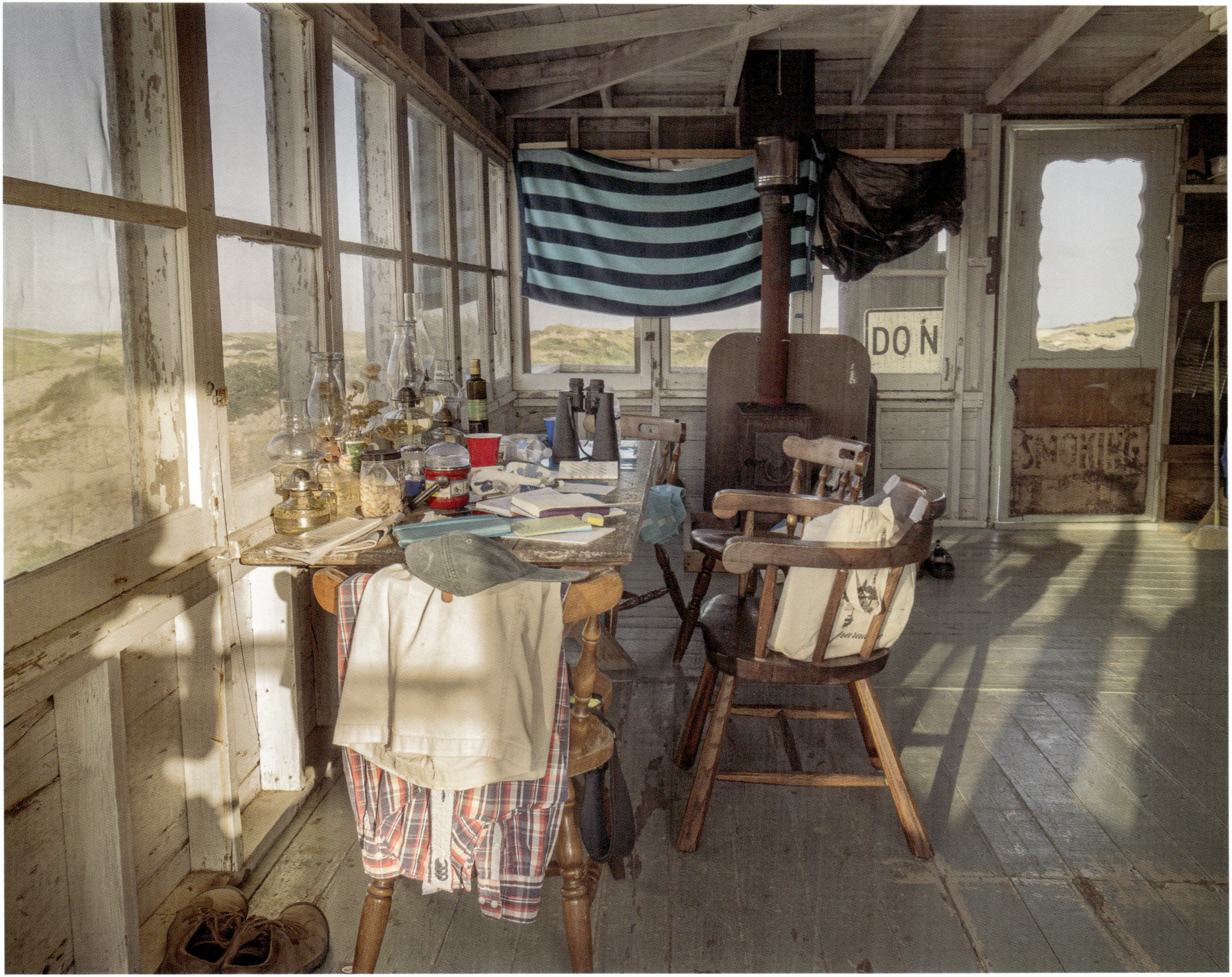
DON
SMOKING

It’s all just beach and ocean. That’s it.

ROB COSTA

owner of Art’s Dune Tours

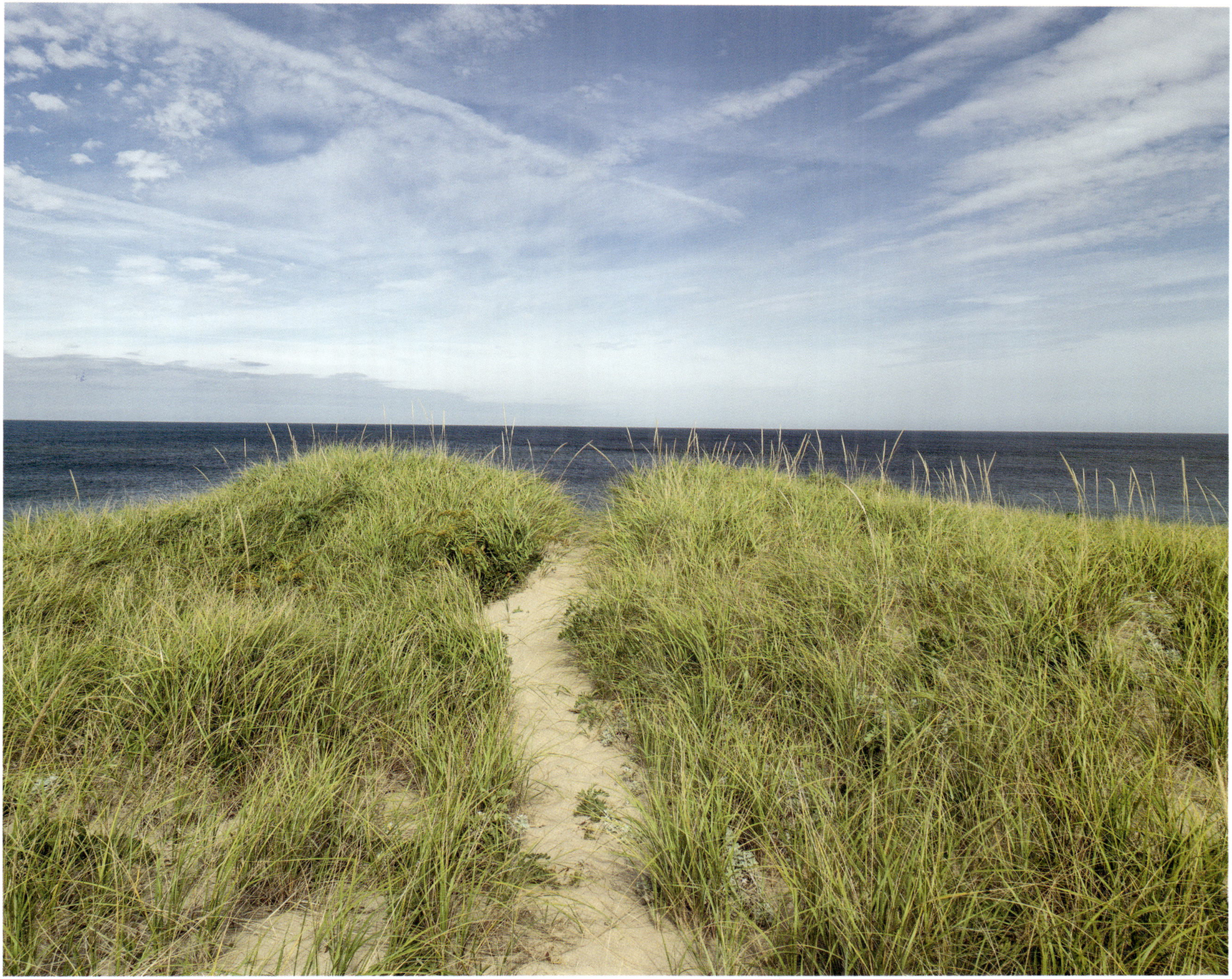

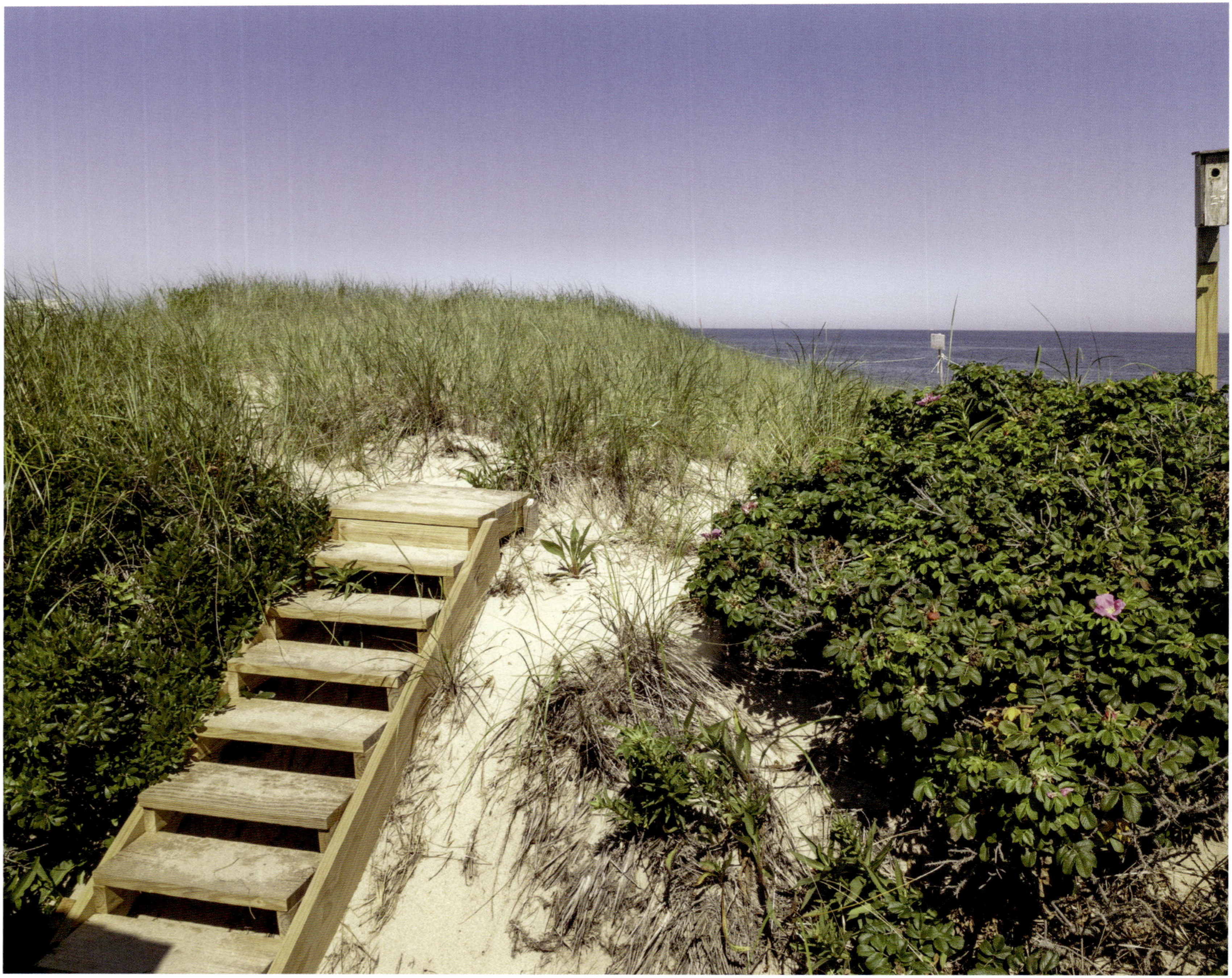

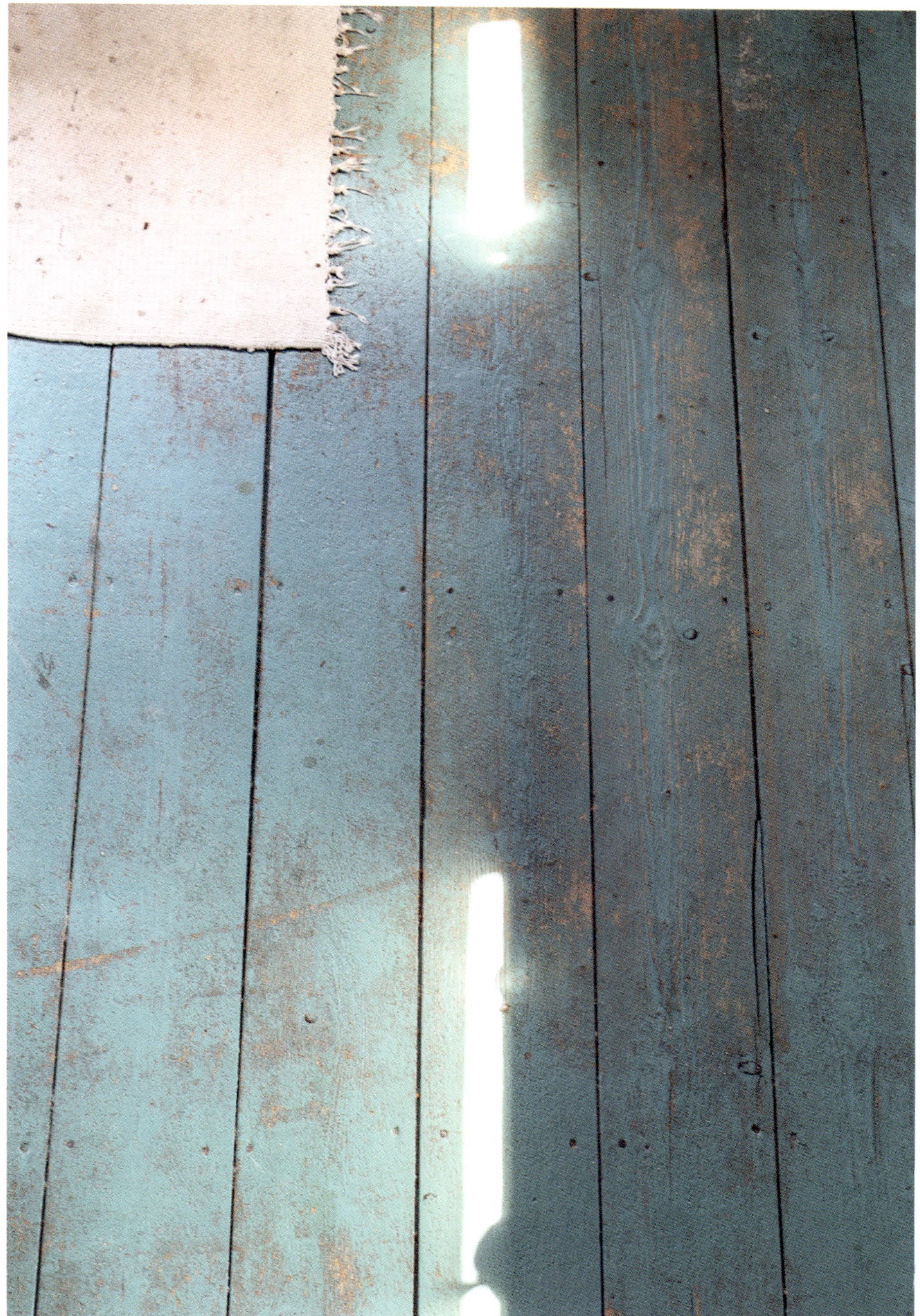

What you have to look at here is a way of life. This is what we are trying to save.

JOSEPHINE DEL DEO

dune shack dweller, writer, historian, author of *The Watch at Peaked Hill*

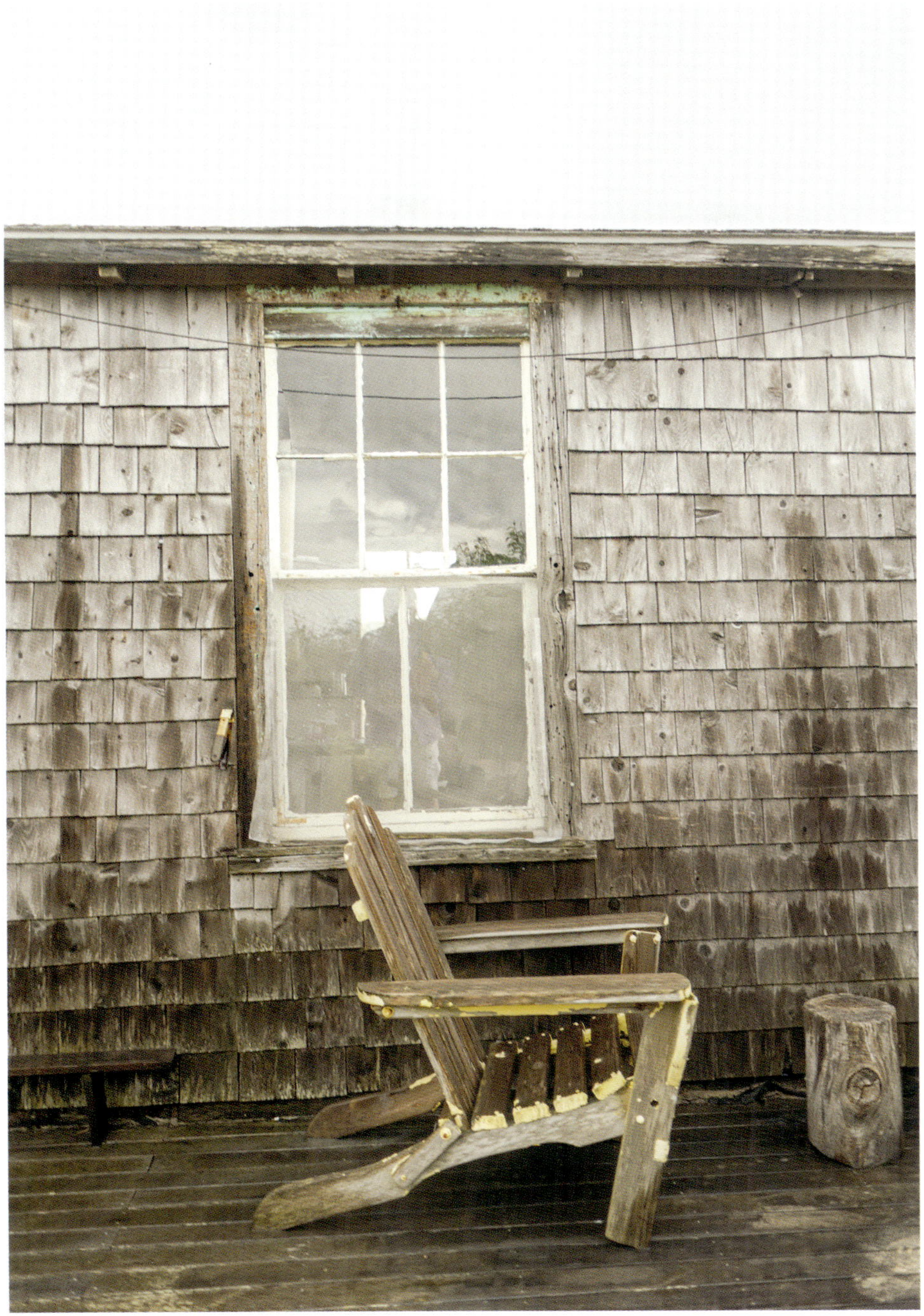

It's the focus of the universe. It's our passion. It's the focus of our lives.

MARIANNE BENSON

dune shack dweller

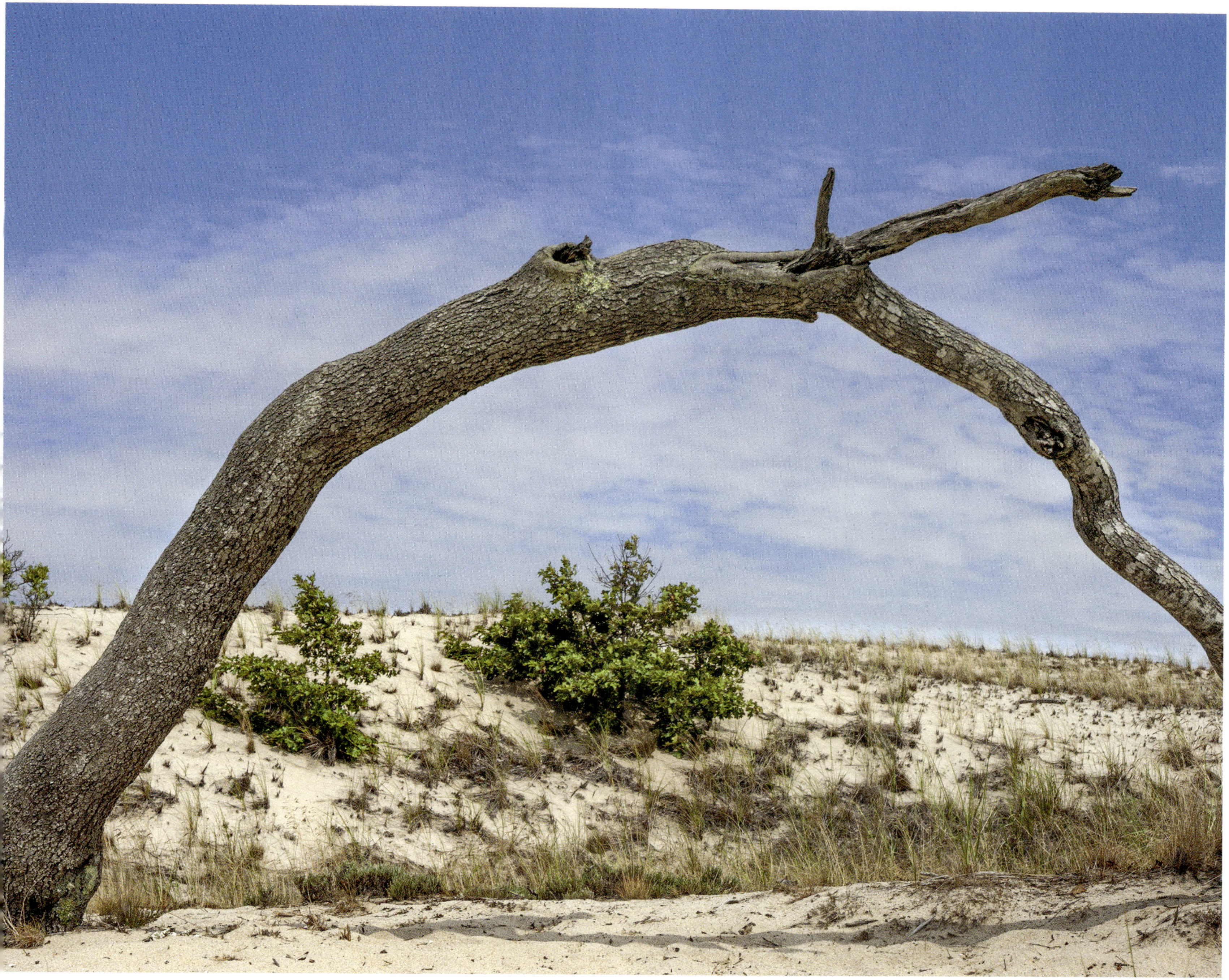

Whoever will forget those dunes—once having seen them and the great rumbling, dramatic "outside" as it was called—the ocean itself, the long stretch of lovely sands, and nothing else.

MARSDEN HARTLEY

artist, poet, essayist

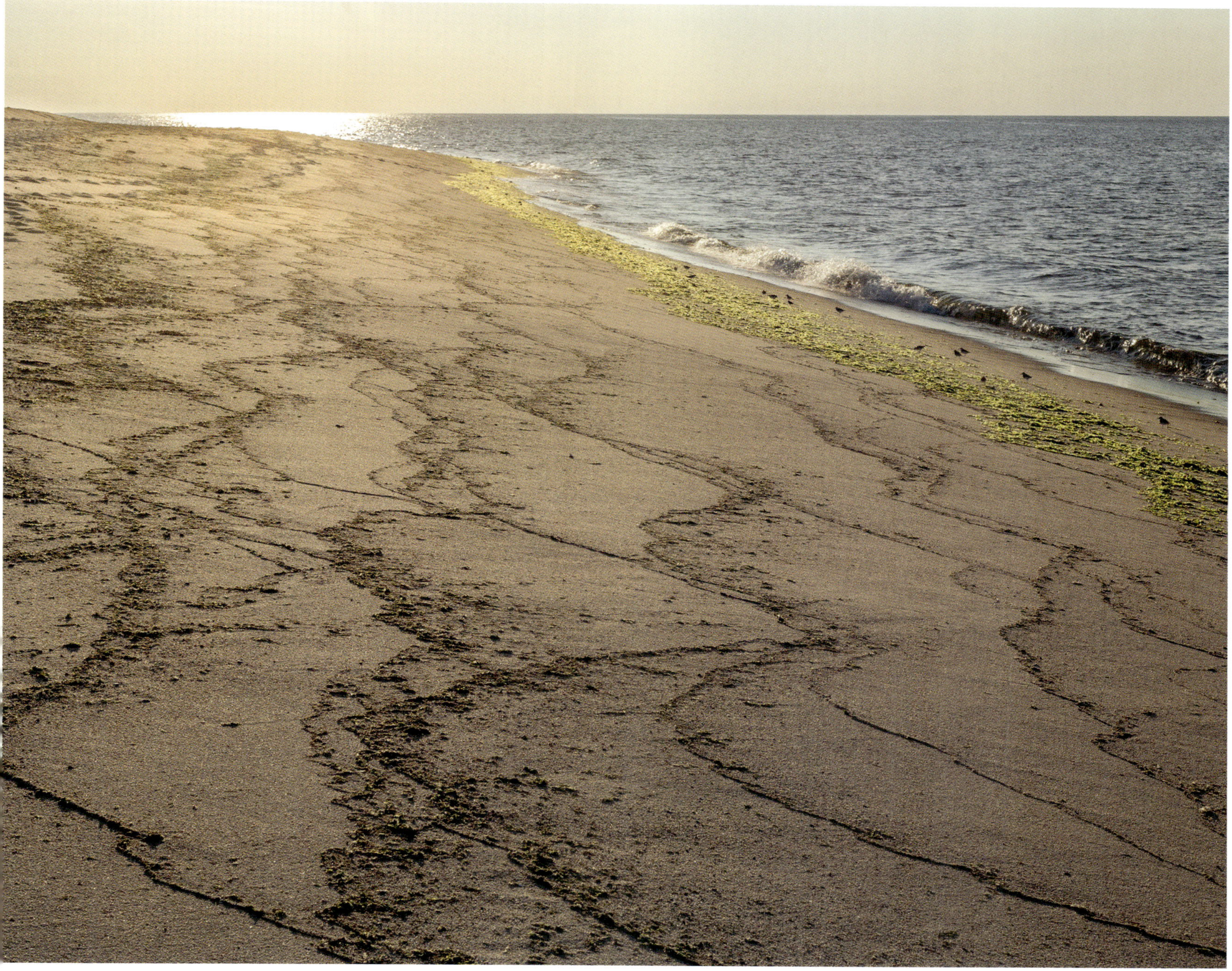

I have loved the solitude. . . . I need to breathe and stretch out. Have some time to finish a thought and not speak.

DEBORAH ROSS

wildlife artist, artist-in-residence

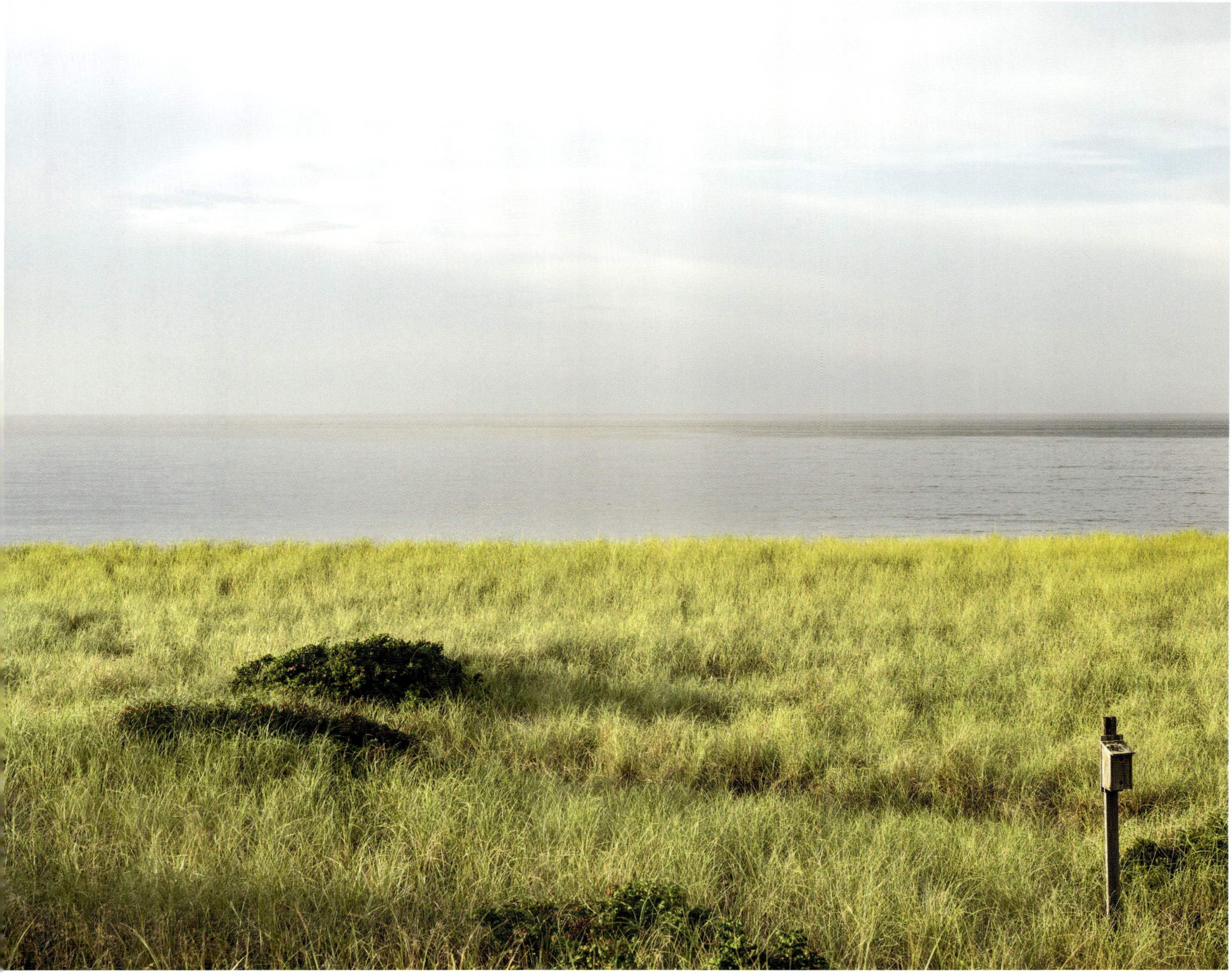

You can still come out here and sit down here in the sun
and enjoy yourself, and kind of forget that that whole world exists.

PAUL TASHA

dune shack dweller

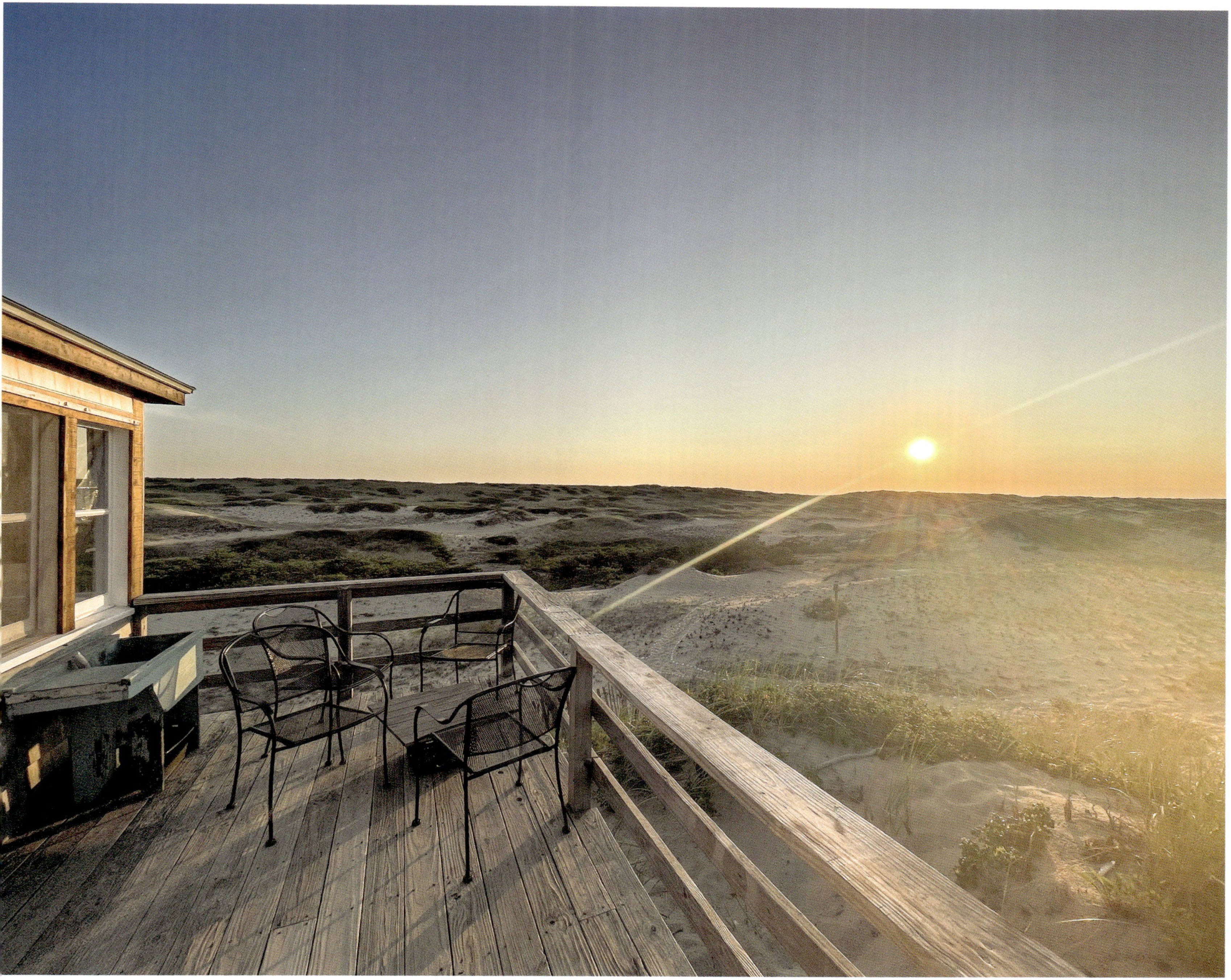

If I am feeling magnificently bundled, I walk through the Beech Forest and over the weird lunar landscape of the dunes, where the sand sweeps and piles, shapes and un-shapes and reshapes itself, so that I know to look very carefully, since I will never see this particular vista again. And yes, it's cold. Damn cold. But you bless the cold that has swept most tourists all the way down Route 6 and back across the Sagamore Bridge.

ANN PATCHETT

author

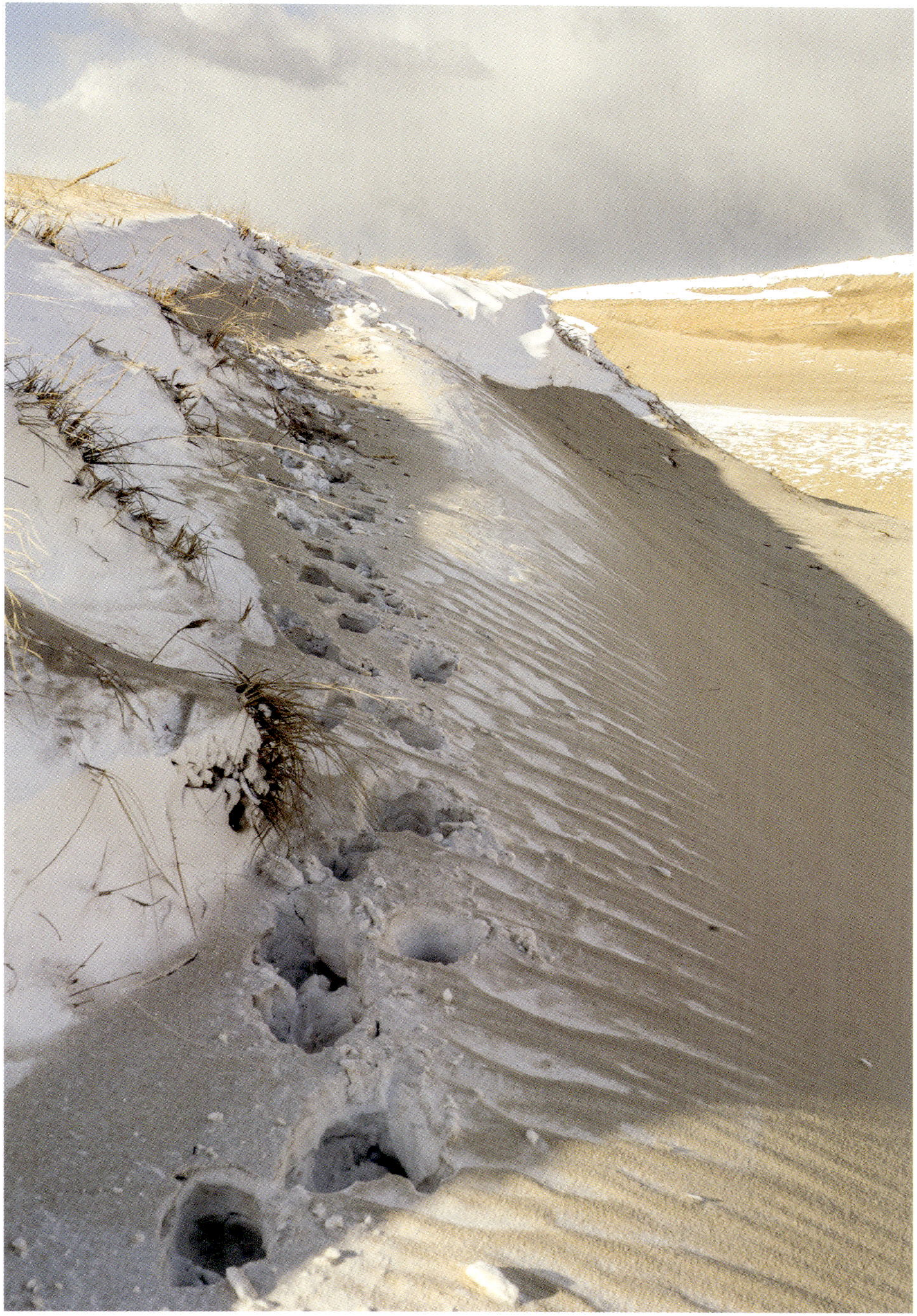

I scattered my uncle's ashes out in these waters,
and that's where my ashes will be joining him when the time comes.

JANET ARMSTRONG

dune shack dweller

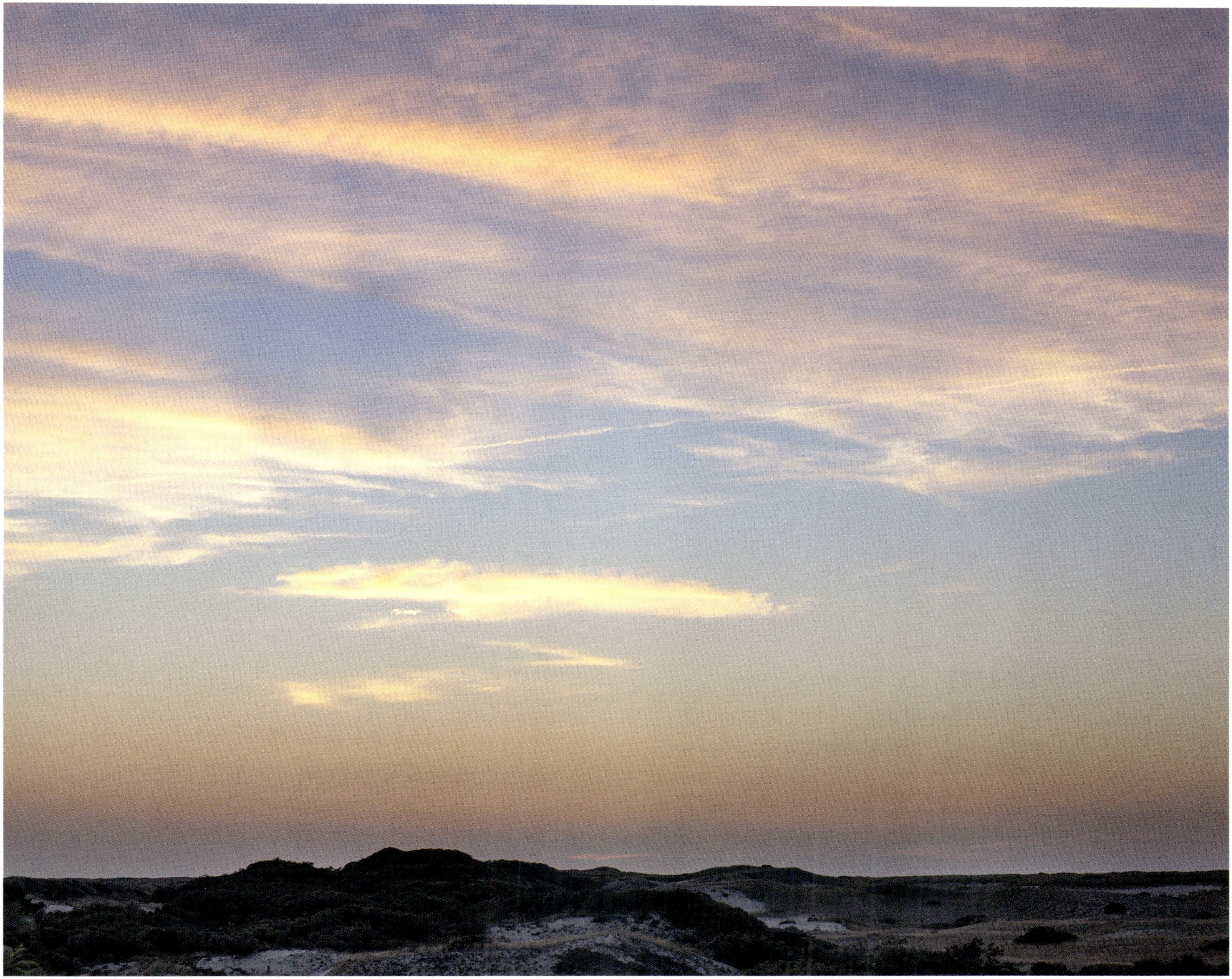

By any natural law, Dune Charlie's place should have fallen into the sea long before. It was a driftwood "Lego" set no manufacturer had ever produced, a construction that defied gravity.

JOSEPHINE DEL DEO

dune shack dweller, historian, author of *The Watch at Peaked Hill*

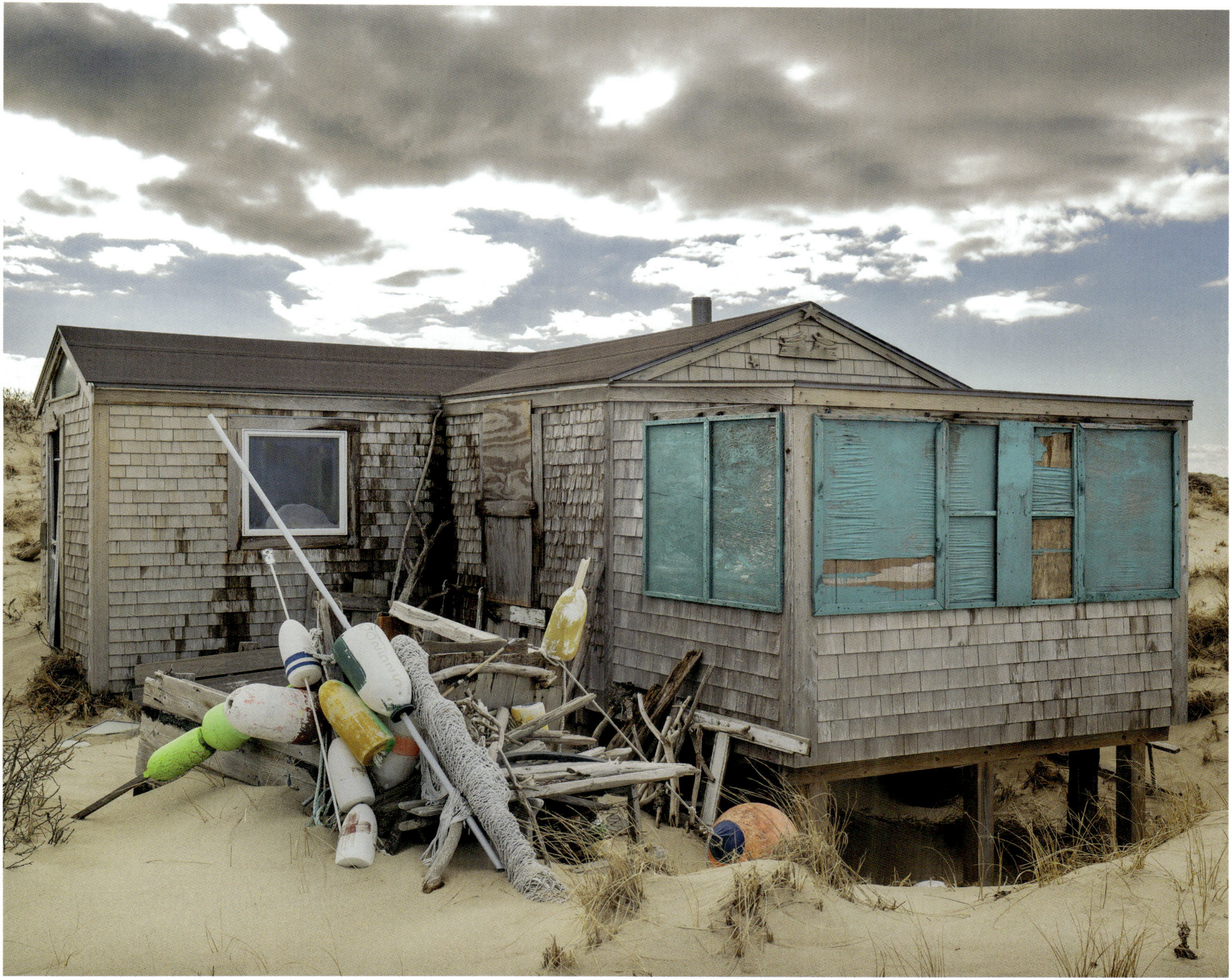

We were pirates, poets, princesses, born on these days of youthful foraging. We were whatever we wanted to be.

KATHIE JOSEPH MEADS

dune shack user

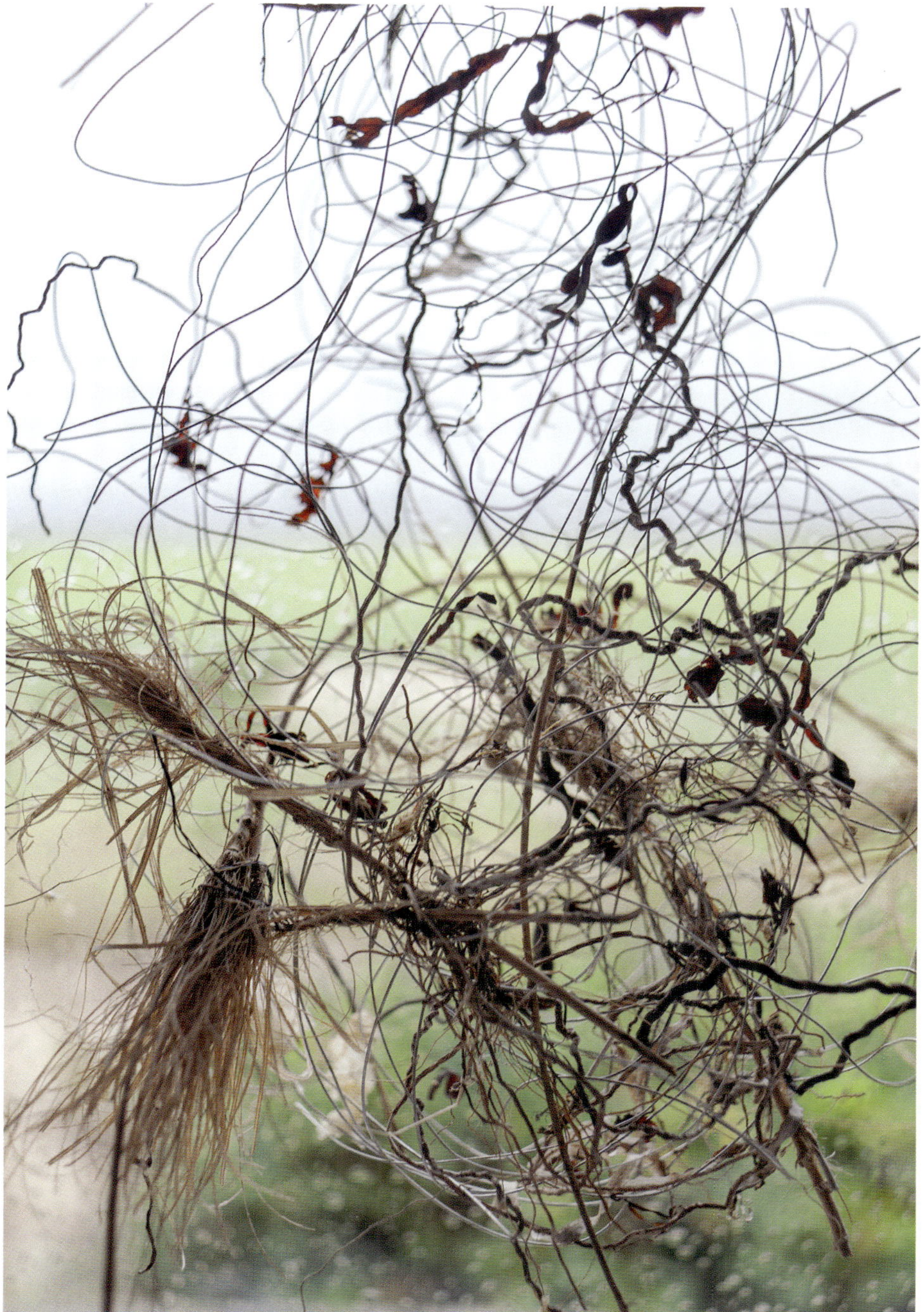

You can't help but feel like an artist, whether you're an artist or not. Whatever you do in your normal day is just magnified by being there.

PETER CLEMONS

dune shack dweller, artist

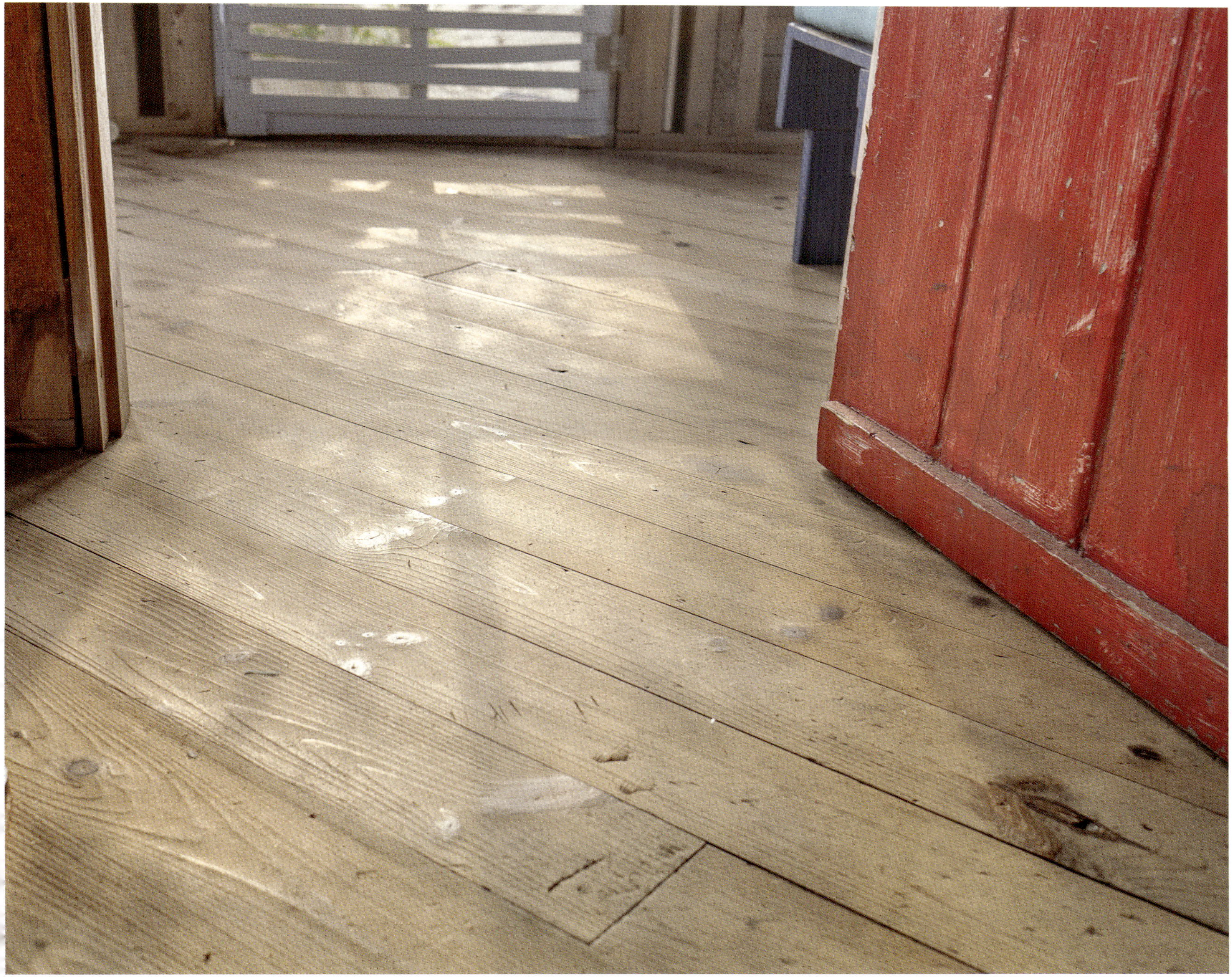

If you want someone to understand the preciousness of water, have them trudge the dewy sand down the hill to fill their jugs at the pump. Have them light the stove and heat the water near boiling, pour it over the night's slicked plates, and plunge the chilled hands into the dishpan steaming now from the morning's cool air, the pleasure of that rusty dune water equal to its cost.

MELANIE BRAVERMAN

writer

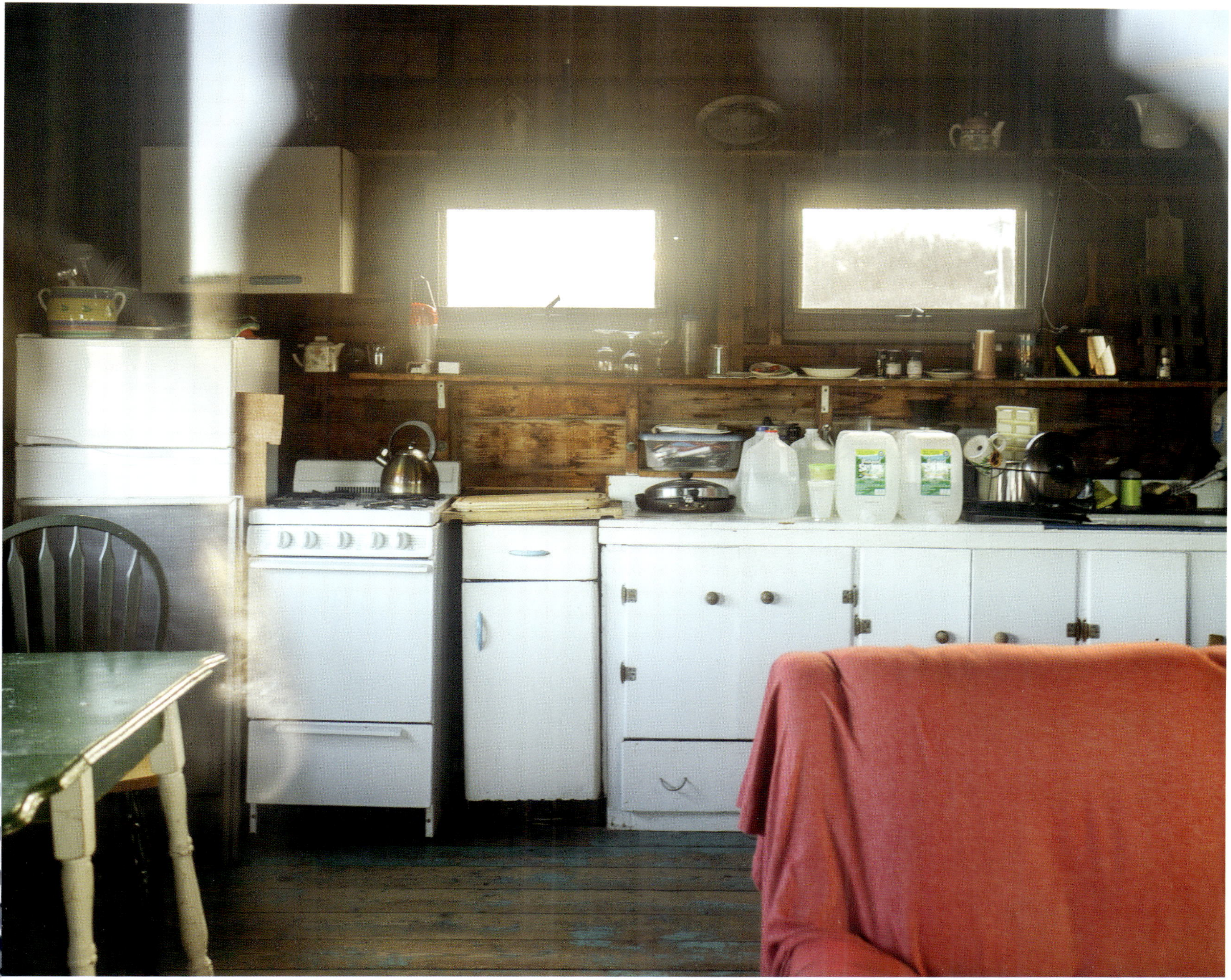

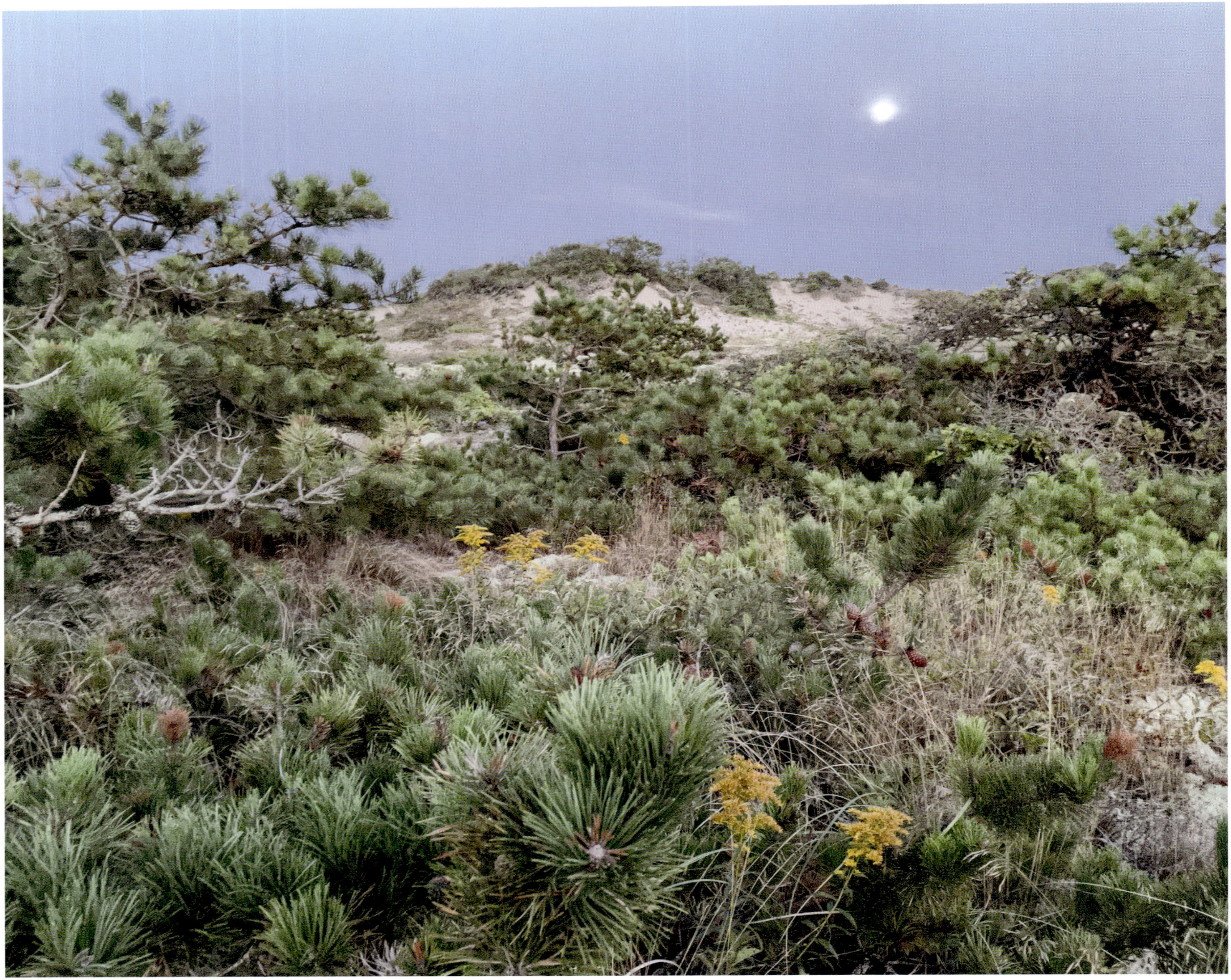

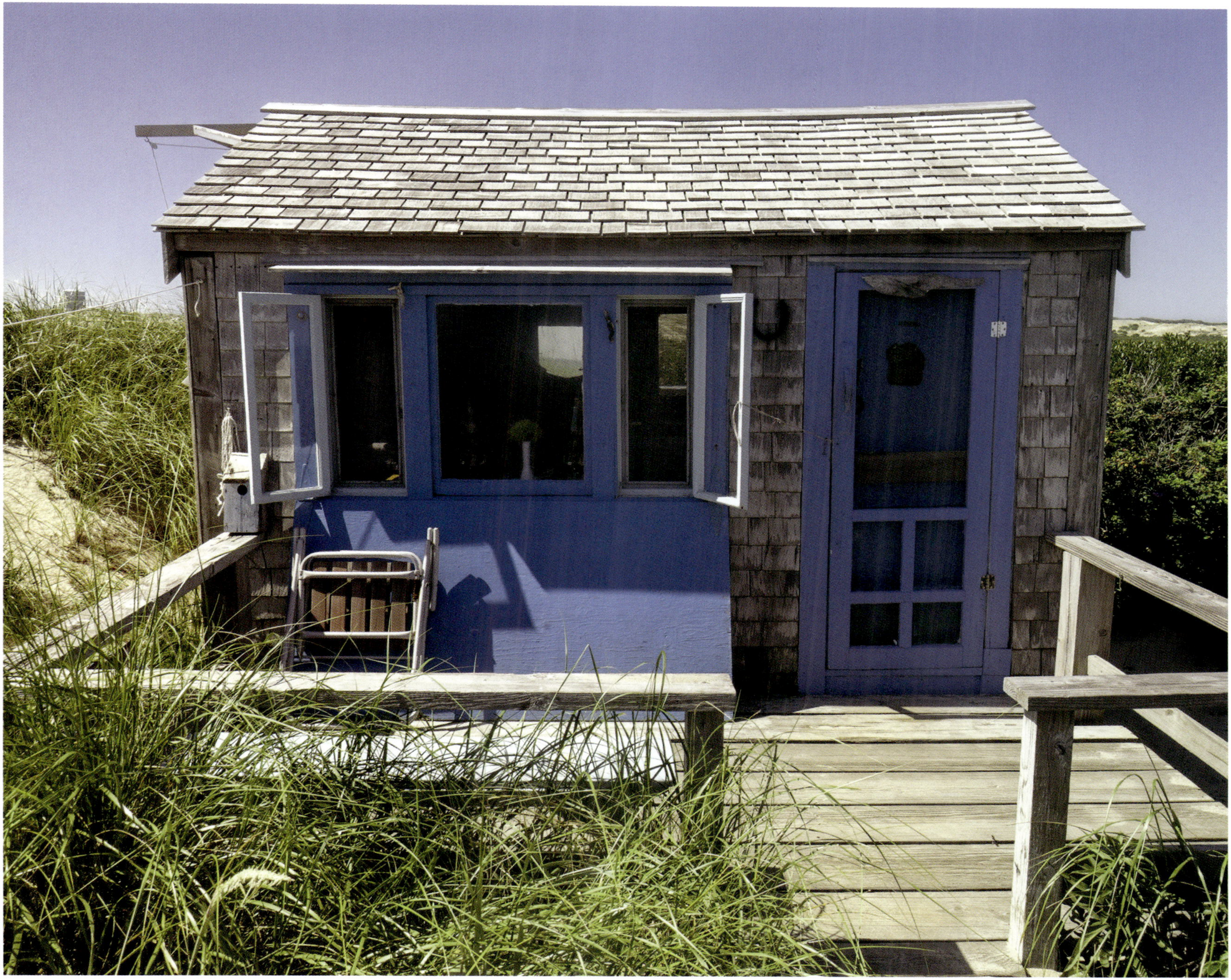

The pump water is sweet beyond belief.

WILLIAM OSCAR JOHNSON

journalist, author, artist

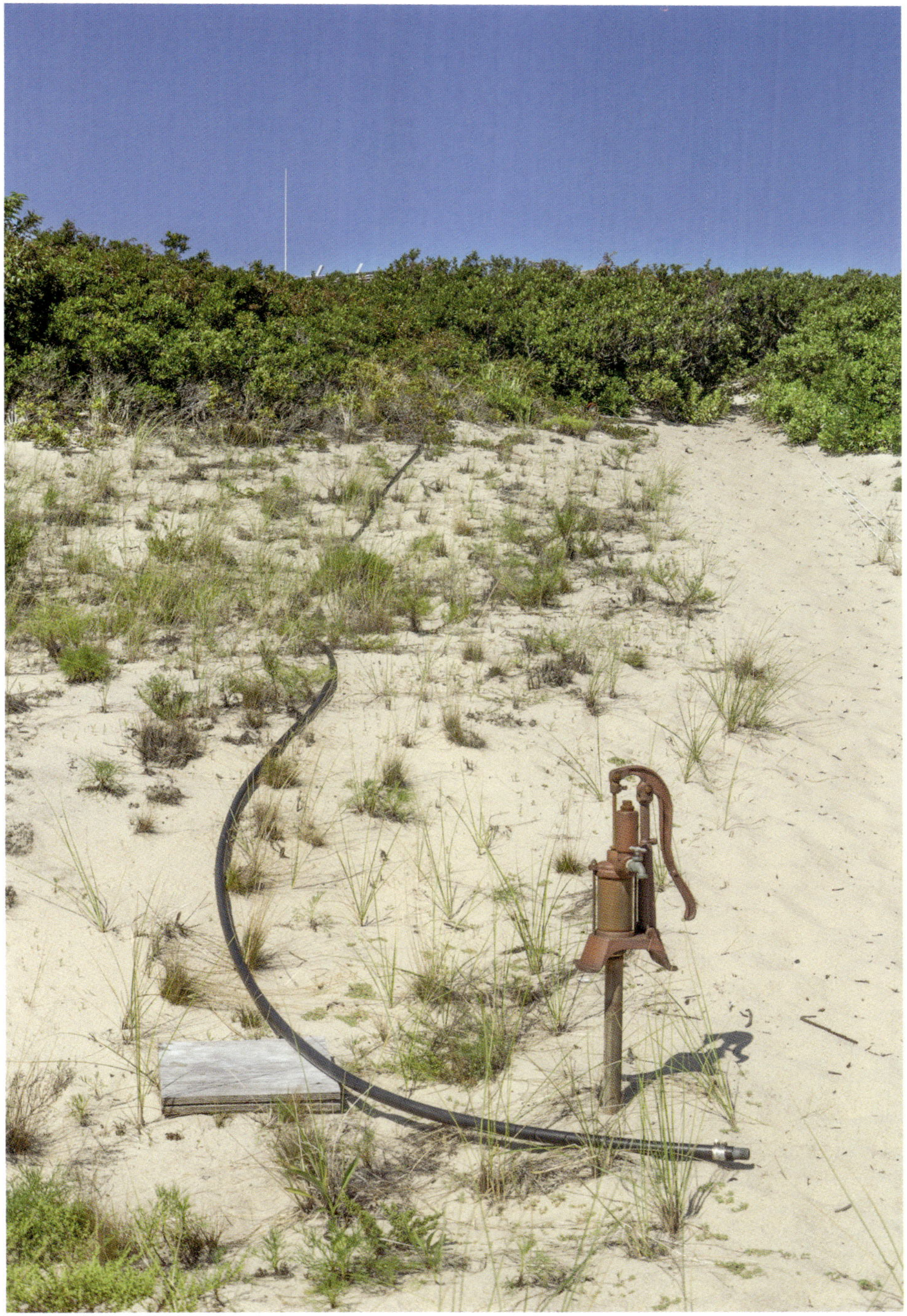

I would love to be able to sit on your beach and look at you [Eugene O'Neill] and be near you in almost silence.

CHARLES DEMUTH

artist

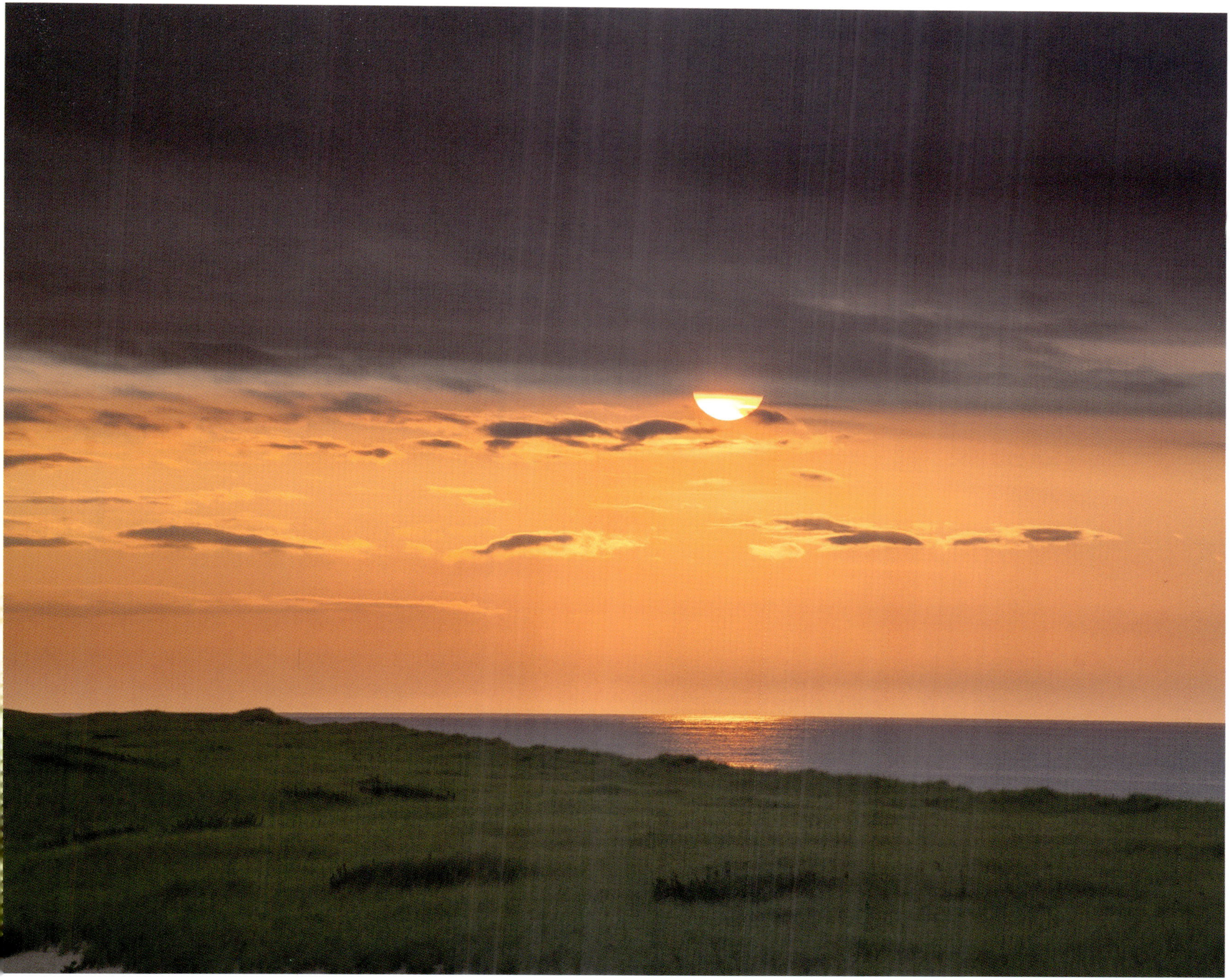

I am moving into a little shanty in the dunes where I can avoid the summer crowds. I find this is a good place to work and think I will get a play off to you next week.

TENNESSEE WILLIAMS

playwright

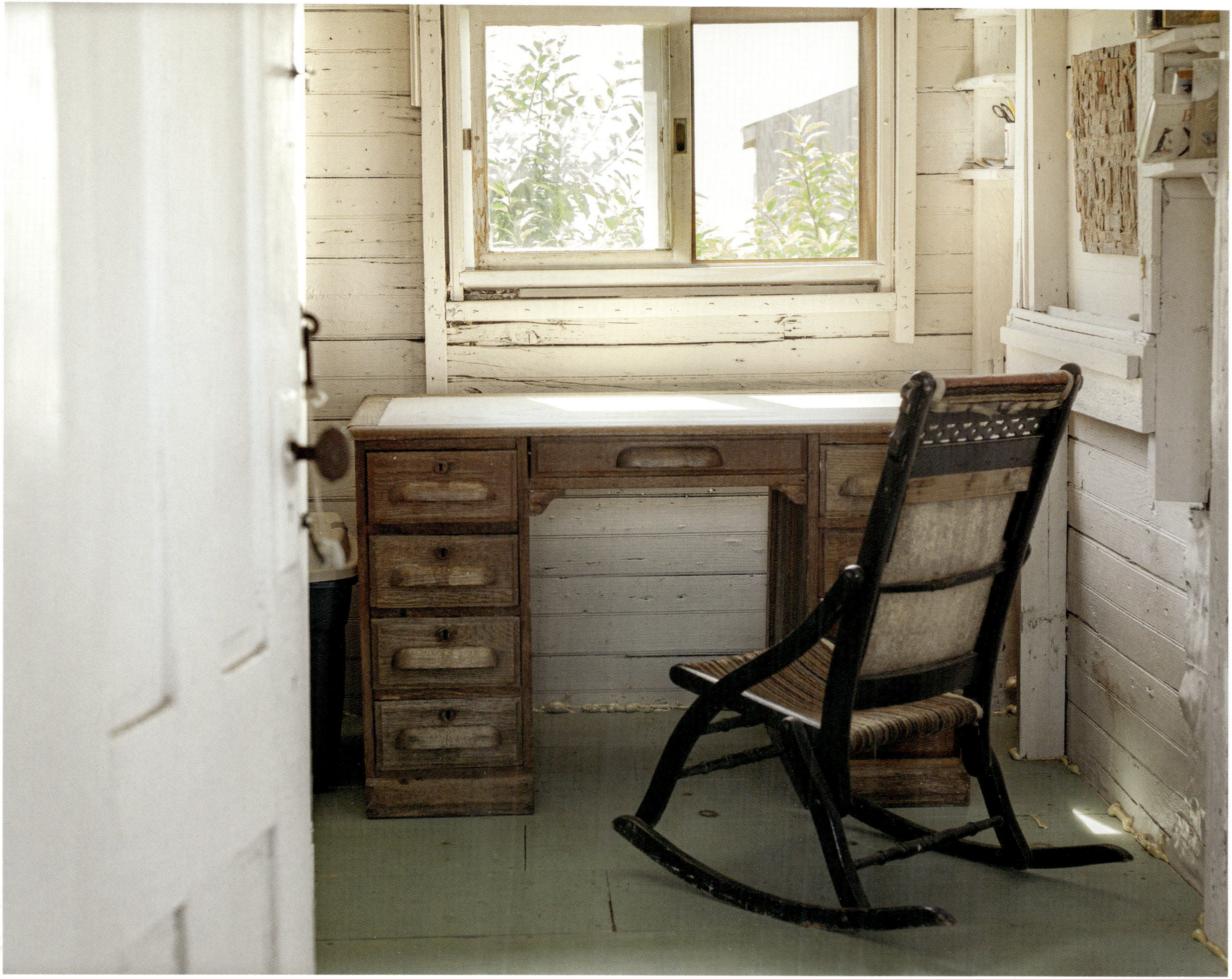

The integration of physics and biology is a beautiful thing, like a flock of birds flying, how they coordinate with each other as they fly. They are responding to the chemistry they sense from the magnetic field of the earth, and they are responding to air currents and gravity, moisture, storms, and weather.

MARK ADAMS

painter, cartographer, coastal geologist

Out of necessity Dad [artist Wolf Kahn] lived frugally and in complete solitude. . . . His time was spent painting and drawing, digging for clams, and foraging off the land and sea.

MELANY KAHN

writer

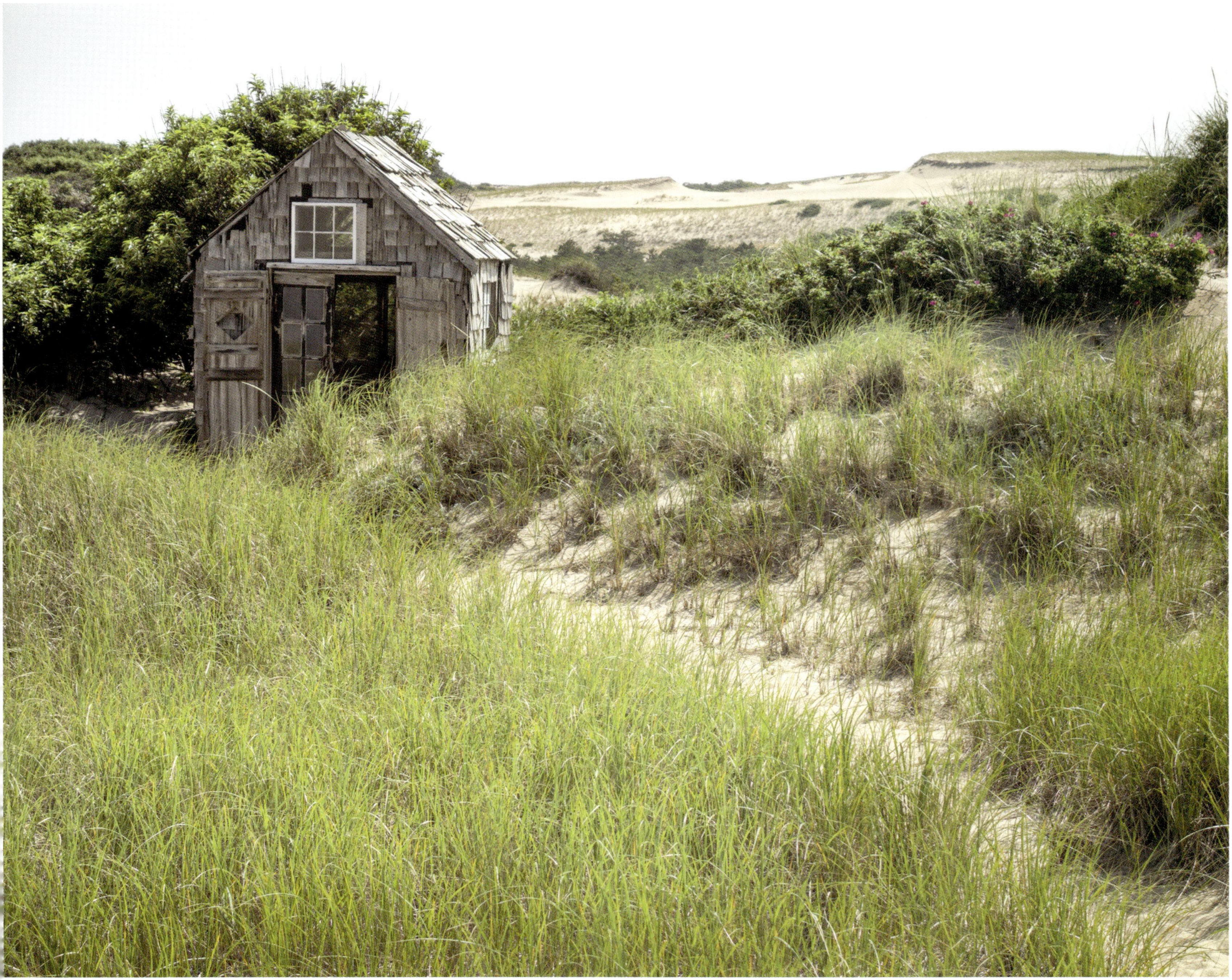

Never saw anything like it and perhaps will never see it again.

FRANK DIGIROLAMO

Provincetown resident

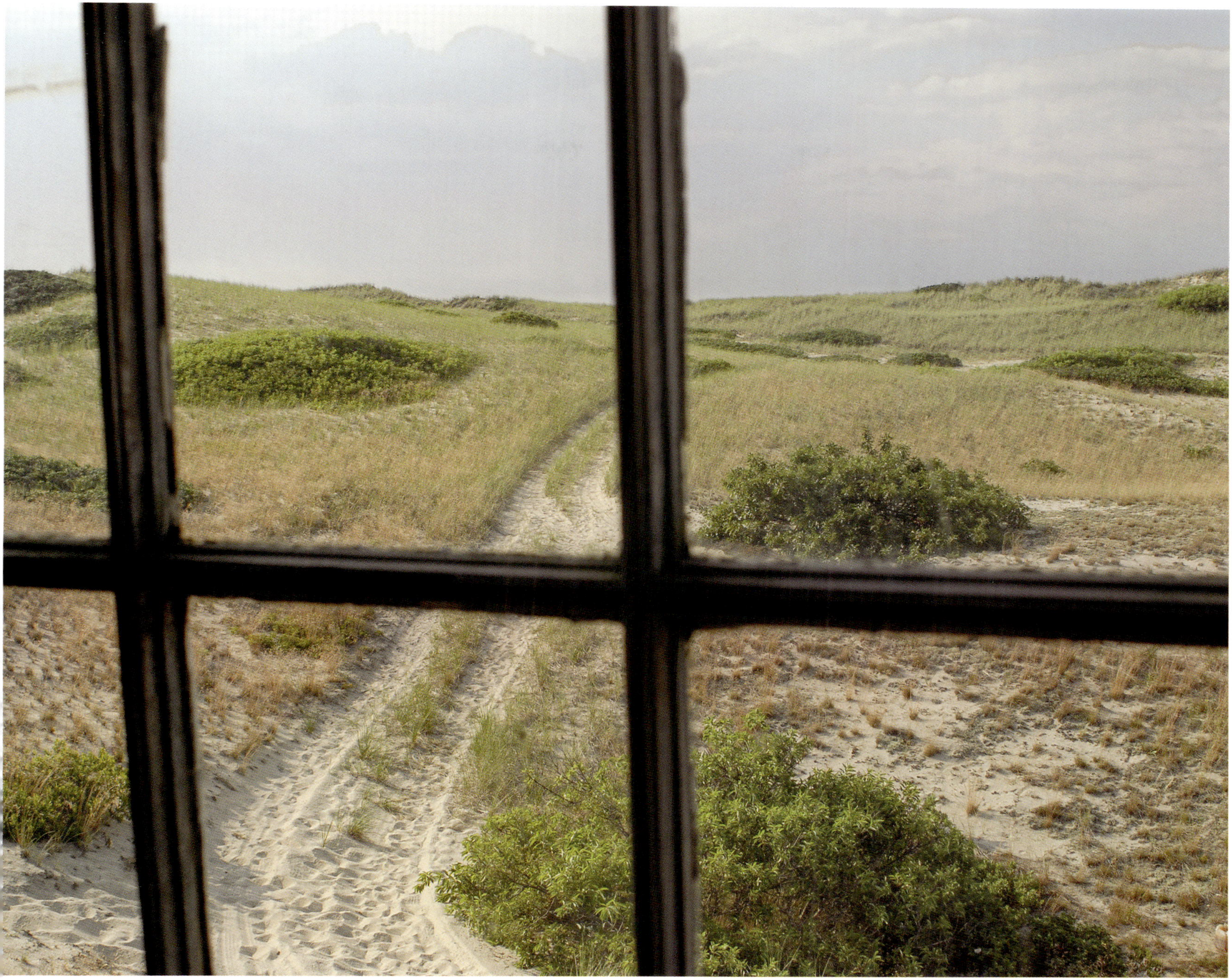

I looked across the rooms to the sea, which shows through the open north door like a piece of blue paper pasted down and, for further security, barred across with the irregular sloping of a dune. When there is a storm and the door is closed, I feel dangerously shut in, and the house seems blinded. I rely a great deal on that door's being open.

HAZEL HAWTHORNE

dune shack dweller and doyenne, author

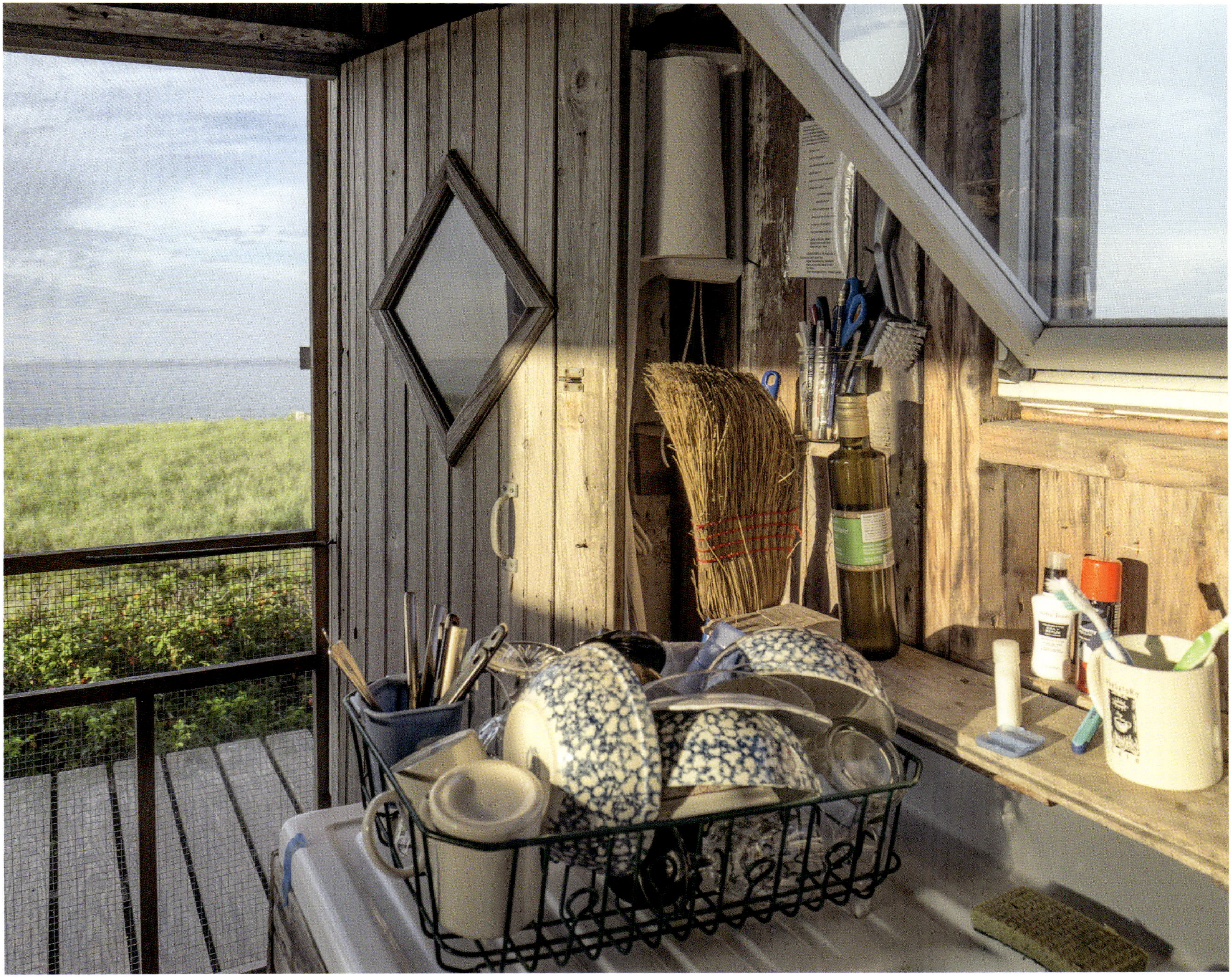

It's just a shack. I could rebuild that shack, without exaggeration, in two days. Maybe the foundation would take a little longer, but the physical building would take a couple of days. So we're not talking about a big deal.

MURRAY ZIMILES

artist

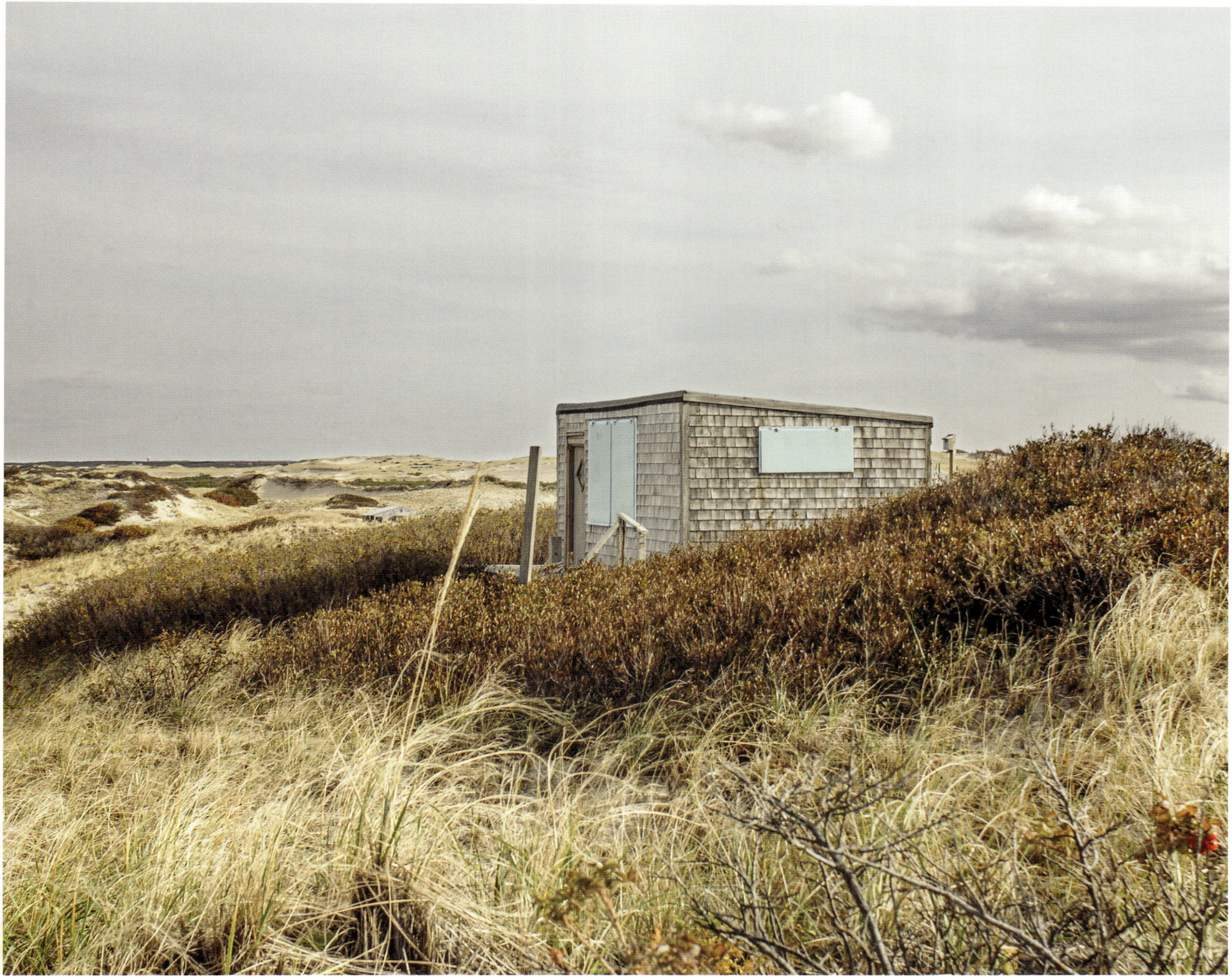

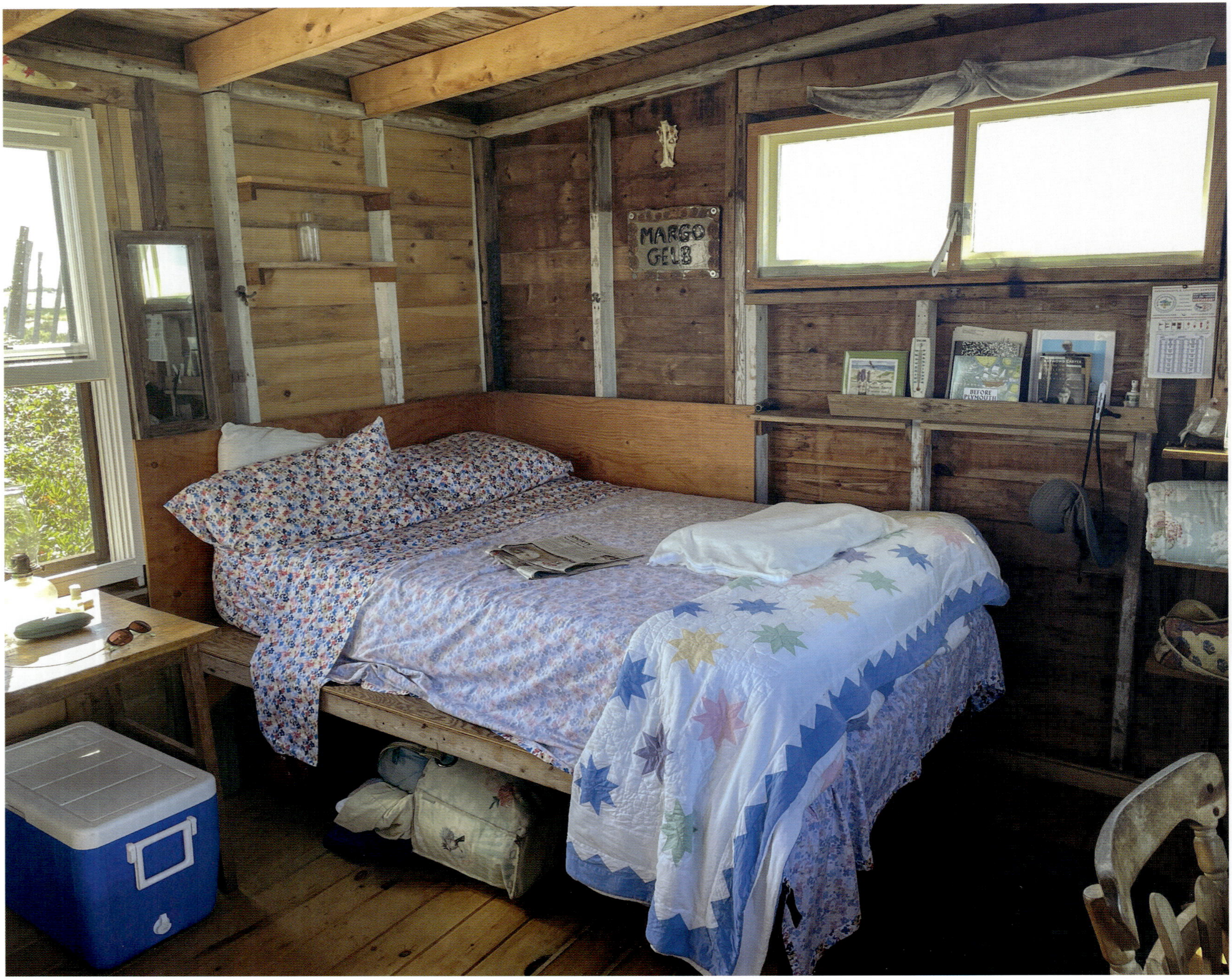
MARGO
GELB
BEFORE
PLYMOUTH

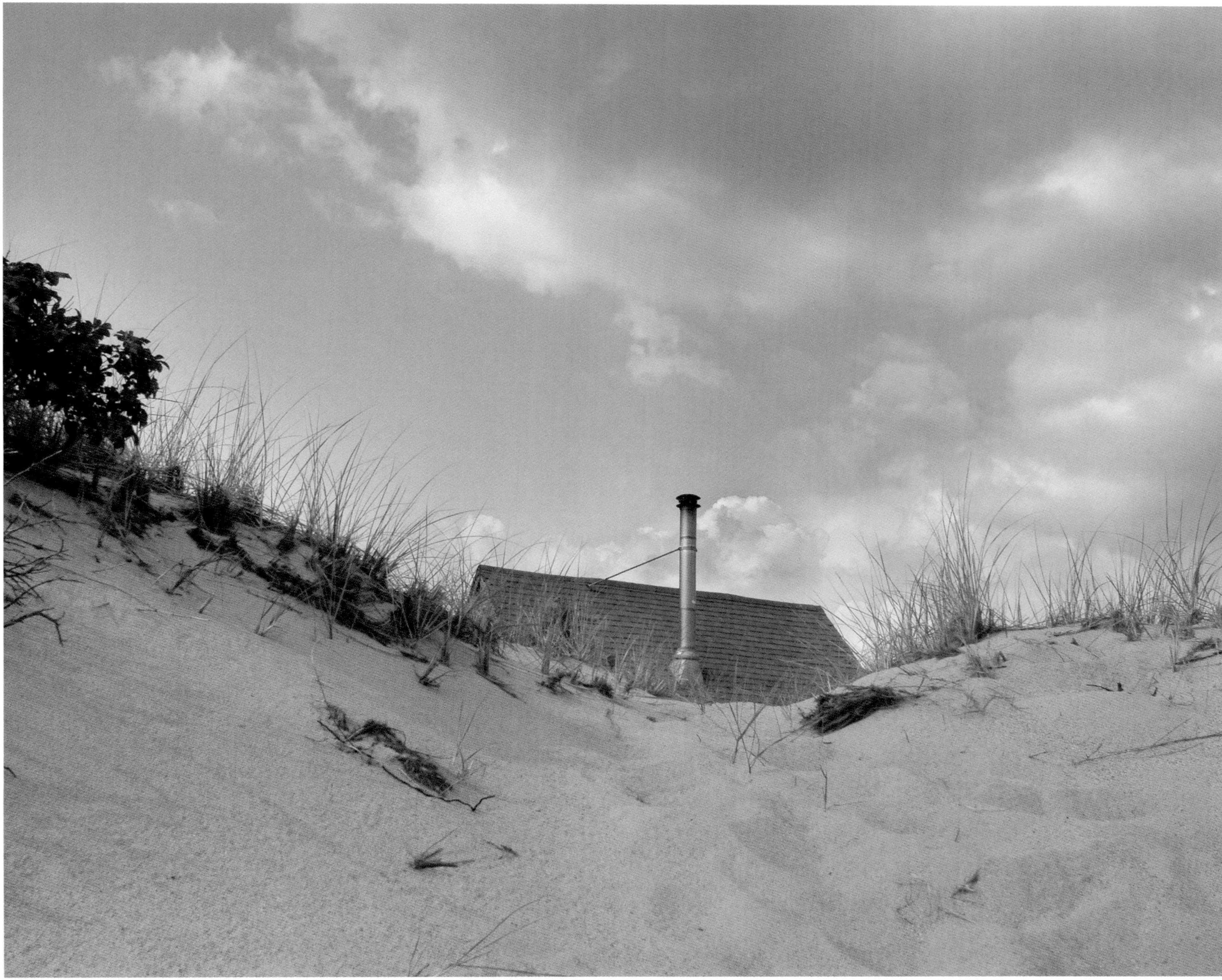

When things are bothering you, you head to the dunes.
When you celebrate, you head to the dunes. It's just a part of our lives.
It's the backdrop. It's the most beautiful backdrop you could ever ask for.
And it's ours.

MAUREEN JOSEPH HURST

dune shack user

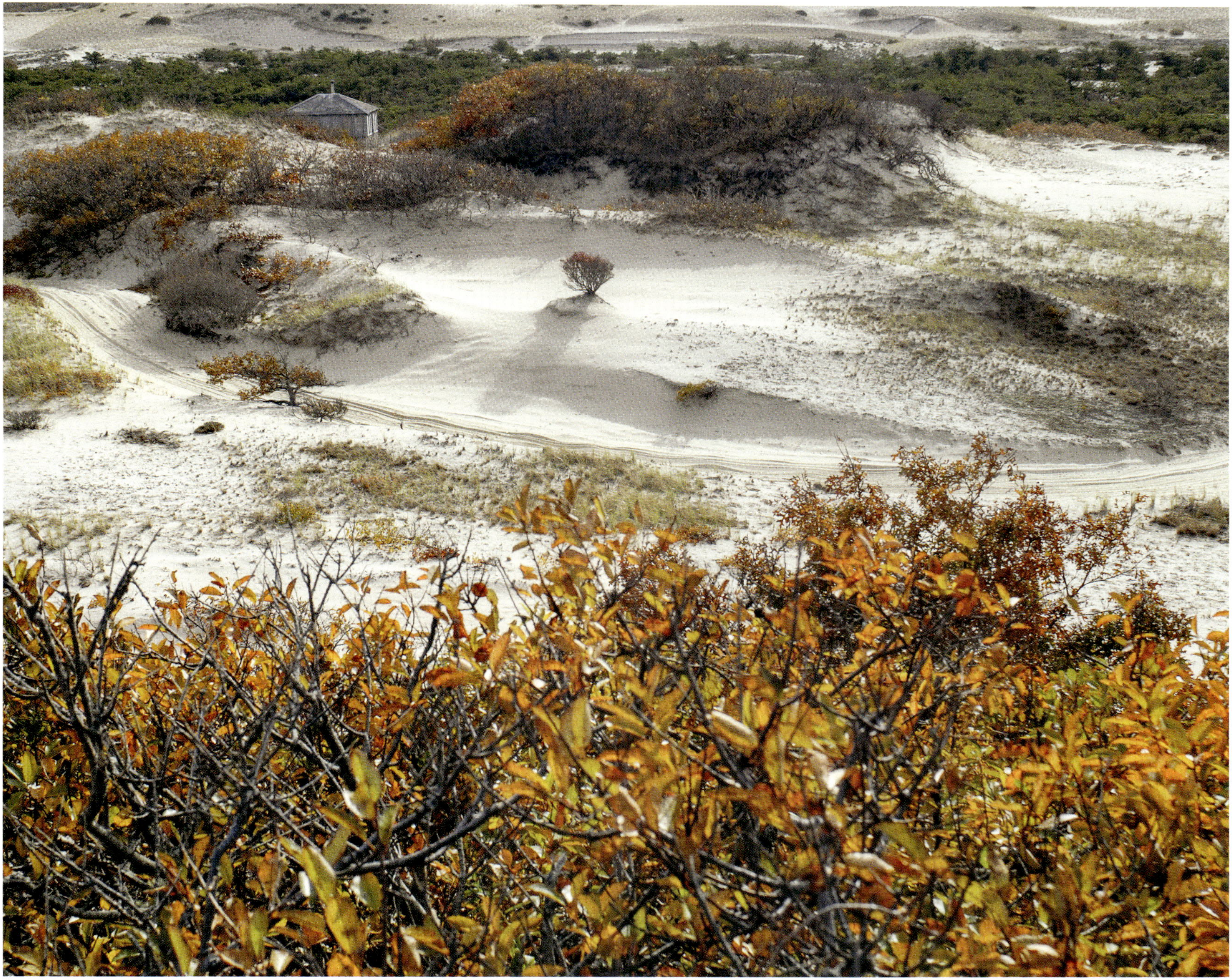

There's a story of a shipwreck that took place right out there. They say they laid the dead men out on the floor of Thalassa. There are people who won't stay out there because they can hear the dead men talking to them.

JULIE SCHECTER

dune shack user, a founder of Peaked Hill Trust

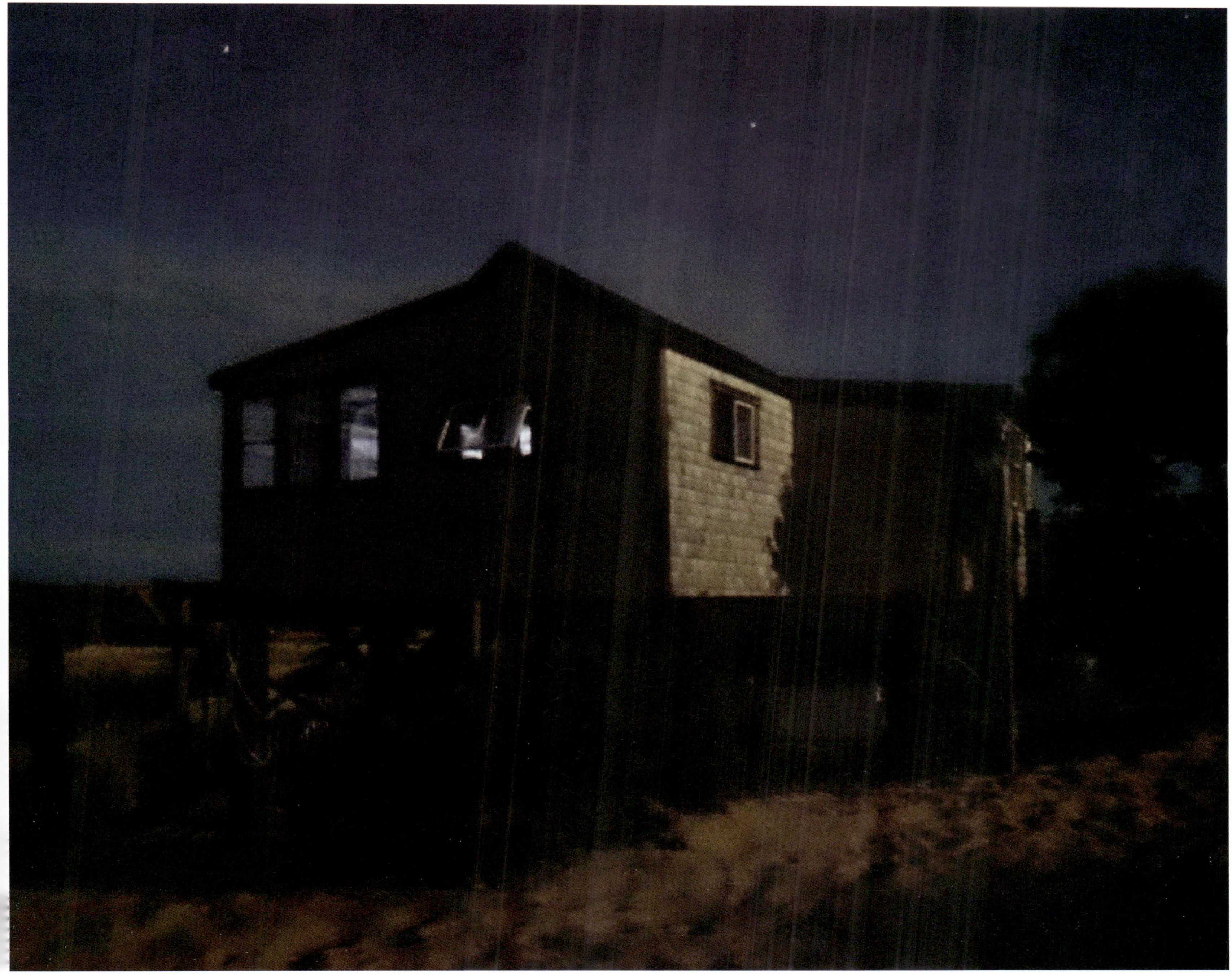

Part of the culture there was this complete care of the natural landscape. The thing is, if you stepped on the dune grass and broke it, the houses would fall down. Part of the way of maintaining the life there was that you had to be careful of everything. This was the feeling there. It was really exciting.

DAWN ZIMILES

artist

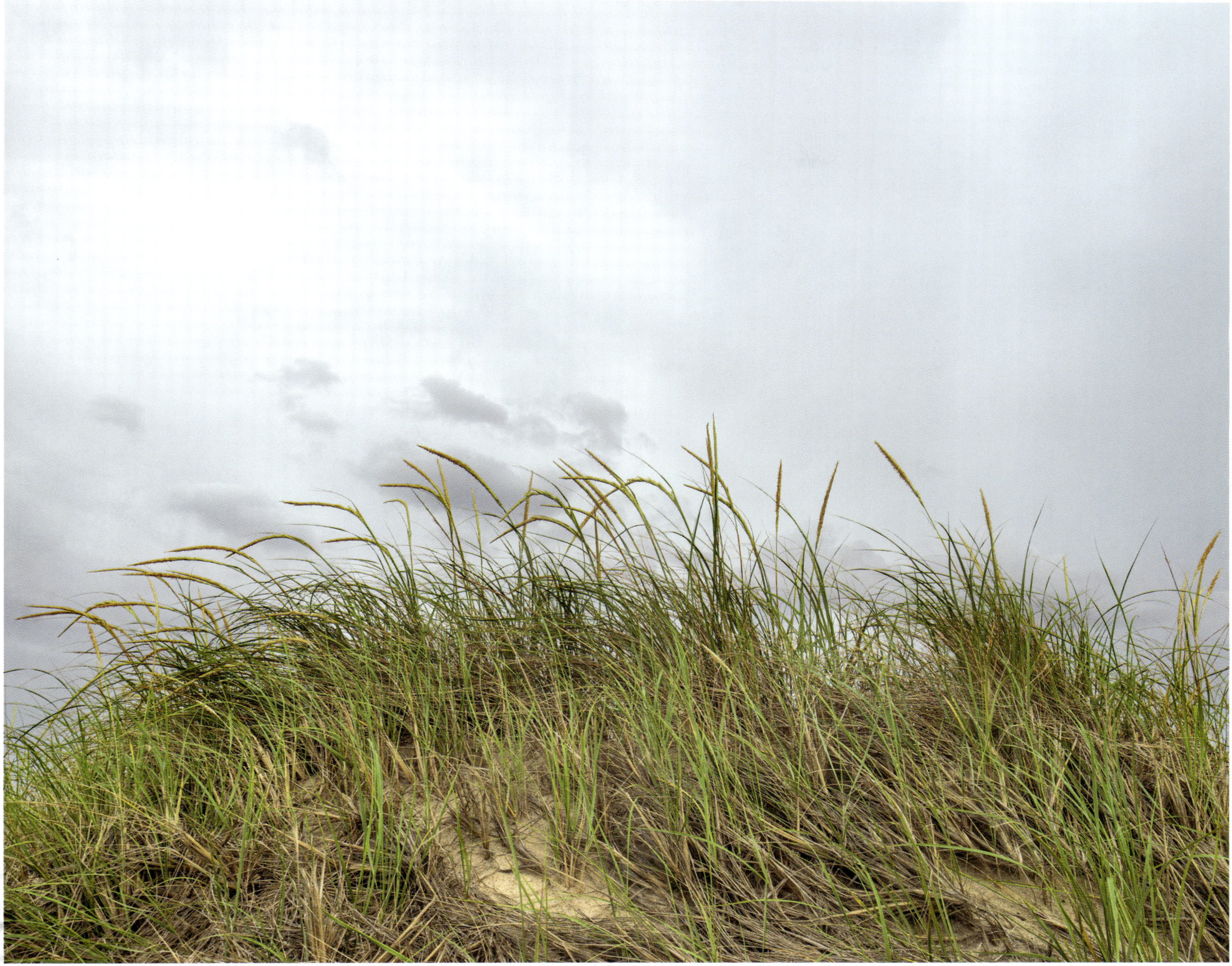

Listening to the waves around the clock from within the thin walls of the shack induces contemplation and a kind of meditation, deep and steadying as a mantra.

RUSSELL STEVEN POWELL

artist

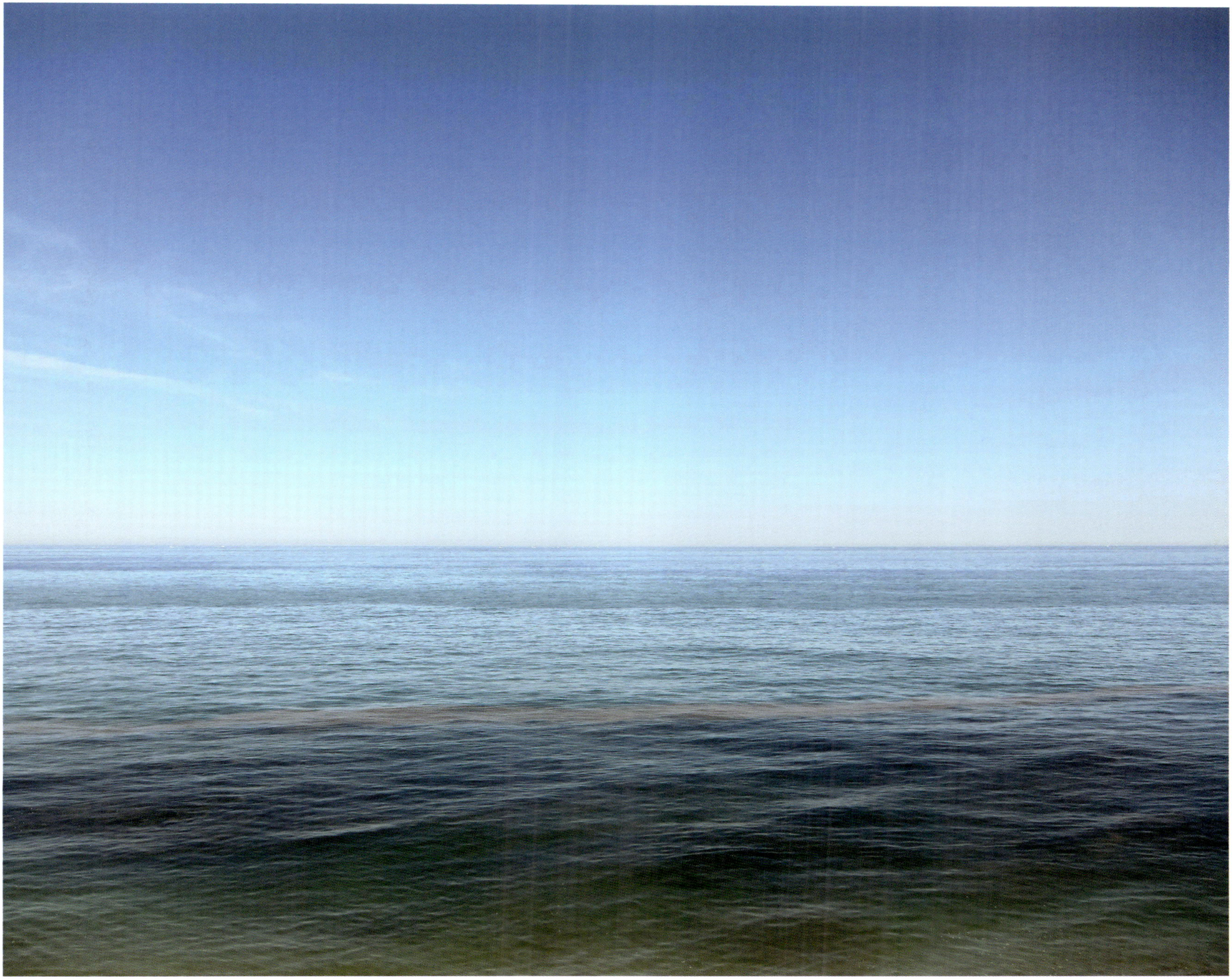

The windows are held open with a wild cacophony of hooks and latches, each one requiring a separate ritual of opening. I reach high on my toes to secure them. They are a constant visual meditation.

JOANNE DUGAN

visual artist, author, artist-in-residence

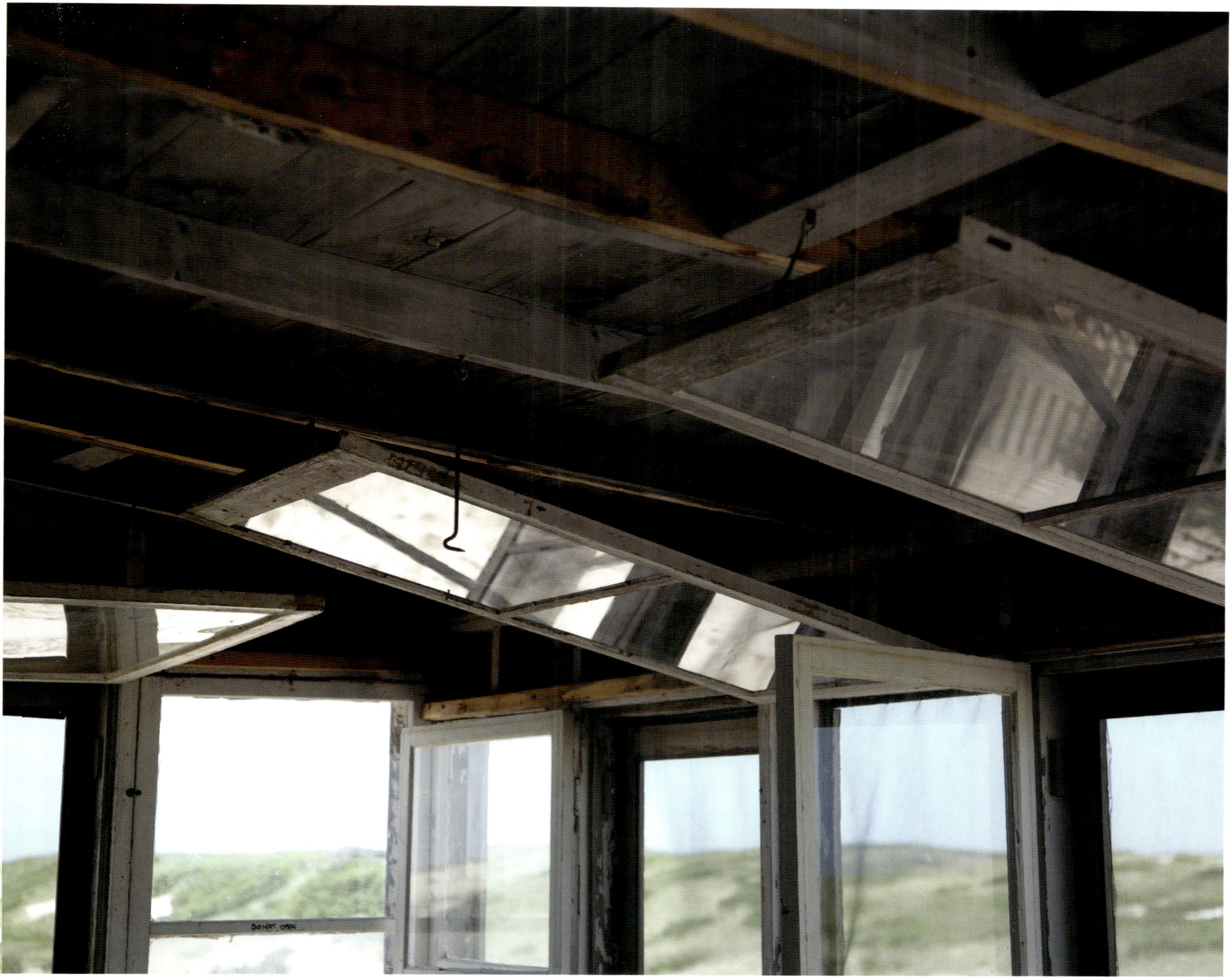

Go mindless here, save enough to sense and perceive. Go naked here, empty and newborn, breathing in the sky and surf, expelling nothing. Lay face down and drink in the tender sand, unangered by the wind. Lay face up and let the stars pierce your soul, feeling them burn their infiniteness into your fleeting existence. Be cleansed by the awe of the dunes and float above them, untethered yet enslaved to their majesty, their simplicity, their fragility.

ROBBY MCQUEENEY

"The Dune Tramp," photojournalist

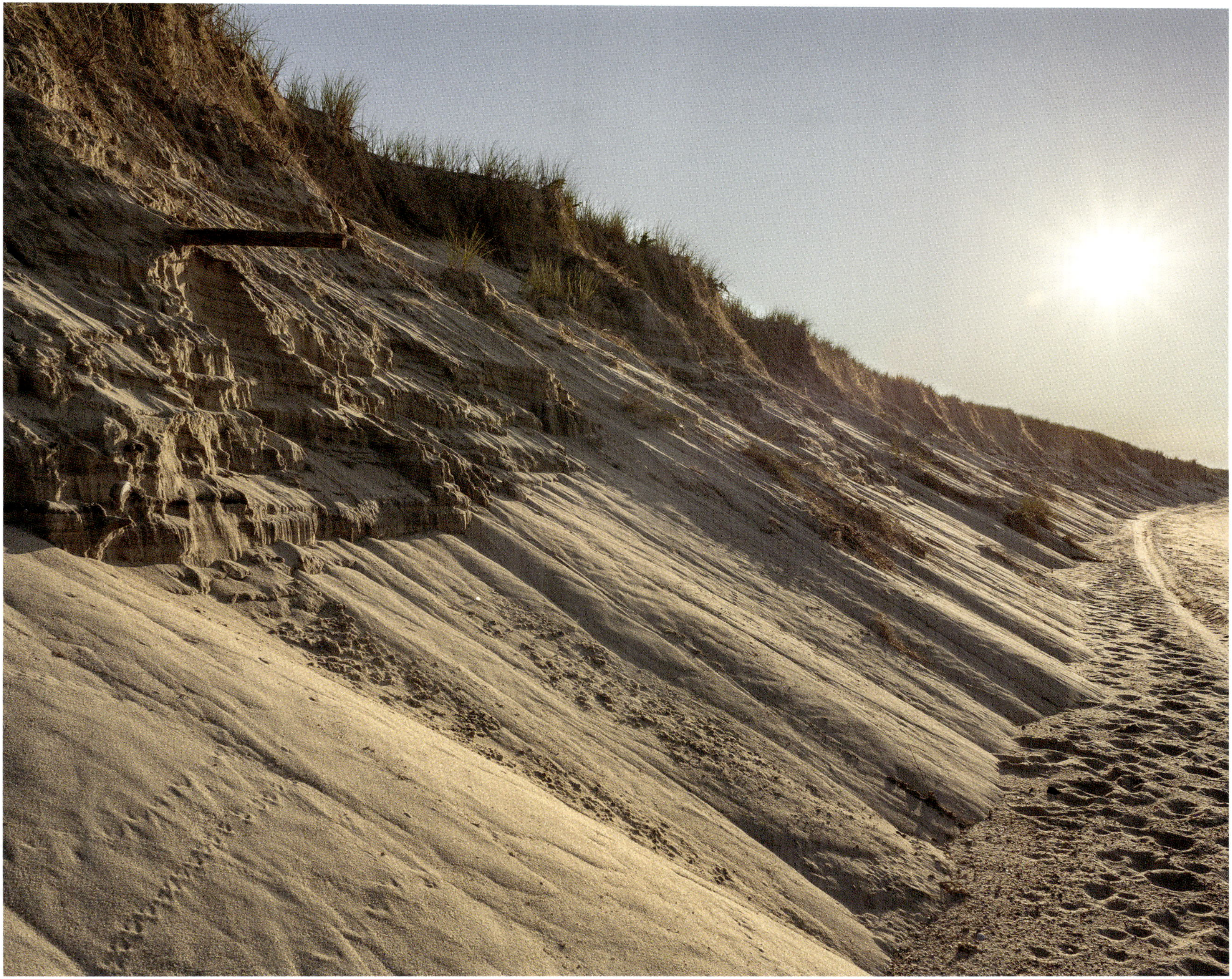

The dunes always give back.

BETTE WARNER

Executive Director, Peaked Hill Trust

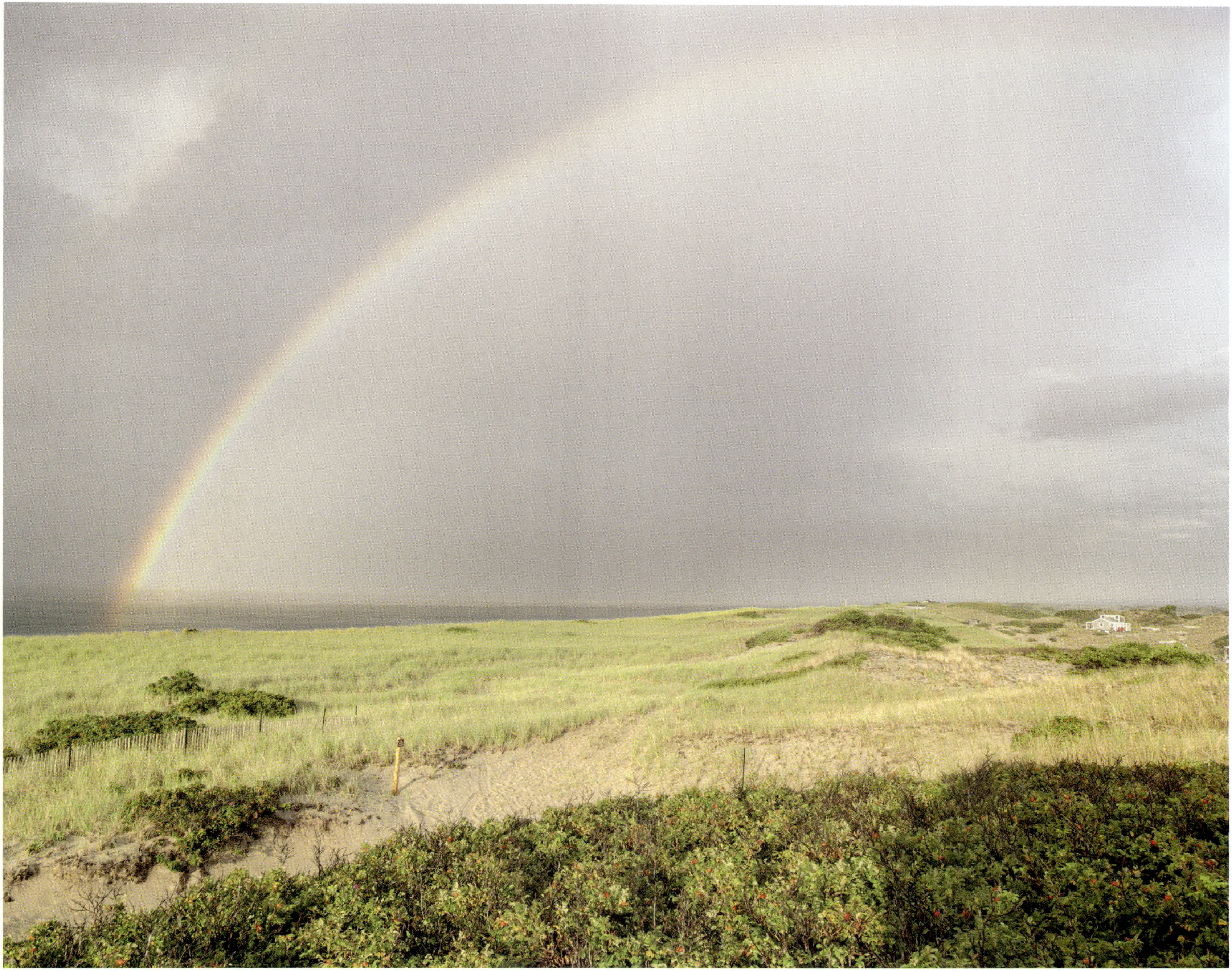

The description of the property lines in the deed used words which, in a very real sense, also describe the boundaries of the murky, lost world of Eugene O'Neill and his plays: "Bounded on the East by lands unknown . . . on the South by lands unknown . . . on the West by lands unknown . . . bounded on the North by the Atlantic Ocean . . ."

CROSWELL BOWEN

author, journalist

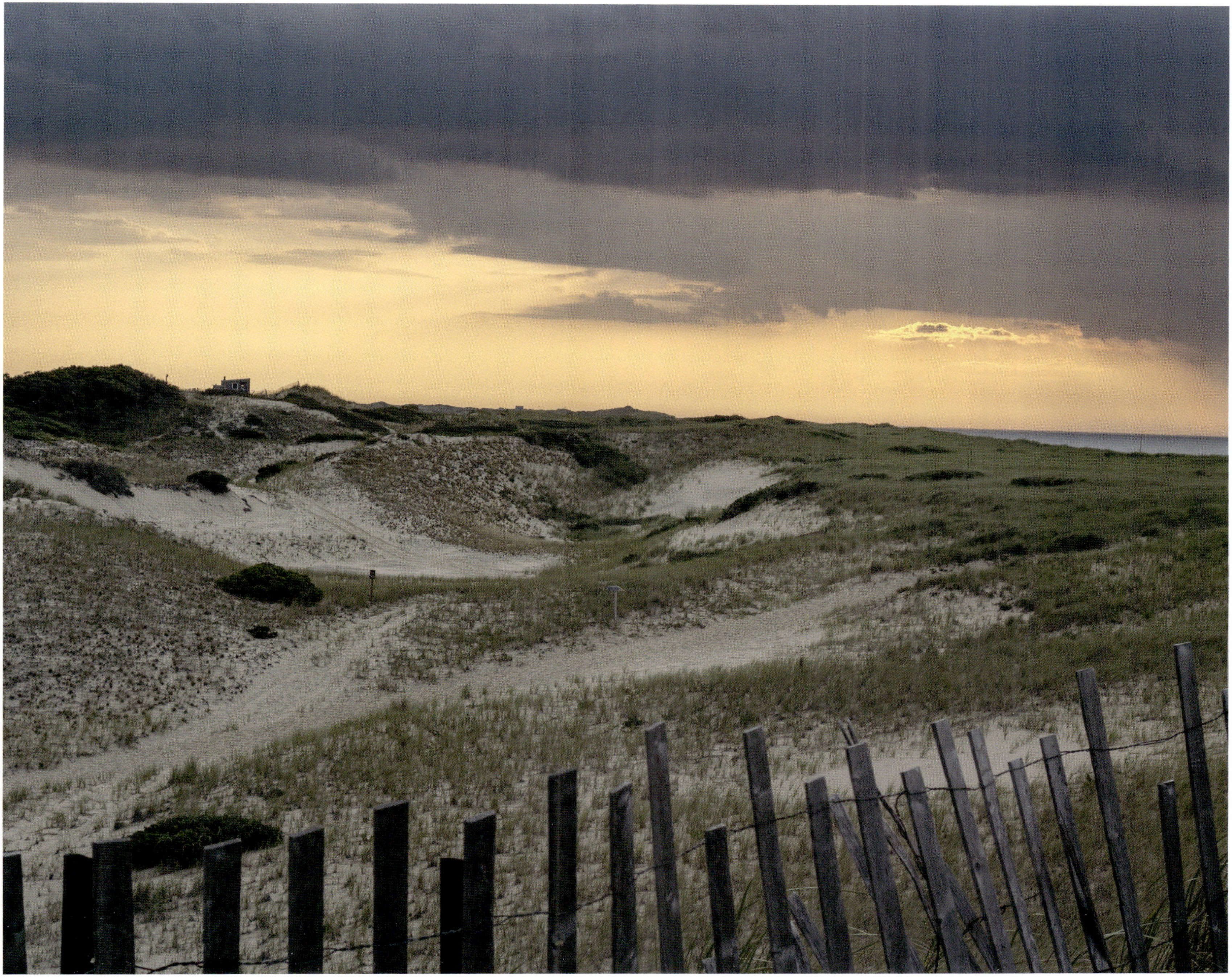

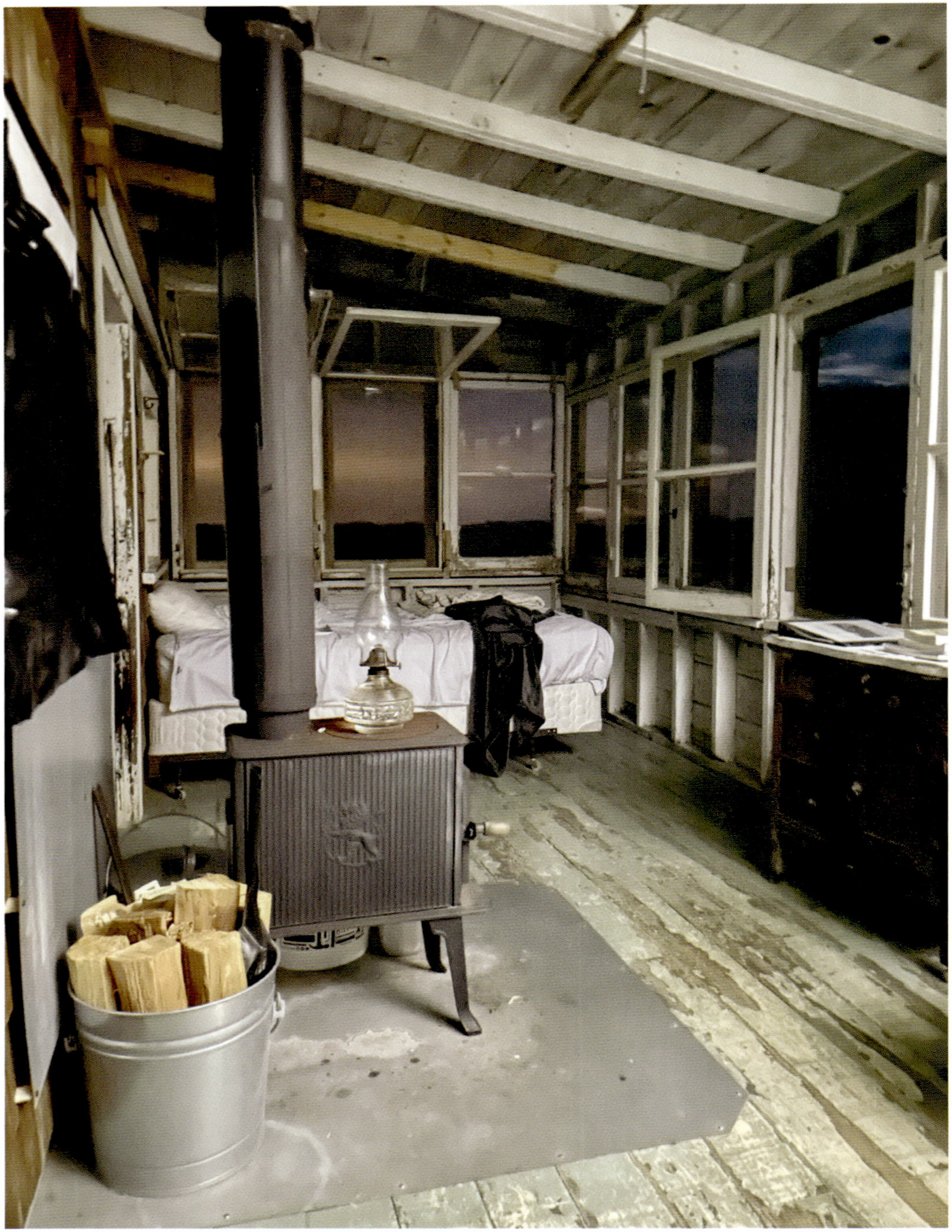

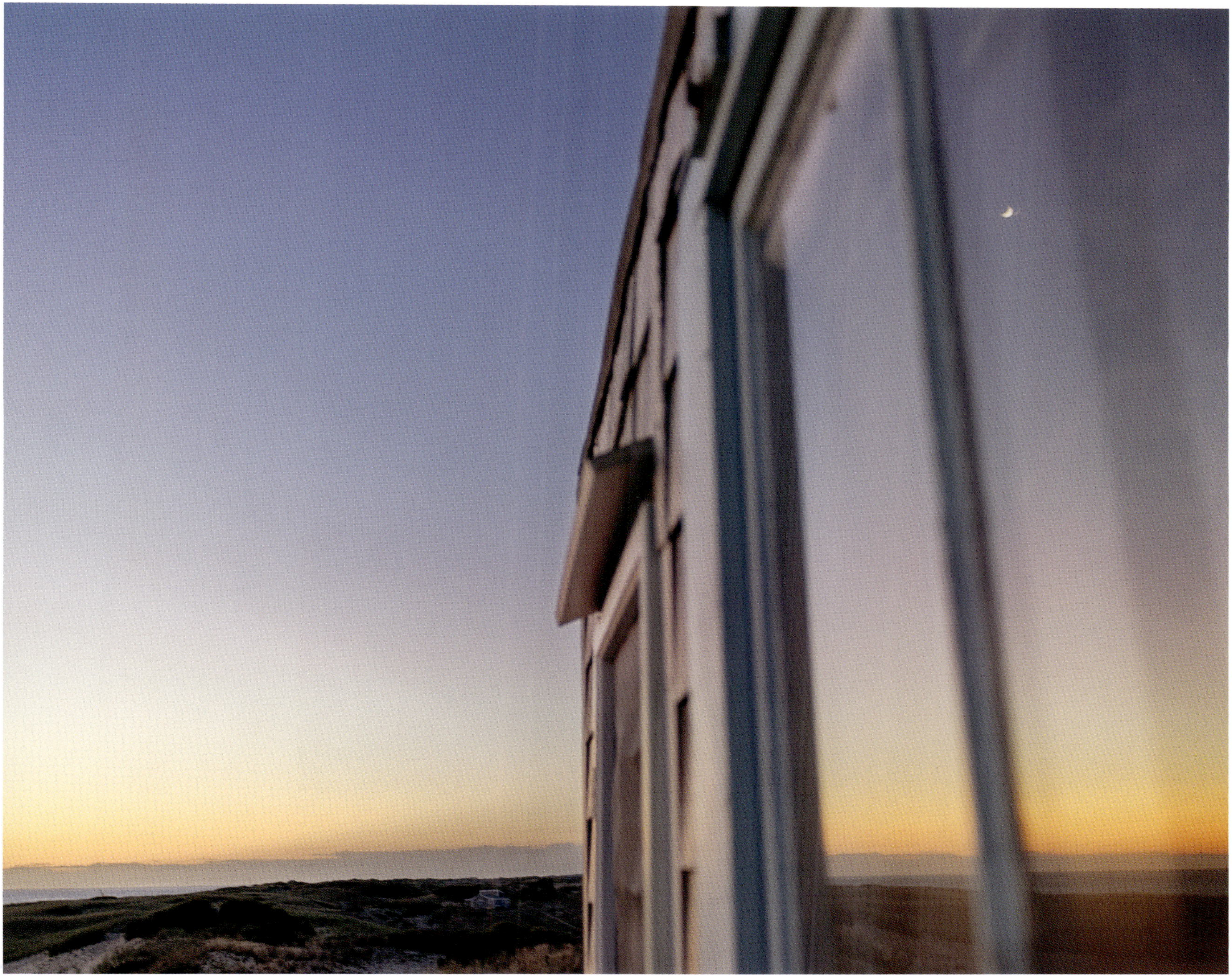

Away from the din of ordinary life, you hear your own music—
the self, stilled, and then, beyond the self—what we call "art."

CANDICE REFFE
poet

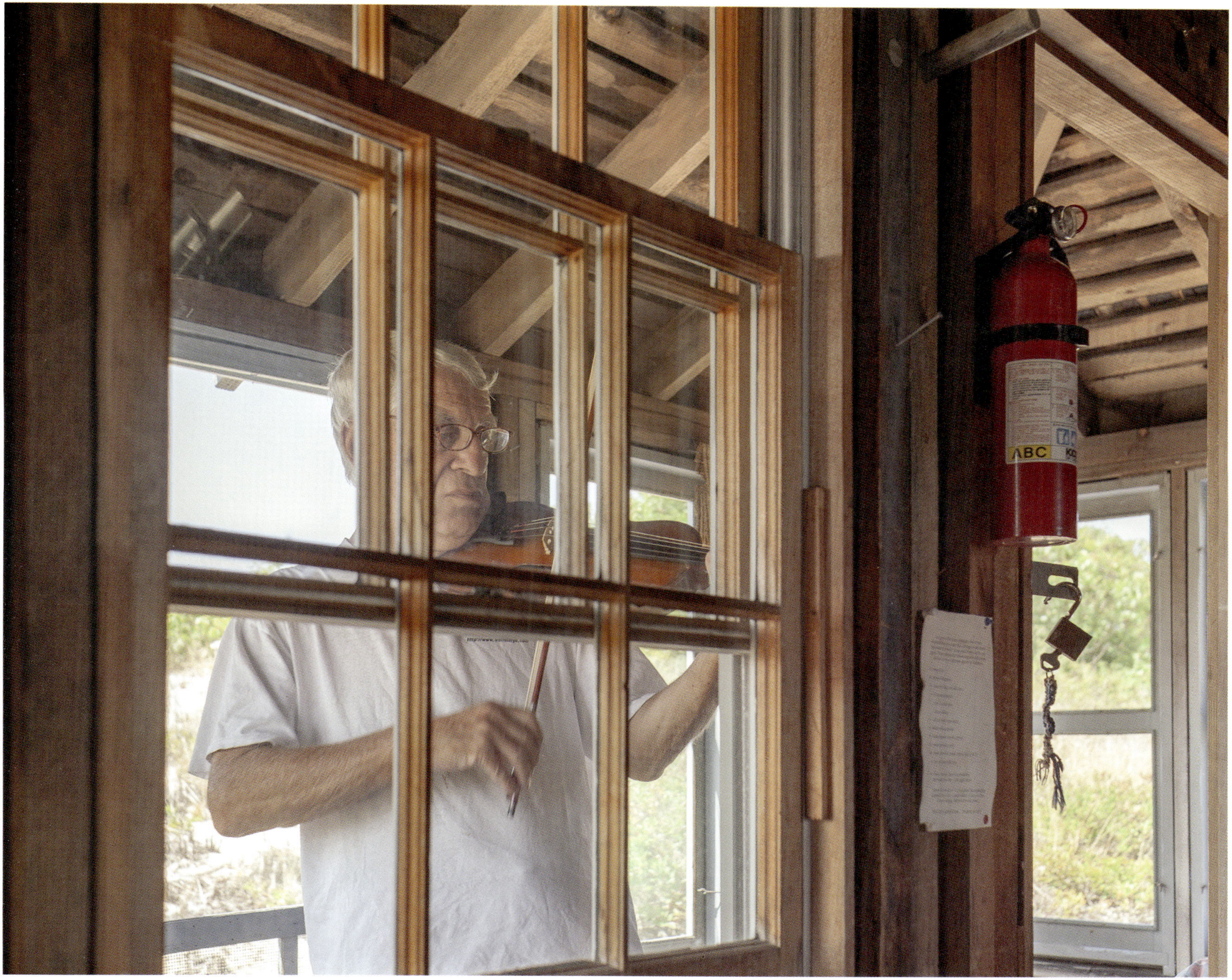
ABC

One day we saw a black spot. . . . It was a kitchen stove in good repair . . . there it sat for no good reason at all, near no road, near no wagon track, a fine kitchen stove. There it remained year by year and rusted away and the sands covered it.

MARY HEATON VORSE

labor activist, journalist, author

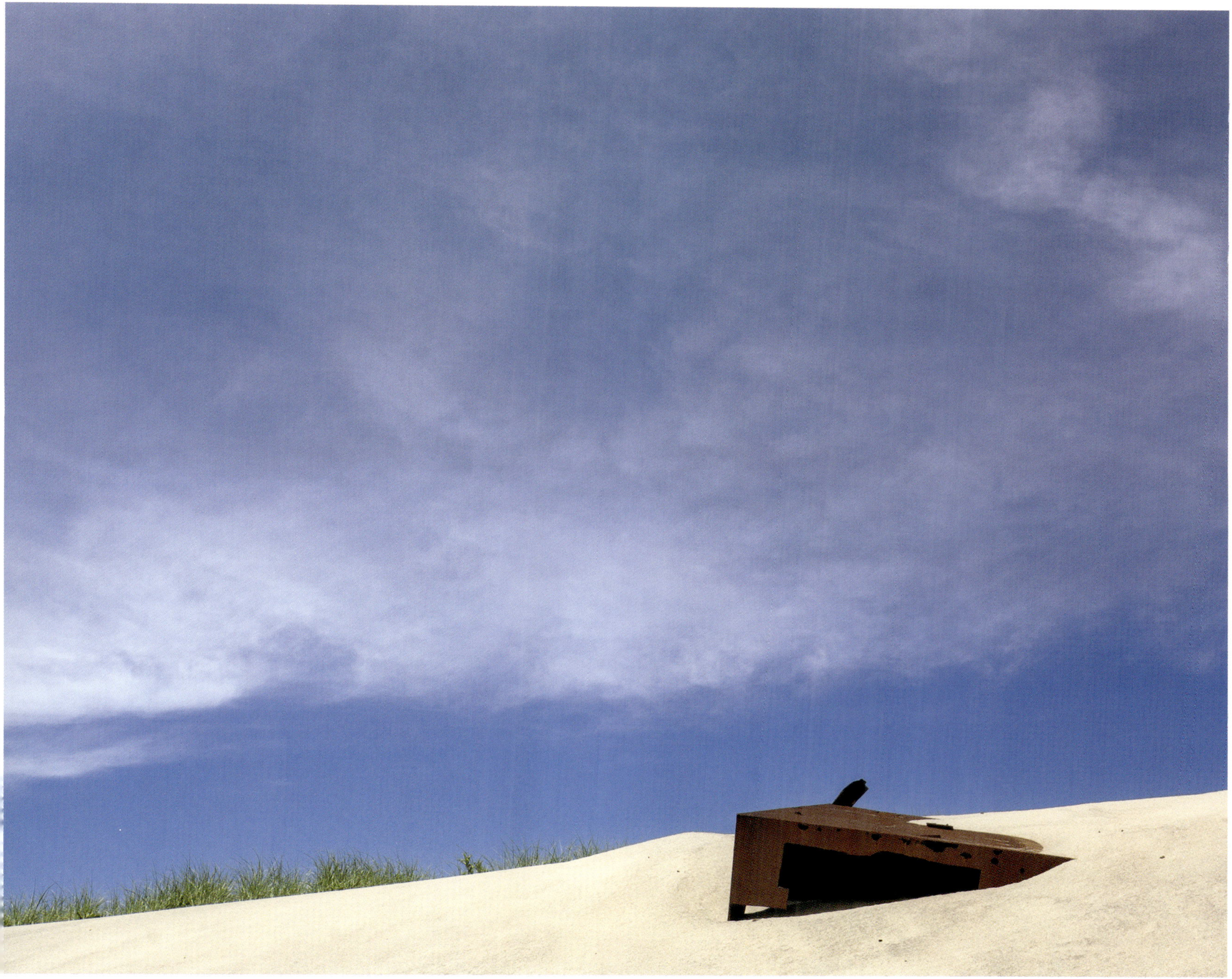

This is not a zoo. This is a private residence. I ask you to respect that.

LAWRENCE SCHUSTER

dune shack dweller

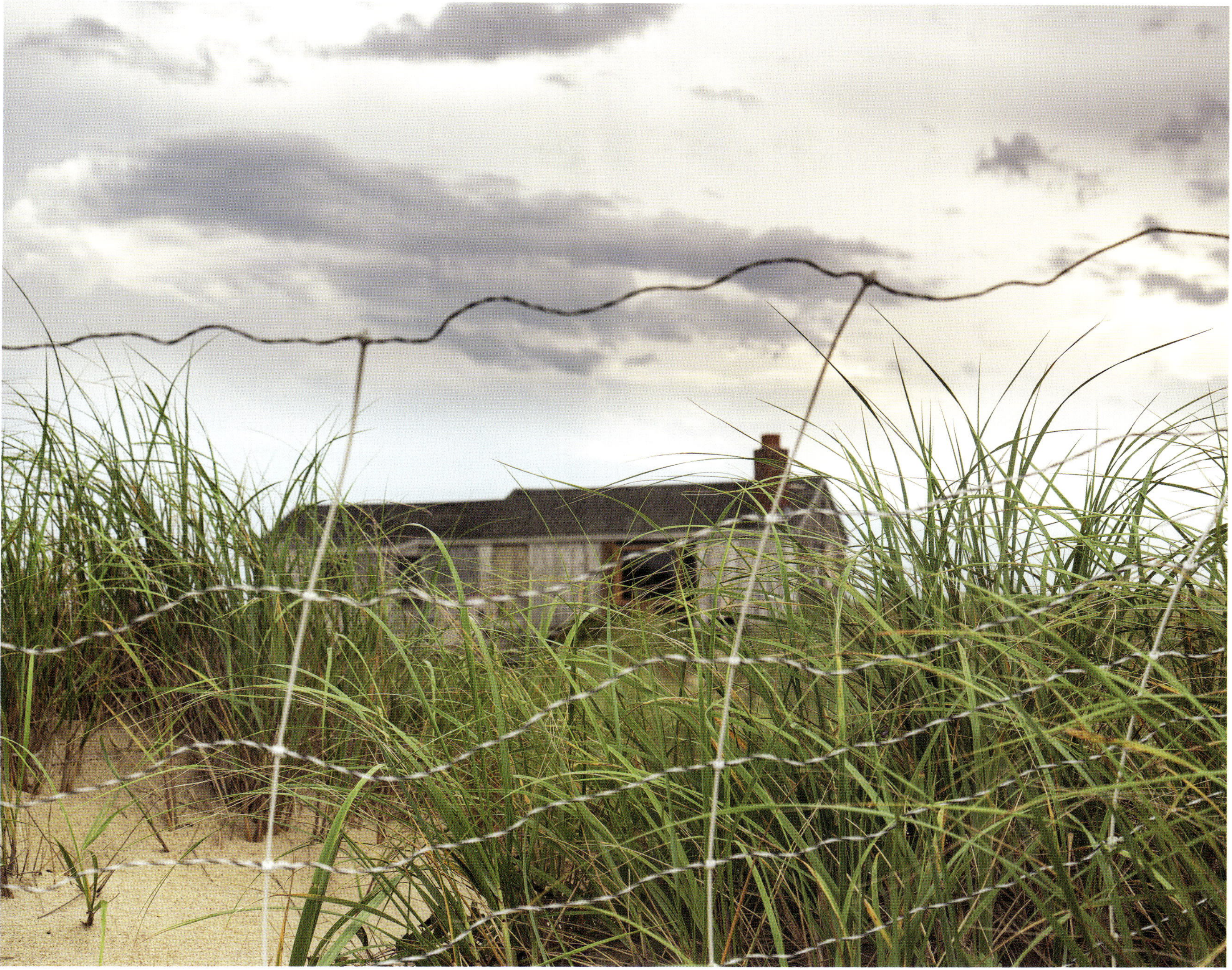

I felt like a combination of Apollo I moon explorer and Lawrence of Arabia as I wandered the sand hills all around.

ANONYMOUS

shack guestbook

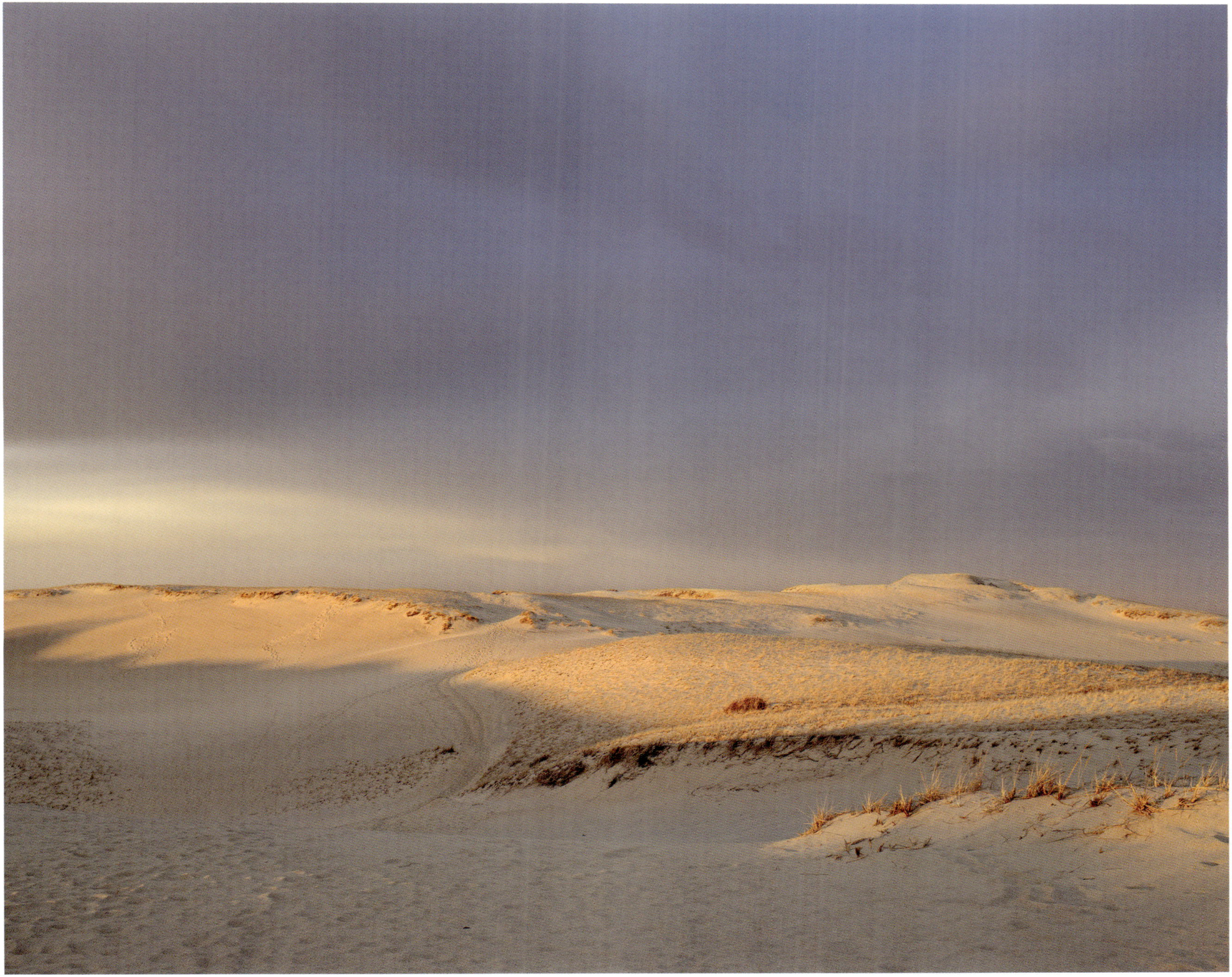

When I sit down to write at this hand-hewn desk, pen in hand and guitar in lap, I think about who built these shacks, the free spirits who lived here and dreamed here. I wonder who else has sat here looking out this window, watching the light change.

PATTY LARKIN

singer-songwriter, guitarist

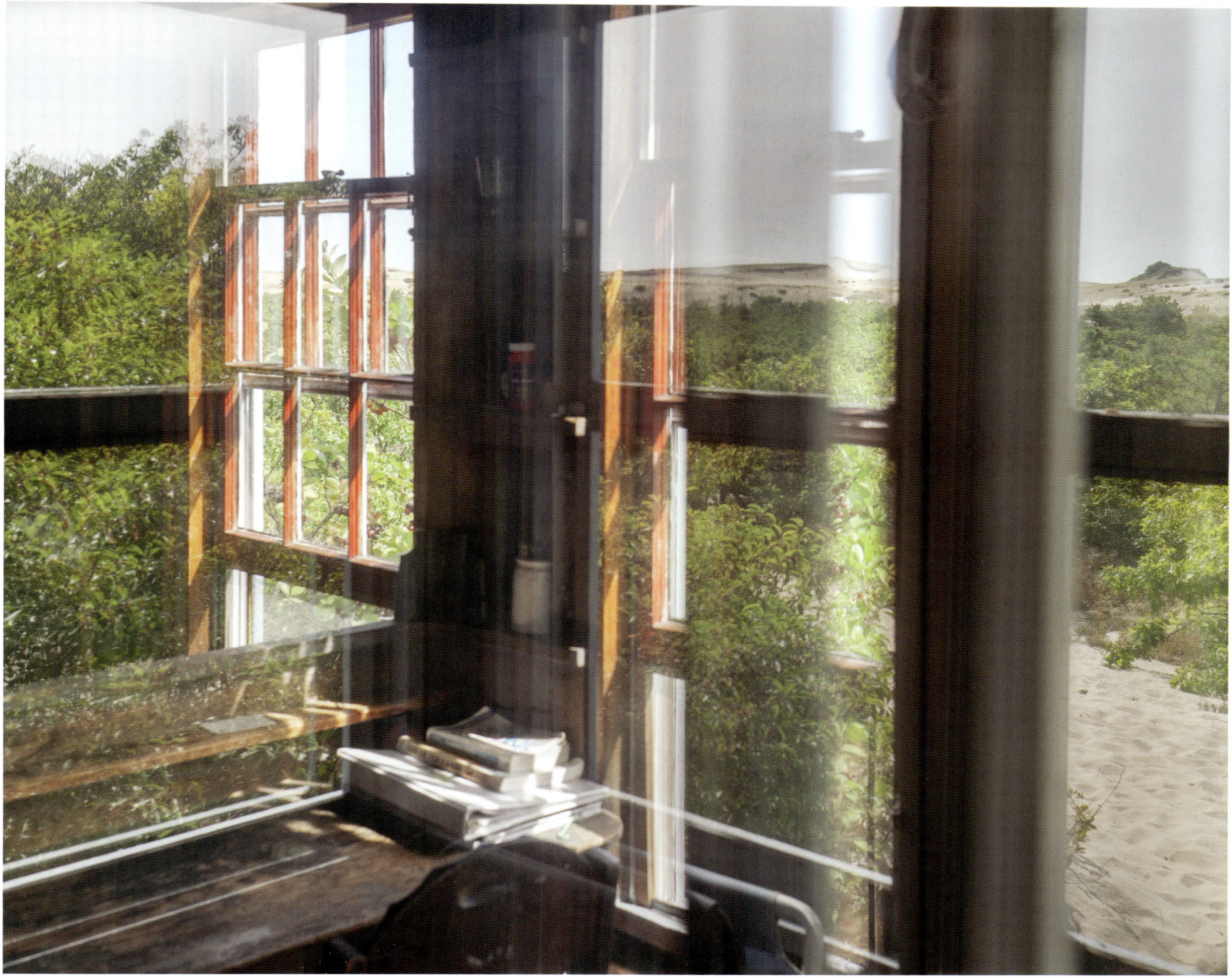

Hans Hofmann used to go out every morning as soon as it was bright, around four o'clock, in the dunes, and you know, he went on foot, he had to travel light so he had just a big pad of paper about 8" x 10" and a bunch of children's crayons. He did the most beautiful dune scenes I've ever seen.

PEGGY HUCK

Hans Hofmann book translator, artist, educator

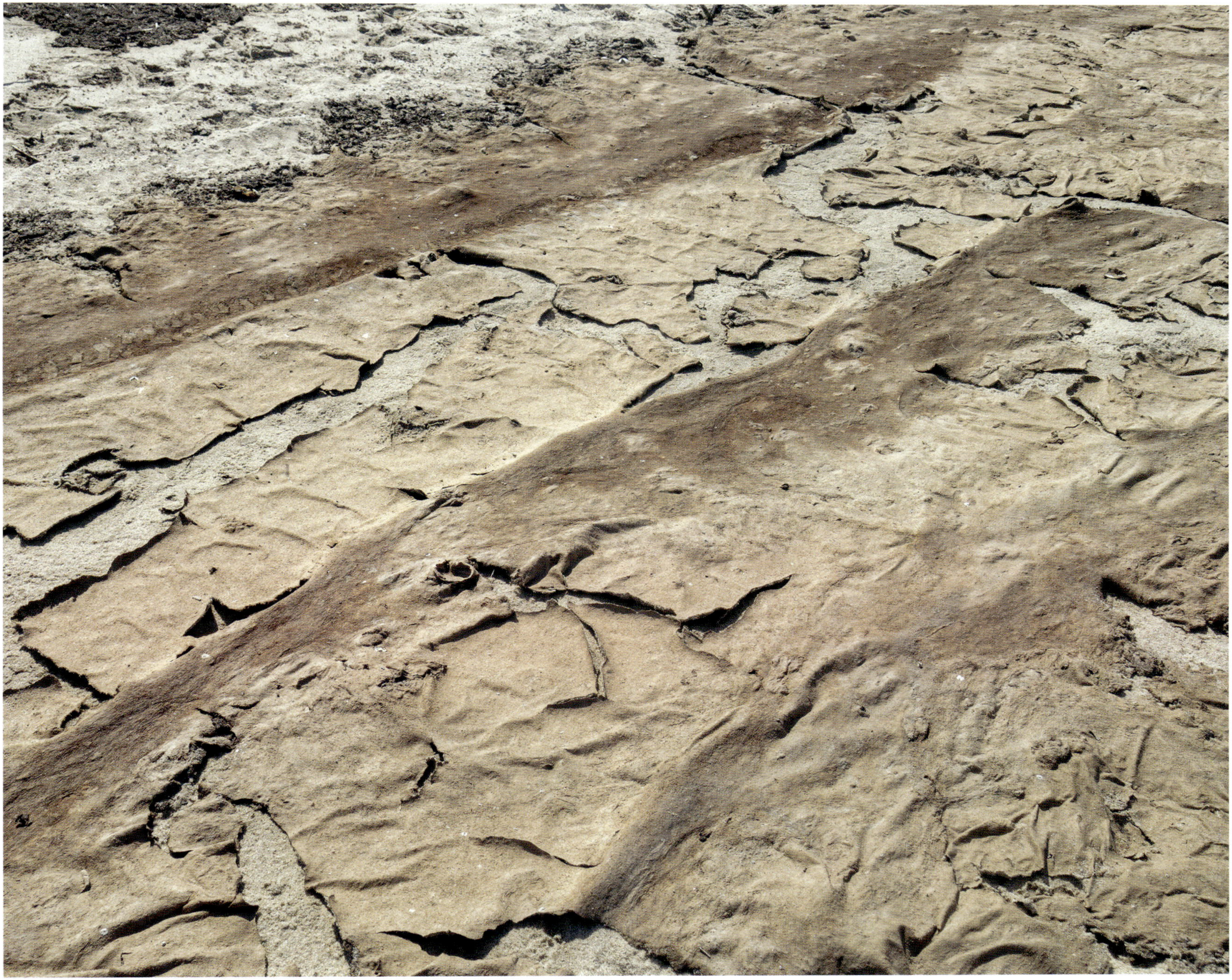

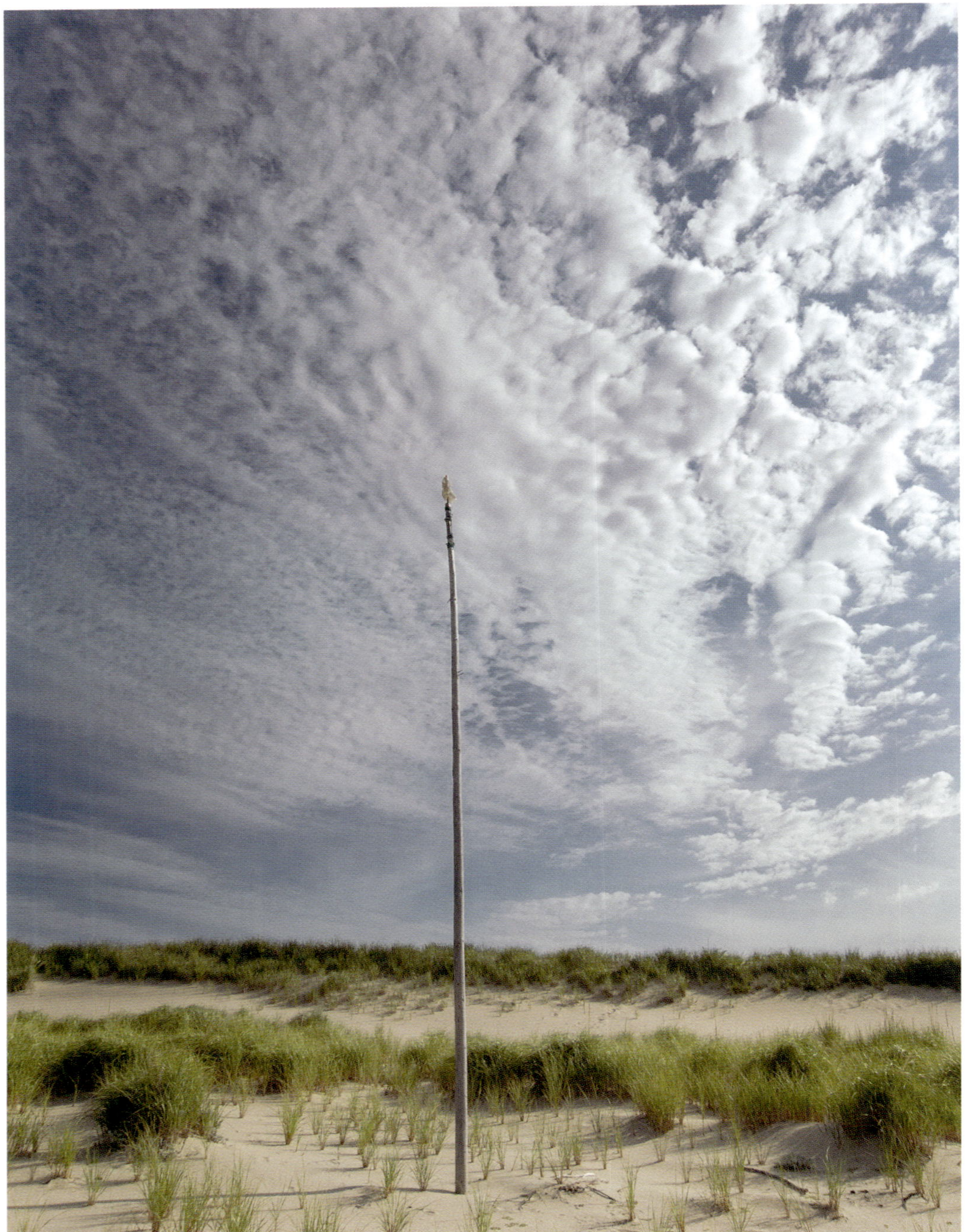

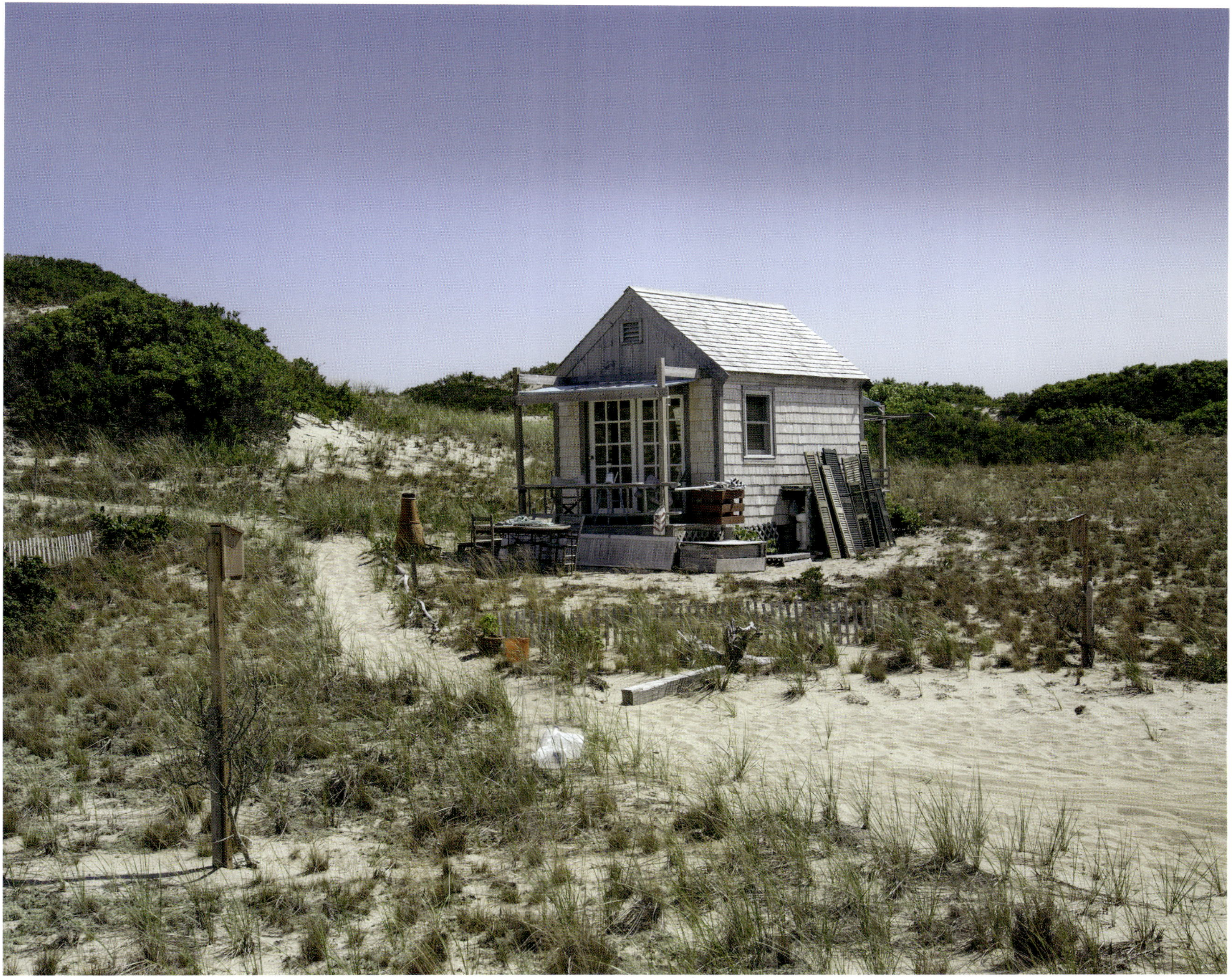

I was told that there were some really, really wild parties.
The Howling of the Moon, they would call it.

JULIE SCHECTER

dune shack user, a founder of Peaked Hill Trust

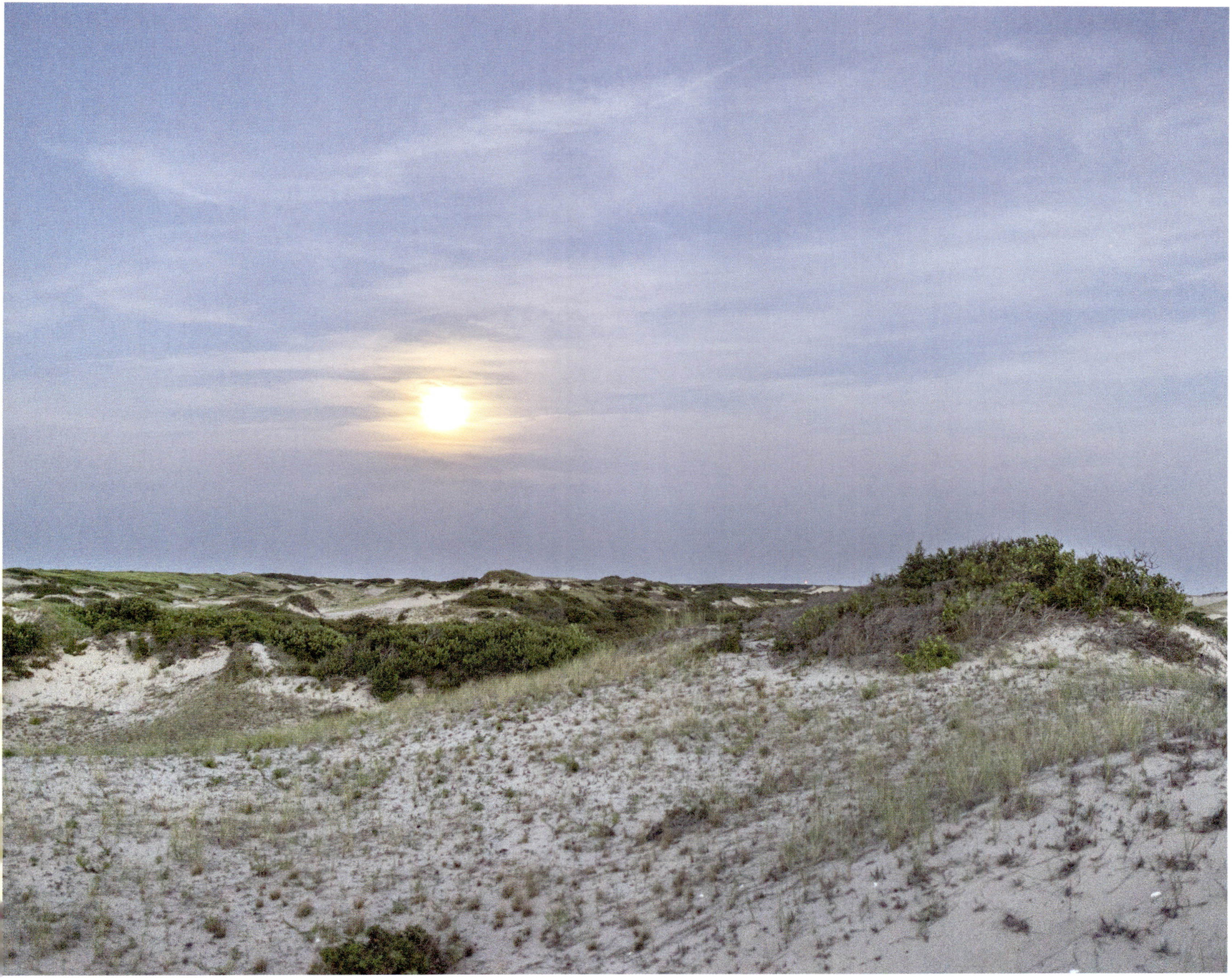

I like to think of our community as a tapestry, with the families and individuals as the warp, some long threads, stretching back over a half century, some a bit shorter, but just as important in the overall pattern. The weft is the associated way of life that we have had in common, raising our families, creating beautiful things, working hard at the tough problems we all face in the unique landscape.

MILDRED CHAMPLIN

dune shack dweller

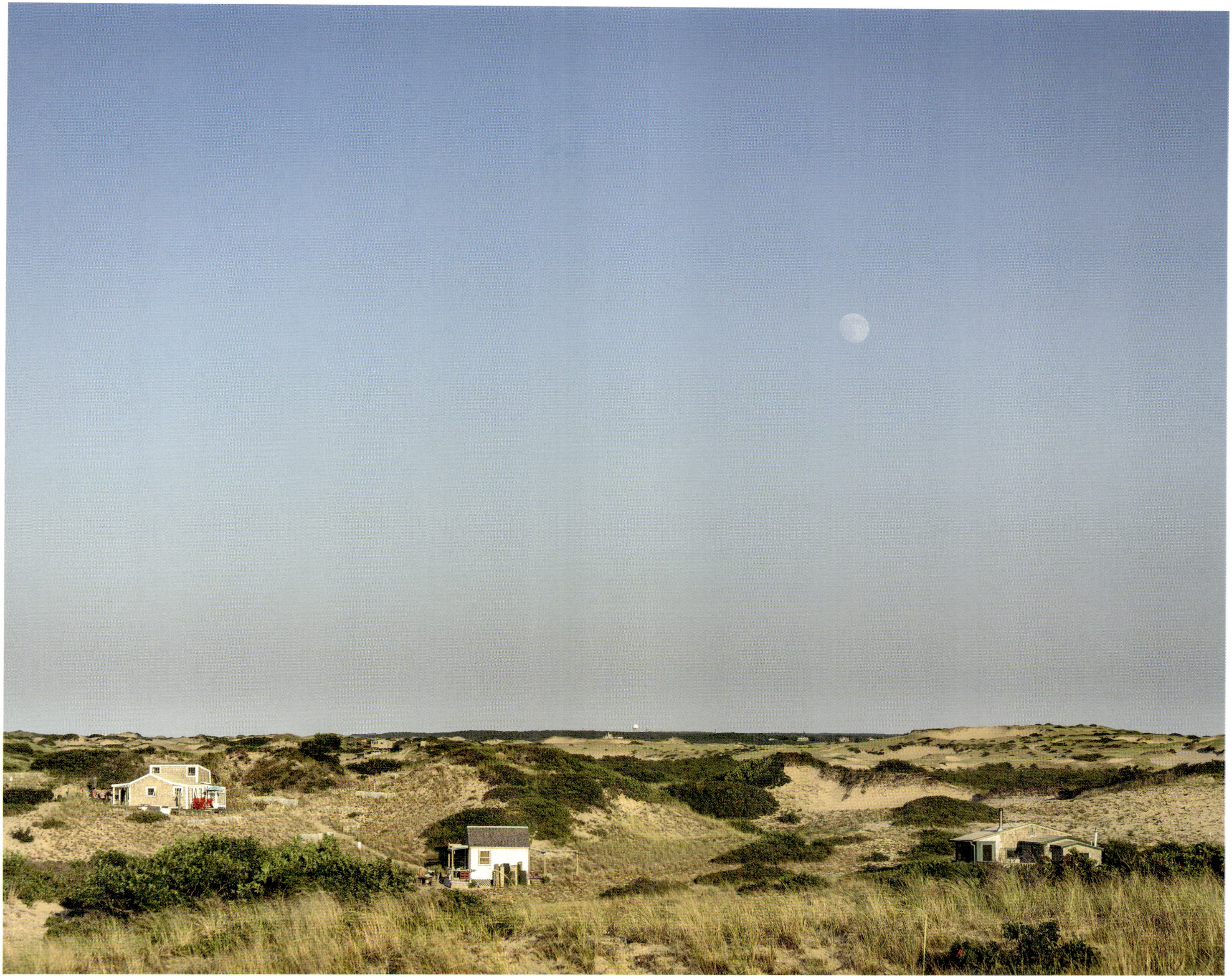

Here is a simple truth: the wind is the sculptor of the dunes.
Wind is the dominant force out here. You know it, shack dweller,
when even the smallest blow hums all around you in your tight little nest;
back in town you probably wouldn't even notice.

DENNIS MINSKY

writer, naturalist

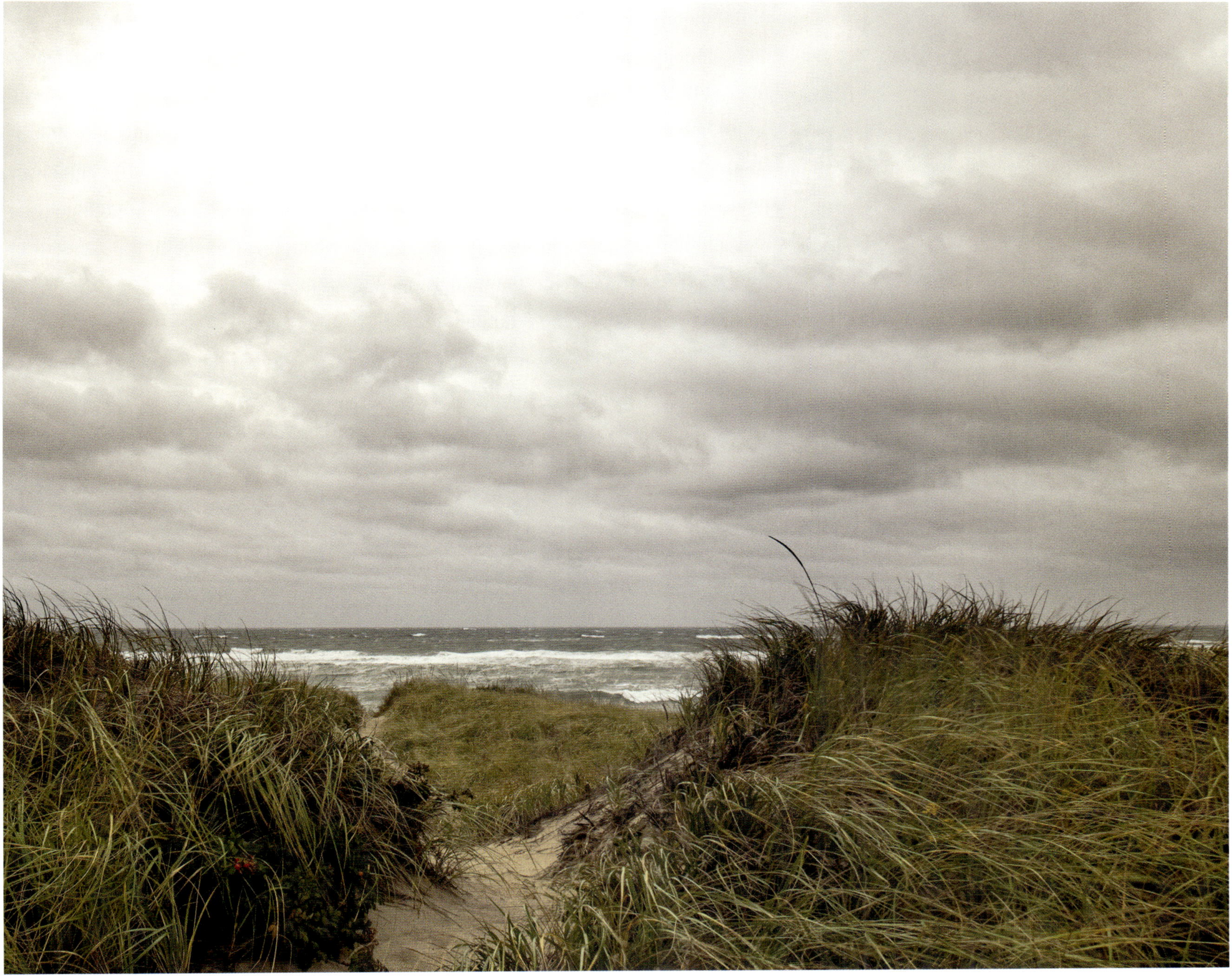

People seem to like to leave something behind;
it seems no one can bear not to make that small claim on departing.

CYNTHIA HUNTINGTON

poet, memoirist, author of *The Salt House*

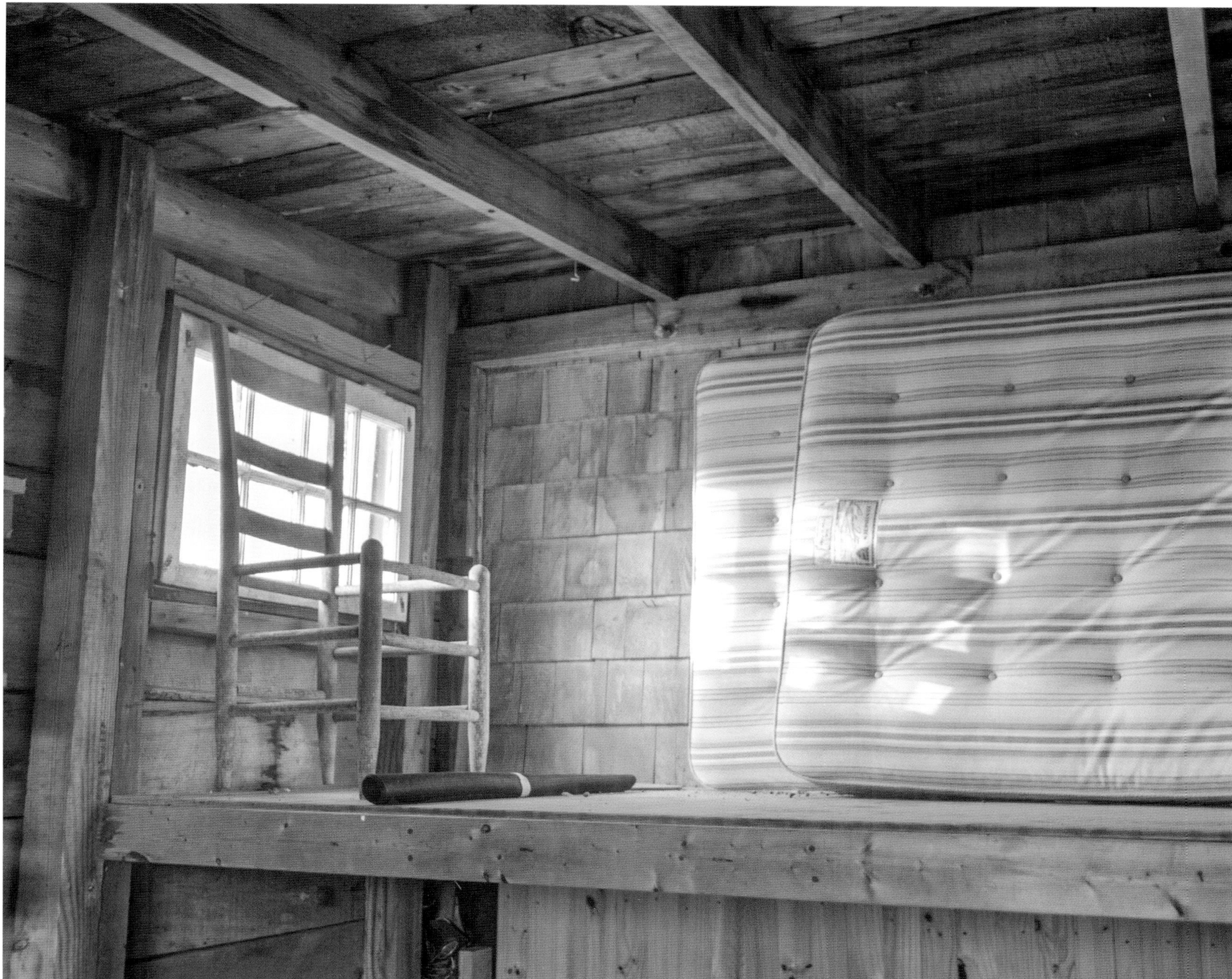

I am leaving with so much more than I arrived with.
My time alone at the . . . shack was two weeks of freedom.
Now leaving, I am full.

JIM BROUSSARD

artist

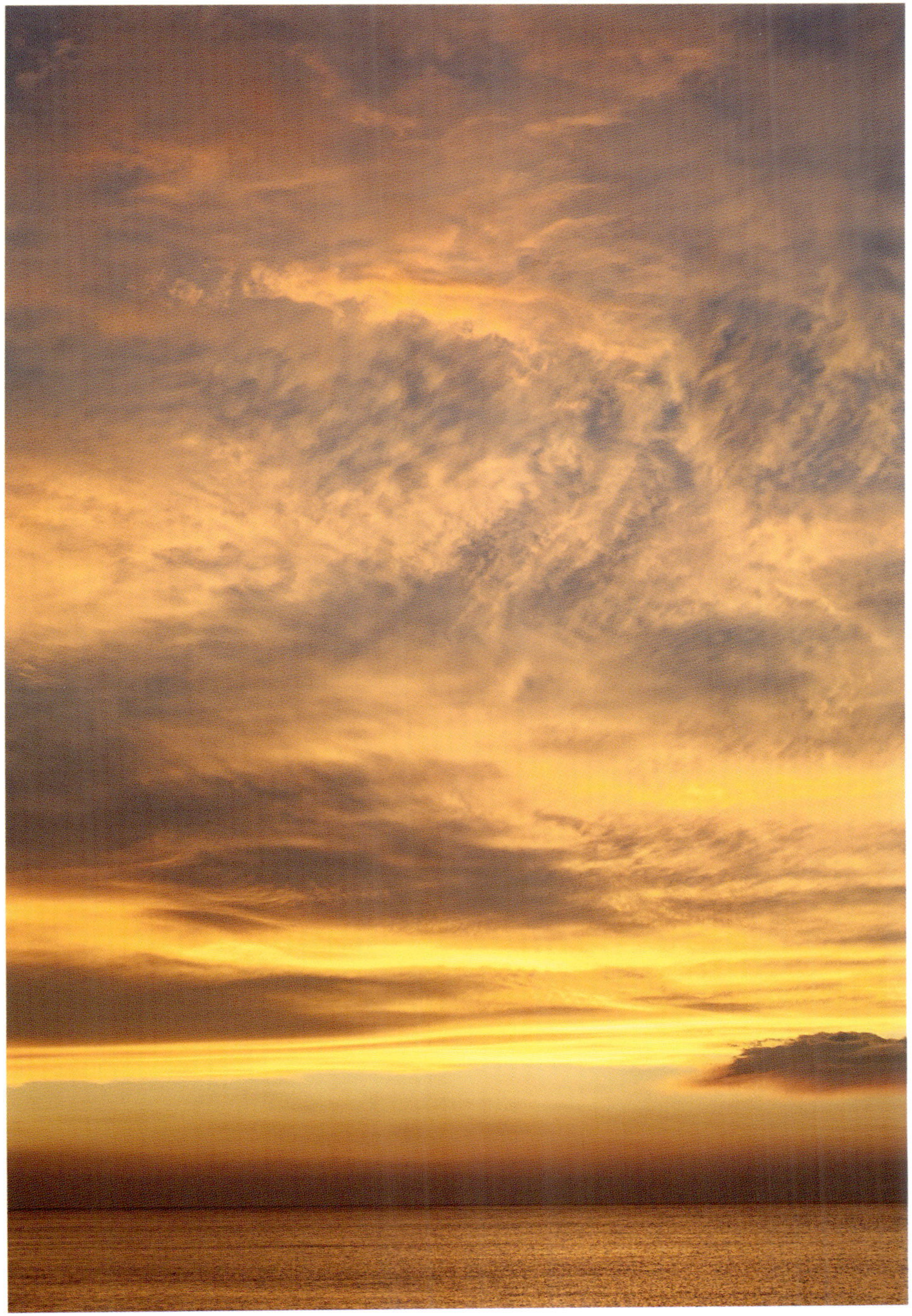

MISSION BELL

My late husband found the house in the early 1950s, abandoned, falling down, no windows or doors, three feet of sand in the living room. He and a couple of fellow veterans tackled this fixer-upper with no money, using old replacement windows and doors and beach wood. All restoration was done with hand tools. It's been a sixty-seven-year labor of love.

The dune shack district has been selected as special because of its "resources"—the houses or shacks. I guess a house can have a history in itself. For instance, think back to when the scavenged windows were put in, when the door was painted yellow, or what year the new roof was put on. Little ugly ducklings in a sublime, often harsh, landscape. Every one of them began its life as an even uglier duckling, lovingly restored and brought to at least a semblance of relative, usually quirky, attractiveness through the hard work and imagination of resourceful and determined real people, who raised families, made art and literature, worked and played.

Each shack is distinct from the others, reflecting the minds, imaginations, and personalities of the people who worked so hard on them.

We feel as part of the fabric of the dunes and ocean, and we enjoy and suffer the myriad aspects of nature there. We live our lives out there by the tides, winds, times of moonrise and sunsets. We love the sound of the ocean and wind and have become storm junkies, appreciating the power of Mother Nature. Except when we've had to run out in the middle of freezing cold to climb the icy dunes to rescue the tattered fencing that protects the barrier between our house and the bottom of the dune. Nature in the raw.

One night a hurricane passed by that was expected to miss us. I spent the night listening to one shutter after the other being torn loose, banging and slamming away. I was in my early eighties and had to take care of it myself because my husband was in the later stages of dementia and pretty frail. I had to climb the long ladder to the second floor. The other dune shack dwellers have had to do the same kind of thing, some much more.

I mention those really difficult problems because it's necessary to get a fully rounded view of life out there. We do all the rhapsodizing of the artists and short-term visitors, but we're lucky enough to spend months and years experiencing the wonderful environment, the reward for the dues we pay in hard work.

The problem-solving and time-consuming labor are worth it. Sunrises, sunsets, remote beach living, raising kids in the old-fashioned free-range style, where they learn to appreciate nature firsthand, become self-sufficient and capable of solving problems on the spot, because you're the one there to do it. We lived for a year almost year-round with our four year-old daughter in that uninsulated cottage, out of contact with the rest of the world. No phones then. I guess it's my favorite year!

The houses were built in response to a certain environment. It's the residents who have been able to restore, maintain, and improve the homes in continued response to the environment, each with its own emphasis.

MILDRED CHAMPLIN

dune shack dweller

QUOTE SOURCES

The following people contributed quotes directly to me: Mark Adams, Melanie Braverman, Mildred Champlin, Peter Clemons, Rob Costa, Frank DiGirolamo, Joanne Dugan, Melany Kahn, Zehra Khan, Patty Larkin, Ellen LeBow, Russell Steven Powell, Daniel Ranalli, Candice Reffe, Elia Sinaiko, Tabitha Vevers, and Bette Warner

The following were quoted from Robert J. Wolfe's "Dwelling in the Dunes: Traditional Use of the Dune Shacks of the Peaked Hill Bars Historic District, Cape Cod," National Park Service, US Department of the Interior, August 2005: Connie Armstrong, David Armstrong, Janet Armstrong, Emily Beebe, Marianne Benson, Irene Briga, Paul Champlin, Jay Critchley, Josephine Del Deo, Hatty Walker Fitts, Maureen Joseph Hurst, Conrad Malicoat, Genevieve Martin, Kathie Joseph Meads, Deborah Ross, Julie Schecter, Paul Tasha, Dawn Zimiles, and Murray Zimilies

Additional sources:

Ann Patchett, "Cape Cold: The Quiet Joys of Winter," *Travel & Leisure*. April 28, 2009.

Anonymous, "Ray Wells Dune Shack Guestbook," Provincetown, MA, 2015.

Charles Demuth, quoted in a letter to Agnes and Eugene O'Neill, in Bruce Kellner, ed., *Letters of Charles Demuth 1883–1935*. Philadelphia, PA: Temple University Press, 2000.

Charles Hawthorne and Mrs. Charles Hawthorne, compilers, *Hawthorne on Painting*. New York: Dover, 1960.

Croswell Bowen, *Curse of the Misbegotten: A Tale of the House of O'Neill*. New York: McGraw-Hill, 1959.

Cynthia Huntington, *From the Peaked Hills, a Collection of Writing and Drawing*. Provincetown, MA: Peaked Hill Trust, 1988.

Cynthia Huntington, *The Salt House*. Hanover, NH: Dartmouth College Press, 1999.

Dennis Minsky, "Little Sister Sand," 2019.

Harry Kemp, quoted in Wainwright J. Wainwright, *Provincetown in Pictures and Story*. Cotuit, MA: The Picture Book Company, 1953.

Harry Kemp, quoted in Frank Cotty, "Provincetown Profiles and Others on Cape Cod," *Barre (Mass.) Gazette*, 1958.

Hazel Hawthorne, *The Salt House*. New York: Frederick A. Stokes, 1937.

Henry Beston, *The Outermost House: A Year of Life on the Great Beach of Cape Cod*. New York: Henry Holt, 1980.

Henry David Thoreau, *The Writings of Henry David Thoreau*, Vol. 4: *Cape Cod and Miscellanies*. New York: Houghton, Mifflin, 1989.

Houghton Cranford Smith, *The Provincetown I Remember.* 1991.

Jack Kerouac, "Residents Move to Preserve Historic Shacks among Provincetown Dunes," *New York Times*, October 19, 1986.

Jeanne Chanel and Josephine Del Deo, quoted in Josephine Del Deo, *The Watch at Peaked Hill: Outer Cape Dune Shack Life, 1953–2003*. Atglen, PA: Schiffer, 2015.

Jim Broussard, "Margo Gelb Dune Shack Guestbook," Provincetown, MA, 2011.

Josephine Del Deo, *Compass Grass Anthology: A Collection of Provincetown Portraits*. Provincetown, MA: 3 Dunes Press, 1983.

Joyce Johnson, quoted in Bryan Marquard, "Joyce Johnson, 84; Sculptor and Defender of Cape's Dune Shacks," *Boston Globe*, May 12, 2014.

Lawrence Schuster, quoted in Victoria McKee, "Provincetown Life Information," *Boston Globe Correspondent*, April 1, 2006.

Marsden Hartley and Susan Elizabeth Ryan, ed., *Somehow a Past: The Autobiography of Marsden Hartley, 1877–1943*. Boston, MA: MIT Press, 1998.

Mary Heaton Vorse, *Time and the Town: A Provincetown Chronicle*. New York: Dial Press, 1942.

Michael Cunningham, *Land's End: A Walk through Provincetown*. New York: Crown, 2002.

Norman Mailer quoted in Olmstead Center for Landscape Preservation, "Cultural Landscape Report for Dune Shacks of Peaked Hill Bars Historic District, National Park Service," Boston, MA, 2011.

Peggy Huck, "Huck Papers, 1931–1996," Smithsonian Institution, Archives of American Art, March 3, 1991.

Robby McQueeney, "Return to C-Scape, Thursday, April 19, 2007," *Dune Tramp* (blog). www.dunetramp.com/stories.php.

Robert Finch and Ralph MacKenzie, *The Cape Itself.* New York: W.W. Norton, 1991.

Tennessee Williams, *The Selected Letters of Tennessee Williams*, Volume 1: *1920–1945*. New York: New Directions, 2000.

US Department of the Interior, "National Register of Historic Places Continuation Sheet, Areas of Significance, Criterion C, Architecture."

William Oscar Johnson, *Smithsonian*, August 1975.

Zara Ofsevit Jackson and Ray Wells, quoted in Russell Steven Powell, *Shack Time* (DVD). Northern Star, 2001.

ACKNOWLEDGMENTS

I am indebted to all the generous people and their relatives who allowed me to use their words in this book. This story would not be so rich without the quotes that give life to the dunes and the shacks.

This book would not exist without Joanne Dugan, my creative director/editor and friend. I am so grateful for her wisdom and tenacity.

My heartfelt thanks go out to my key assistant and friend Zehra Khan, who was invaluable, and also to Haley Robinson, who kept me moving forward.

Thank you to the following people who have provided unwavering encouragement and friendship over the years: Lois Hessert-Blawie, Sharys Wheeler, Regina Casciato, Erika Gentry, Jane Hee, Pat Medina, and Jimmy Swift.

Thank you for your support and kindness: Ann Jastrab, Paula Tognarelli, Aline Smithson, Christine McCarthy, George Slade, Hannah Frieser, Kate Gartside, Joseph Cooper, Godofredo Torres, and all the staff from the Mews Café and Restaurant, Mac's Fish House Provincetown, Napi's Restaurant Provincetown, and the Provincetown Art Association and Museum (PAAM).

Thank you to Amanda Young (who has become a dear friend) and her daughter Evelyn for being such great companions to my husband, Frank, who has Alzheimer's. They bring out his humor and playfulness and allow me to work and have some downtime. He so looks forward to "the girls."

I so appreciate all the photographers, instructors, and reviewers whom I have met along the way, especially at portfolio reviews; your encouragement and advice had a significant impact on my career. Thanks to the Houston Center for Photography, and Fernando Castro, for giving me my first exhibit in 2009. Thank you to Galatea Fine Art in Boston and Alden Gallery in Provincetown, as well as their directors, Marjorie Kaye and Howard Karren, for representing me and supporting my work through the years.

Special thanks to the National Park Service, especially Bill Burke, the Provincetown Community Compact, Jay Critchley and Tom Boland, the Peaked Hill Trust, and the Outer Cape Artist Residency Consortium.

Thank you to my Provincetown and San Francisco book club and community of friends for always inspiring me and keeping me sane.

Thank you to Mark Adams, artist and geologist, for his incredibly beautiful artwork that graces the end sheets.

Thank you to the people who follow me and support my work on Instagram and Facebook. It has really helped me keep pressing on.

Final thanks to my family, to whom I am eternally grateful, especially my parents, for instilling in me a deep love of the Outer Cape and its endless wonders.

Thank you to Schiffer Publishing.

I want to thank everyone else who helped along the way—you know who you are.

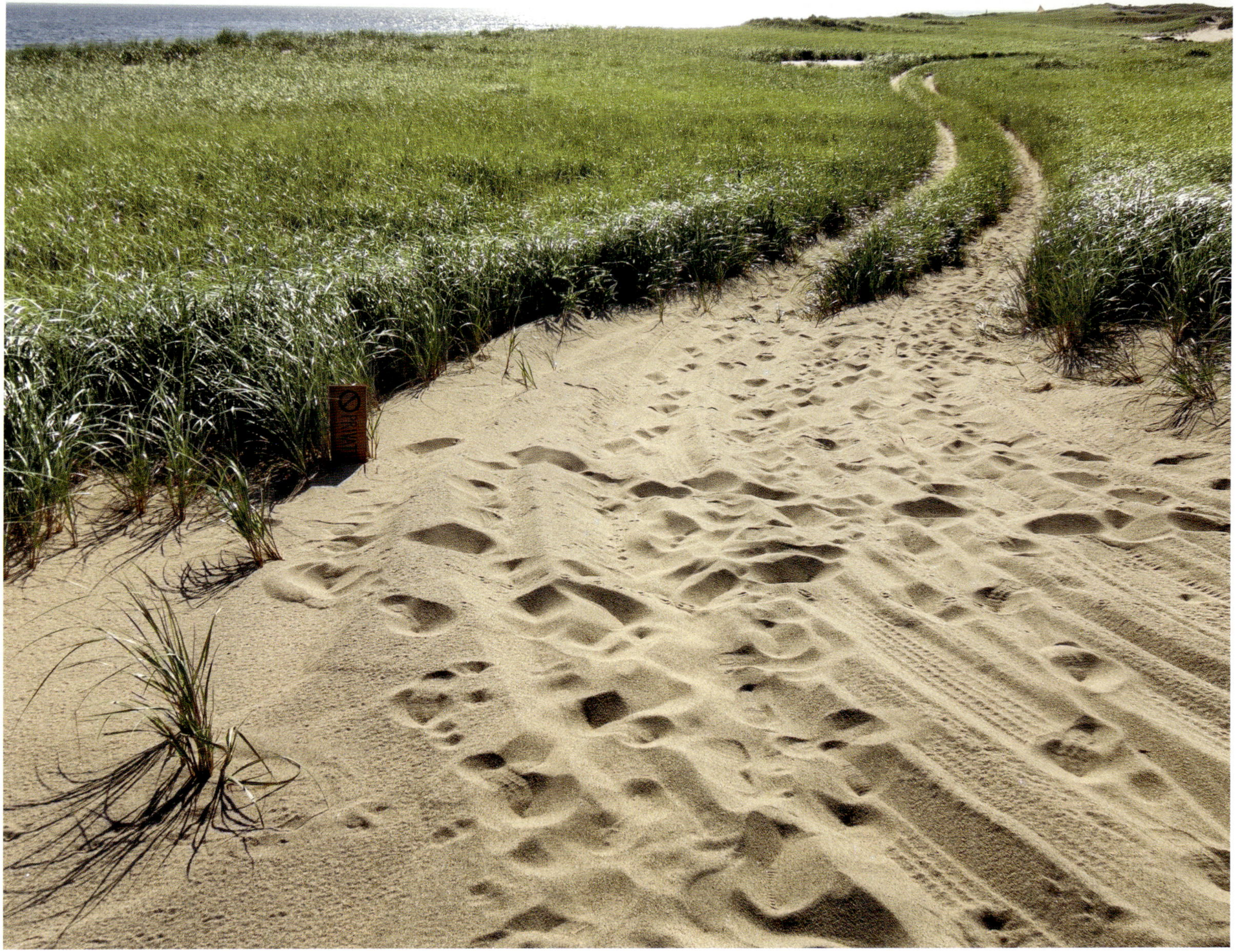

Schiffer Books on Related Subjects

The Cape Cod National Seashore: A Photographic Adventure & Guide,
Christopher Seufert, ISBN 978-0-7643-3995-0

Art from above Cape Cod, Christopher S. Gibbs, ISBN 978-0-7643-5747-3

The Watch at Peaked Hill: Outer Cape Cod Dune Shack Life, 1953–2003,
Josephine Breen Del Deo, ISBN 978-0-7643-4978-2

Library of Congress Control Number: 2021942595

Creative Director and Editor: Joanne Dugan
Design by Ann Lemon
Production design of cover and interior by Molly Shields
All photographs by Jane Paradise, except page 153 by Joanne Dugan
Endsheet map by Mark Adams
Type set in Brandon Grotesque / Century725

ISBN: 978-0-7643-6361-0
Printed in China
5 4 3 2

FSC www.fsc.org MIX Paper | Supporting responsible forestry FSC® C104723

Published by Schiffer Publishing, Ltd.
4880 Lower Valley Road
Atglen, PA 19310
Phone: (610) 593-1777; Fax: (610) 593-2002
Email: Info@schifferbooks.com
Web: www.schifferbooks.com

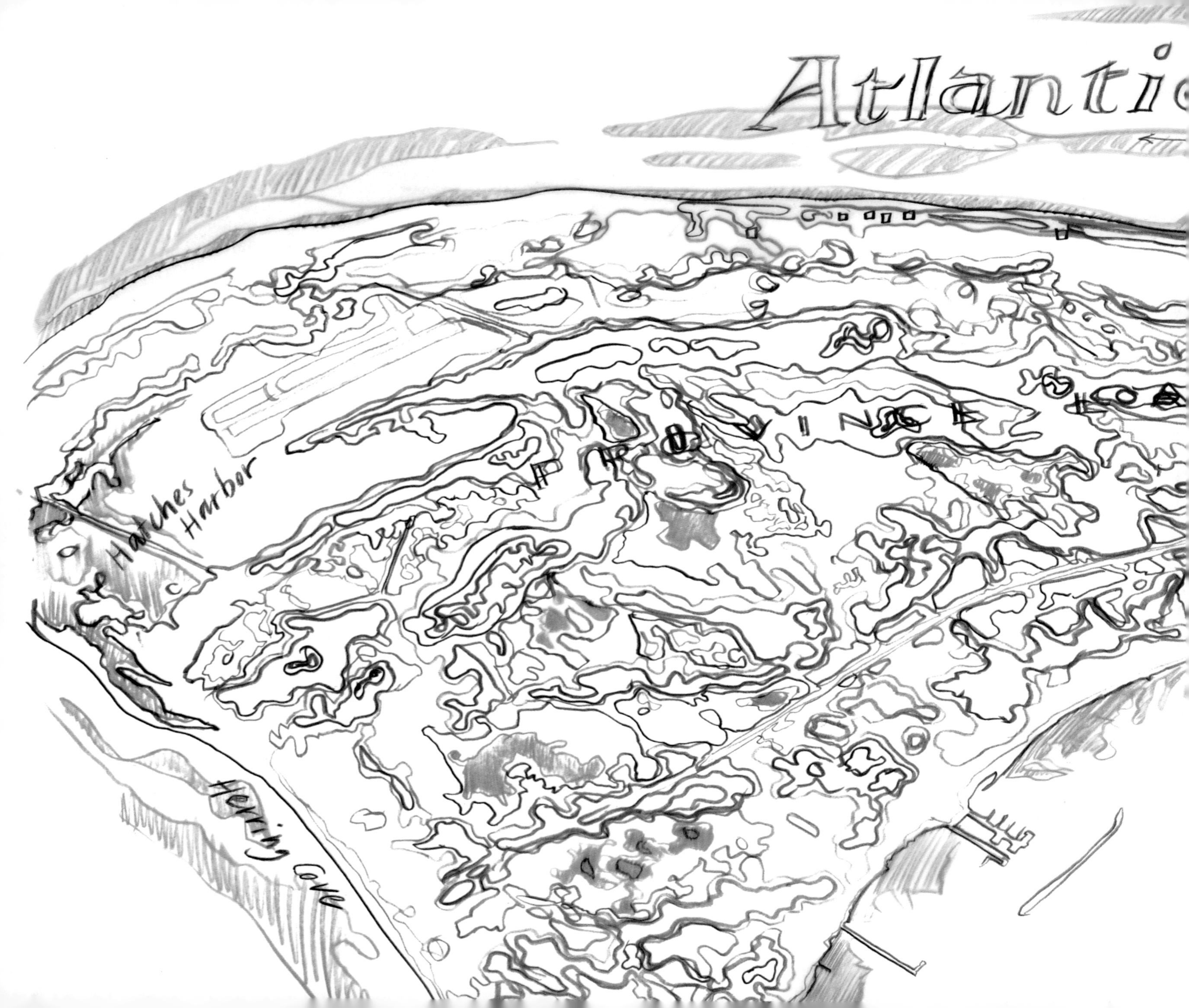

Atlantic
Hatches Harbor
Herring Cove